Rethinking the Way We Teach Science

Offering a fresh take on inquiry, informal and readable, this book draws on current research in science education, literacy, and educational psychology, as well as the history and philosophy of science, to make its case for transforming the way science is taught. It addresses major themes in national reform documents and movements—themes teachers are keenly aware of in their day to day work: how to place students at the center of what happens in the classroom; how to shift the focus from giving answers to building arguments; how to move beyond narrow disciplinary boundaries to integrated explorations of ideas and issues that connect directly with students; and most especially, the importance of engaging students in discussions of an interactive and explanatory character.

Rethinking the Way We Teach Science:

- Is grounded in actual teaching episodes
- Provides a much needed foundation for STEM and interdisciplinary study as ways to deeply transform how science is taught
- Shows how teachers might teach a wide range of science topics from elementary school through high school—is relevant across grade levels and subject matter
- Is highly interactive—in keeping with the pedagogical argument at its core about the value of talk and dialogue

The premise of this book, with its sense of humor and of pathos and its passion for the promise of good schools, is this: If teachers work at having things make sense, students will join them in that work. But this is complicated: Teachers will find themselves in the intersection of three conversations, the interplay of science content, the teaching of science, and the nature of science; they will also need to consider their students, who are often alienated and uncertain of their place in school or society. As the book addresses these issues, it is, above all, about choosing to place the authority of reason over that of right answers.

Lou Rosenblatt is a teacher with over 30 years of experience, chiefly at The Park School, but also at The Baltimore Freedom Academy, Johns Hopkins University, The University of Leeds, and Gallaudet College. He is a consultant with TIES, having worked chiefly with Baltimore City Public Schools and STEM schools in North Carolina. He has published several articles and presented at numerous conferences, and he was a member of the design team which secured funding from the Bill and Melinda Gates Foundation among others to establish The Baltimore Freedom Academy.

Teaching and Learning in Science Series
Norman G. Lederman, Series Editor

Visit **www.routledge.com/education** for additional information on titles in the Teaching and Learning in Science Series.

Rethinking the Way We Teach Science

The Interplay of Content, Pedagogy, and the Nature of Science

Louis B. Rosenblatt

Routledge
Taylor & Francis Group

NEW YORK AND LONDON

First published 2011
by Routledge
270 Madison Avenue, New York, NY 10016

Simultaneously published in the UK
by Routledge
2 Park Square, Milton Park, Abingdon, Oxon OX14 4RN

Routledge is an imprint of the Taylor & Francis Group, an informa business

© 2011 Taylor & Francis

The right of Louis B. Rosenblatt to be identified as author of this work
has been asserted by him in accordance with sections 77 and 78 of the
Copyright, Designs and Patents Act 1988.

Typeset in Minion and Gill Sans by
Florence Production Ltd, Stoodleigh, Devon
Printed and bound in the United States of America on acid-free paper
by Walsworth Publishing Company, Marceline, MO

Library of Congress Cataloging in Publication Data
Rosenblatt, Louis Barry.
  Re-thinking the way we teach science: the interplay of content,
  pedagogy, and the nature of science/Louis B. Rosenblatt.
    p. cm.—(Teaching and learning in science series)
  1. Science—Study and teaching (Elementary). 2. Science—Study and
  teaching (Secondary). I. Title.
  LB1585.R54 2010
  507.1—dc22   2010018615

ISBN13: 978-0-415-87733-6 (hbk)
ISBN13: 978-0-415-87734-3 (pbk)
ISBN13: 978-0-203-84327-7 (ebk)

Contents

Preface
Statement of Intent

Not too long ago I attended a meeting where a publisher's representative was urging the adoption of a series of textbooks. After 10 or 15 minutes of describing various advantages of the books, he came to a new feature. Teachers could access a web-site where lesson plans were available. One needed only to specify the number of days to be spent on a given chapter, and out would come a breakdown for lessons: 5 minutes here, 10 for this activity, and another 15 for that . . . In addition, each specified chunk of time would be related to state learning objectives and national education standards. I could feel the energy in the room. Clearly, the teachers were pleased by the notion of a web-site that would virtually write their lesson plans. But there was more. The sales representative went on to say that these lesson plans were especially good for new teachers, who have a tendency "to get bogged down explaining things." That was the part I loved. Here was help making sure you wouldn't waste your time explaining things.

It is my intent here to praise the virtues of getting bogged down. There is more here than a question of speed. Choosing to go "slowly," that is, choosing to stop for questions, to explore what it all means, and to lay out a map, is also choosing to have things make sense. In the end, it is placing the authority of reason over that of right answers.

Everything in the chapters that follow comes down to this: if we work to have things make sense, students will join us in that work. But it is complicated. We will find ourselves in the intersection of three conversations. There is the science we seek to teach, such as the material in our textbooks. There is, as well, a body of pedagogical notions about how best to go about teaching. To these we may add the history and philosophy of the sciences, which help us appreciate both the nature of science and the problems and issues that shaped the modern understanding. Together these three make a good story.

Acknowledgments

Before anything else, a word of thanks. I am indebted to so many who listened, laughed, argued, read, and critiqued . . . to family, Bon, Pete, Kate, and Shanna . . . to colleagues from Park, especially Marshall Gordon and Jan Morrison . . . to Fouad Abd El Khalick . . . to students, especially Dale Beran and Paul Nestadt, but also Stephen Conn, Rebecca Derry, Brian Eden, Liz Eisenberg, and Matt Raifman . . . to a lost friend, Peter Reed . . . and to Marty, who told stories.

Chapter 1

On Wonder

Some time ago Jesse, a kindergarten child, and I were scurrying through a heavy rain on the way from my car to his classroom. I remarked that it had been raining pretty heavily for some time and over a large area. That was a lot of water and it must be very heavy. Had he ever lifted a bucket of water? Yes, he had, and it was really heavy. So what did he think about how all this water could stay up in the sky? By this time we had entered the building and he looked at me and proceeded to explain that there was a great big glass or plastic ceiling in the sky. Moreover, that's what thunder was—when it would crack. This was a wonderful theory, and I said so; but it occurred to me that he had recently flown for the first time. Did he think the plane had broken through the glass barrier? He didn't say anything at first . . . you could see him thinking about things, and of course the most striking feature of flying is looking down on the clouds. Then he said that he hadn't thought of that. Maybe his idea wasn't right. Maybe something else held the water up. "Wonder what it is," he said. "Yes," I agreed, "wonder what it is."

When Jesse had paused before he went off to join his kindergarten class, when he paused to say "Wonder what it is," the wonder he expressed was not so much a wonder of nature as a wonder of the human imagination. It was not the rain he was wondering about, but the intricacy in thinking through how it might work. This is an important distinction. Often people take science to be about nature's wonders, but it isn't. Science is not a series of National Geographic specials on volcanoes or the fantastic world within a microscope or the birth of stars. It's how we understand these things.

Of course, in seeking to understand nature we need some experience, but too often science class becomes a time to marvel at the world when it ought to be a time to marvel at reason and the power of the imagination.

There's a lovely story about the connection between reason and the imagination that comes from the latter years of the eighteenth century and seems exactly right here. James Hutton, a Scottish man of science, had proposed that we link the hard, crystalline rocks so abundant in the Earth's crust, rocks like granite and marble, to volcanoes and fires deep within the Earth. This was a remarkable hypothesis. The only rocks clearly derived from volcanoes are rocks like pumice, rocks that are porous and brittle with a dull, matte-like finish—utterly different from the granites and marbles Hutton proposed also came from volcanoes.

Hutton ably made his case and deeply transformed the way we understood the Earth's history. Before Hutton, the story of the Earth was the modest tale of a gradual wearing down, as the wind and elements eroded its bolder features. With Hutton, things opened up dramatically. Different parts of the Earth could be different ages, depending on the play of igneous forces. Whole mountain ranges and continents could be relatively old or young. The Rockies, for example, are only about 40 million years old; while the Appalachians are around 300 million years old. Moreover, in a given place the layers of rock may reveal a history of the rise and fall of landscapes as complicated as the rise and fall of the kings and queens of medieval Europe. This was immediately clear to Hutton and his colleagues on a trip into the field when they came to Siccar Point, which juts out into the North Sea some 30 miles east of Edinburgh. There they found two beds of sedimentary rock, each one representing a long stretch of time when this region had been below sea-level so that sediment could accumulate and compact into rock. Furthermore, the fact that the lower, older bed was vertically standing meant that it had been upended from its original horizontal lie by powerful forces long before the younger bed had been formed above. Here is a lovely photo of Siccar Point from the geology department of Lawrence University in Wisconsin.

Figure 1.1 Siccar Point. By permission of the geology department of Lawrence University.

Reconstructing the likely sequence of events that had produced this vista—two separate events of uplift and vast spans of time for erosion and the accumulation of sedimentary rock—John Playfair, one of the group wrote: "The mind seemed to grow giddy by looking so far into the abyss of time, . . ." and then he added "we became sensible how much farther reason may sometimes go than imagination can venture to follow" (Playfair, 1822, vol. 4, p. 81). When we marvel at the intricacies of the world of electron-microscopy or at the vastness of distant nebulae "dying in a corner of the sky," we are carried to these fantastic worlds, not by the imagination of the poet, but by the careful reasoning of the scientist making sense of the world.

"Excuse me, but don't you have that upside down? Everyone knows that poets are imaginative and carry you to exotic places like Xanadu; while careful reasoning only gives you whatever fantasy you can find in the fine print of a footnote."

"Oh, hello. I know what you are talking about, but if you stop to consider the proportions of modern science from black holes to the 'charm' of quarks, isn't it clear that reason sometimes goes far beyond footnotes or Xanadu?"

"You make science out to be a something like the *Twilight Zone*. But isn't it all about the facts? What about careful observation and the scientific method, meter sticks and triple-beam balances?"

"Facts and observation are there, but they're a small part of things. There are always two stories to tell. There's the one that features the thing itself. You know, the 'Wonders of Nature'—from the intricate lace-like patterns of snowflakes to the dramatic images of nebulae billions of light years away. These are the stories we find on public television specials. They're great, but there is another kind of story. It's the one we invent in order to understand. It's the one with all those wonderful notions about things we can't even see—such as atoms, the double spiral of the DNA molecule, evolution . . ."

"Whoa! Do you mean atoms and evolution were just made up?"

"Certainly! Evolution is far too slow to see, and atoms are far too small for us to experience. You can't pick one up, hold it to the light to see what color it is, or place it on a scale to weigh it. The atom was invented, not discovered. The key here is a matter of how we see things. Let me tell you a story . . ."

"Some time ago I went hunting for dinosaurs. As I went, I remembered the *Golden Book of Big Dinosaurs* I'd read as a kid: their monstrous size, the violence of their eyes, their fierce step, and their great jaws. It was a completely foreign and exotic world. Yet, it was also a *real* world. Perhaps this is the key to their mystique; here were dragons that actually stomped about and breathed their fiery breaths. That's why you get all those marvelous tales, such as Michael Crichton's *Jurassic Park* (1990), where hidden away in lost corners of the globe are descendants of the lumbering beasts of the Mesozoic. We are captivated by the thought that they were real.

"On my expedition, we went back to the mid-Jurassic, to the Morrison formation—rocks of a characteristic type deposited 150 million years ago but presently found all around you, if you happen to be in parts of Colorado and elsewhere. We can all conjure up the lost world of the dinosaur. A typical scene might involve great beasts lumbering through swamps, or locked in deadly combat, and of course, there are volcanoes smoldering in the background (this is the cover illustration by Joel Snyder of David Eastman's *Now I Know: Story of Dinosaurs*, 1982).

"What an extraordinary contrast this is with the modern scene, the one that shows a barren and bleak hillside, no volcanoes, no swamps. We had gone to

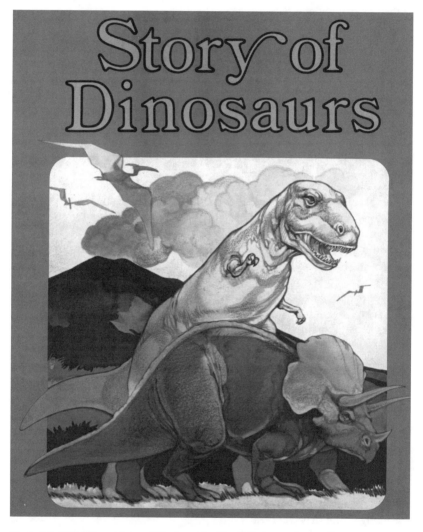

Figure 1.2 *Now I Know: Story of Dinosaurs* by David Eastman. Cover illustration by Joel Snyder. By permission of Scholastic Inc.

Figure 1.3 Dinosaur fossil site in Colorado. Author's photograph.

a site near Grand Junction, Colorado, in the Western range of the Rocky Mountains, not very far from the Utah border, a most prosaic patch of arid land.

"If you could superimpose these two scenes, you would have the measure of the difference between facts and theories. Here we are, reason tells us, knee-deep in the world of the Iguanodon and the Apatosaurus, with Pterodactyls in the skies, flanked by Tyrannosaurus Rex in battle with a Triceratops, the great plebeian warrior. Giant ferns grow around us, while volcanoes are smoldering, and what do we see? What are the facts? A bleak, bleached out hillside!

"At a certain point in our scouring of the hillside, I realized that everyone else had found a fossilized morsel to relish, and that all I had been able to do is swat at the predatory gnats that are a large part of the modern environment. Determined not to let the moment escape, I opted for the beaten path and began to search for some sign of ancient life in the rocks just a few feet to the right of another find.

"I clambered along the slope, chose my spot a respectful distance away, and began to scrape at the surface. Success! I found two small lumps of dark rock! I called out to my friend, a paleontologist, and he came over right away. 'Ah,' he said, 'a great find. It looks like two vertebrae of a Camarasaurus.' I had done it! I had found the remains of a dinosaur. The Camarasaurus was a beast of that broad, sleek Apatosaurus design, though quite a bit smaller. Its remains are not uncommon in the Morrison, and there are some lovely specimens on display at Dinosaur National Monument not too far away in Vernal, Utah.

"Then, right at the height of my joy over my great discovery I learned we had to go. I was shattered. One of our party was, unfortunately, quite ill, and ought not to have gone out in the first place. And so everyone packed up their goods and made for the car and the ride back to town. I was left standing there in a daze, staring at my two lumps of dark rock; since that was all they were. I wasn't going to have the chance to bring them to life. The reality they constituted would continue to be a private affair between them and their setting. I hadn't found vertebrae, I'd found two dark rocks. To make them the vertebrae that they really were would require work, and that's the moral of the story. All we experience is the appearance of things. The real world takes time and work and analysis and a well-schooled, disciplined, imagination. But I was already lagging behind. So I too picked up my gear and headed back toward the car."

"That's really a drag, but I think I see what you mean by the difference between what we see with our eyes and what we see with our understanding."

"No problem . . . I'll just carry on."

There are wonders to nature, such as the Grand Canyon or the Great Barrier Reef, where we are overwhelmed by nature's colors and proportions. But there are other wonders, such as black holes, ice ages, and the intricacies of molecular genetics, where the color and proportions rest in our reason, in our capacity to conjure up what things must be like in keeping with argument and analysis. Without the reasoned imagination Playfair spoke of, our world would be bleak and bleached out.

Years ago, T.H. Huxley suggested that, for most of us, the world is like walking through an art gallery where most of the paintings have been turned to the wall (Huxley, 1907, #80). We lack the feel, the insight that can evoke the wealth all around us. That is what expertise is all about. I had a colleague who had grown up on a farm. He told of watching his father pick up the soil and work it in his fingers, and from that his father could tell what fertilizer to add. Any such expertise will turn some of Huxley's paintings around, but I readily confess . . . the capacity to see the abyss of time, or to know those rocks as vertebrae, that would be especially sweet.

The sciences are filled to the brim with notions like "the Earth is a planet" or that "life has evolved"—notions invented in order to explain phenomena such as those two dark rocks on that bleached out hillside in Colorado. But these ideas are far from obvious. Presented outside the context of the puzzles that prompted them and without the support of the arguments that carry them, these ideas lose their vitality. We don't know what we are looking at and we don't know what the theories are really telling us. Science becomes at once inert and exotic, like a display case of butterflies or tropical birds. There remains nature's artfulness, its design, its color, but we miss the life within. We miss the movement reason provides, the argument that would have coursed through the veins, as it were. And so we are left with landscapes that do not present the "abyss of time." We are left with dark rocks, instead of the vertebrae of dinosaurs. Our task, as teachers, then is straightforward. It is to connect answers to puzzles, theory to experience. It is to see the wonder of reason's imagination, to see the argument—and, of course, to share that with our students.

If this were a class or a text in geology or evolutionary biology, this story might lead to an examination of what it takes to see vertebrae where the untutored eye sees only dark rocks. We might examine comparative anatomy—the contours of different bones and how their contours are related to their function—and we might talk about the processes of fossilization. But our focus is quite different. When we ask "What is the significance of the difference between rock and vertebra?", what we are really seeking is the difference between the body's eye and the mind's eye, the difference between what I see and what my understanding can "see." For us, in an essay on the practice of science teaching, we want to know how this should shape what we do in the classroom. How should we talk, so that students see both the two dark rocks *and* how they are vertebrae?

On Talk

We have talked ourselves out of talk. We have seen this already in that publishing representative's remarkable observation that their web-site would help teachers avoid getting bogged down explaining things. We can see it as well in "direct instruction," an approach to teaching that is virtually scripted. As the National Institute for Direct Instruction says on its web-site: "The popular valuing of teacher creativity and autonomy as high priorities must give way to a willingness to follow certain carefully prescribed instructional practices" ("About Direct Instruction (DI)," n.d., www.nifdi.org/15/about-di).

This is not to say there are not a lot of words. There are lots of words in our science programs. Too many. In a delightful paper, Robert Yager (1983) counted the number of technical terms introduced in our science textbooks. There were literally hundreds and thousands more words than the standards set in foreign language study. But these words are answers, and answers are not talk.

This is an interesting distinction. Why would we make it? In an intriguing book, *A is for Ox*, Barry Sanders talks about the importance of story-telling. Children learn by talking. The very sense we have of ourselves as persons, he suggests, is a "sounding or telling through," a *per-sonare* (Sanders, 1994, pp. 45–46). This notion of talk as story-telling is the key. We forge our identity, our person-hood, through the act of telling stories.

What is true of the child is also true of the student. As children shape their sense of self through talking as story, so students shape their identities as reasoning beings through the act of explaining. They forge their intellects by giving shape to arguments. Where a child learns the role of suspense and detail in focusing a tale, so the student learns the role of issues and evidence in focusing an explanation. In both the development of the child's talk into conversation and story-telling and the student's development of explanatory schemes from his or her earliest "essays" to fuller expositions, the individual draws upon their inner self and in the act of drawing . . . gives shape. Consider the name we give to the kind of writing where students explain themselves: "expository writing." The act of explanation is to expose, to reveal, to lay open, *and* at the same time it is to stand out from—to *ex-pose*. That is the great power of making sense of things. It is simultaneously the laying open of what was hidden, and the assertion of self—the standing out from shelter. When we explain, we expose and we are exposed.

Language is a curious thing. A rose by any other name would smell as sweet; yet, there is something to the way we name things. There is something, for example, about naming explanatory essays as "expository" writing that captures the heightened vulnerability of trying to explain yourself. This is underlined when we stop to note that an "essay" is an attempt, an undertaking, and only in the modern era has it come to mean a written piece. There is an essential vulnerability to being a student.

Several years ago I attended a small high school graduation party for the first born child of a family that had immigrated to the United States from Iran. As the father proudly spoke of his daughter's success, he found himself talking with bitterness about a teacher he had had who had not given him the credit that was his due. Such is the pain we suffer as students at the hands of adults through their indifference, their failure to recognize what we have done, that decades later that pain is still with us. Here was vulnerability writ large.

To continue the discussion about the value of talk, how different this talk is from sharing information. Too often we tell students. Too often we make the serious business of the classroom a kind of decanting where we pour information, however elegantly, into their minds. Over the years, I have had many colleagues. Several have stumbled over just this distinction between talk and information. They could see that class was "flat," that students were not really enjoying class or activities, but they couldn't see what the real problem was. One colleague—very bright, with a strong background—kept revising his presentations, his lectures, convinced that if he could just find the right way to organize the material, students would see what was going on, would do well on tests, and would be happy about their learning. But students only became more disenchanted. They hadn't needed a still more elegant essay, a still more refined answer. They needed questions to ponder, seeming contradictions to resolve, and issues to engage and make sense of.

Another colleague often stayed late working and reworking labs for his classes. I'd ask him what he was up to and in the course of his account it became clear to me that he was doing the best part of the lab. He was solving the problem, finding a way to make something work to prove a point. All that was left to the students was to turn some stuff on and collect the data. He needed to hold students responsible for how they could make sense of a puzzle or address a problem. Only when we do this are we nurturing their capacity to reason and so become more fully independently minded—just as story-telling nurtures a fuller sense of identity.

On Perplexity

The importance of talk in the classroom is heightened once we appreciate that the material does not speak for itself. Our textbooks present the material as if what it means and why we would hold these views is obvious; but it is no more obvious than was the claim that those two rocks were vertebrae. I have been there. We have all been there. The material does not speak for itself.

If this is so, then how can we speak for the material? How can we focus the mind's eye of a class full of students, so that they are prepared to see the vertebrae in the rocks? This is a central issue as we prepare for the classroom, and it proves to have many parts; but right in the middle is the notion of perplexity.

Perplexity is the natural companion to that sense of wonder linked to the imagination. When Jesse wondered what held the water up, he was perplexed. Things did not make sense. There is an interesting nuance here. Not all things that don't make sense are perplexing. Perplexity seems really only to apply to those things that we think we ought to understand. So, the classic Norman Rockwell-like image of a father scratching his head while standing in front of the various parts of a bicycle that he's been trying to put together is an apt image of perplexity. On the other hand, the fact that the same father might not know the sequence of nuclear reactions involved in the release of the vast energies of stars is more simply something he does not know. This difference is crucial for the classroom; for perplexity is vital, it enlivens, while information is inert and deadening. If we return to Sanders for a moment, the importance of talk highlights the corrosive impact of television and other modern forms of passive entertainment. Children are being stimulated, but not challenged. Their time is occupied, but their imagination, their own talk and thus their own forging of notions, is not. He offers this striking observation: "Young children need to feel lost, confused, and bewildered enough to concoct their own stories in order to climb out of tight situations. They need to string together narrative threads from here and there to reach meaning in their lives" (Sanders, 1994, p. 47).

As with the development of children, so too with the development of students. The logic of the material, as opposed to the logic of the exchange in a classroom, tends to foster a passive witnessing. Students do not expose. That is the work of the text and the teacher. The material does not provoke. It lies there, inert. The task is not to forge an understanding but to secure identification. Students witness. They watch. And even the various hands-on activities we offer are programmed, formatted to provide a witnessing, a confirmation of the material. There is no driving perplexity.

There is a lovely display of the pedagogy of perplexity in a text as old as they come. Over 2,000 years ago a young Athenian, Plato, established the first recognizable school in the Western tradition. The textbooks at this first school, the Academy, were dialogues he had written that caught the wisdom of his mentor, Socrates. Several of these dialogues are still often read in university study, and the reason is clear. Plato and Socrates systematically examined the most fundamental questions. In the dialogue, *Meno*, for example, the opening line has the character, Meno, asking: Can virtue be taught? Certainly, this is a key issue.

In the course of the dialogue, Socrates' persistent questioning irritates Meno. He compares Socrates to a stingray; for whenever anyone comes into contact with a stingray, they are numbed by it. And that is just what Socrates' questioning has done. It has reduced him to a state of numbing perplexity where he now questions what he had, just moments before, confidently assumed he knew. Socrates acknowledges that there is a certain justice to this charge; for, being perplexed himself, he infects others with his perplexity. Yet, he argues, it is for a noble and just end, as true opinions are aroused by questioning and turned into knowledge (Plato, 1956, 80d).

As we have already talked about the meaning of "expository," perhaps we can venture another such note. Consider the word "perplexity." *Plexus* meant "knot" in ancient Greek and *per* meant "through," so that we might think of a perplexity as being knotted all through, confused by the issues and choices. Socrates would create perplexities by adding ideas and arguments to think about.

The moral then is this: we need to perplex our students, to engage them with a puzzle that strikes them as puzzling. When Socrates first speaks to Meno about virtue, he encourages him to explain his ideas: "What do you think virtue is?" He then takes what Meno offers very seriously. Will this notion do? He finds that it will not. There is now clearly a problem, and the real work may begin. Further notions are offered and carefully considered. What we gain from this as an approach to the classroom is that learning begins with a puzzle, a perplexity—something that doesn't fit—and so, from the beginning, there is more going on than a witnessing. There is a problem to be solved. Perplexity focuses the mind's eye.

This, then, is our first step. In terms of the practice of science teaching we have suggested an orientation. When we walk into the classroom we need a problem . . .

"Excuse me again. I have another question."

"That's fine, but I can see that this is going to be confusing. That is, if you are going to do this very often . . ."

"Well, I don't know, of course, but . . ."

"O.K., let me see . . . we could put this in *italics. That should help; so would names. What should we call ourselves?*"

"*You're the writer. We could call you that, and then I would be the reader.*"

"Yes, that would be fine; though, of course, you're not really a reader. You're more a projected reader, a kind of hypothetical entity."

"What! You mean I don't really exist?"

"No, not exactly. You're more or less an imaginary friend."

"Well, that's not so bad. I'm an imaginary sidekick; so, you may call me Sancho."

"Fair enough, Sancho. Did you have a question?"

"Yes, D.Q., it's that I don't understand how you can start with a problem. Don't problems come at the back of the chapter? How can you start with them?"

"There's a pretty fundamental difference between problems at the beginning and problems at the end of a chapter. To start with a problem is to invite a conversation: as in 'Can virtue be taught?' To end with a problem is to say, in effect, 'You are being held accountable for the following.'"

"Yes, but it's still not clear to me how you can start with a problem. Problems presuppose knowing something and there being issues with it. The material comes first."

"Perhaps, but I tend to see it the other way around, Sancho. The material in the chapter is a set of answers . . . answers to questions that are not made explicit most of the time. This was the argument put forward by an intriguing character, R.G. Collingwood, about a hundred years ago. For Collingwood, the act of understanding was directly tied to figuring out the question a person is answering as they write or say something. He came to this out of an interest in archaeology where he found himself routinely looking at artifacts and asking what problem they had been designed to solve. Only by knowing what it had been for could you understand what it was and with that, what life had been about for these ancient peoples (Collingwood, 1939, pp. 29–39).

"There's a charming book, Motel of the Mysteries, *by David Macaulay (1979) that plays with this. Do you know it?"*

"No, I don't, D.Q."

"The story is set far in the future after our civilization has collapsed. Future archaeologists stumble upon the ruins of a motel and attempt to decipher its meaning. They see it as an elaborate burial chamber, as they found a body on a ceremonial platform (a bed) facing the great altar (a television). Another body was found in an inner chamber (the bathroom) with a still more elaborate, polished white sarcophagus (a bathtub). The opportunities for misunderstanding are staggering and in this case amusing. The point for Collingwood is that we do this all of the time. Early on we develop a mental faculty where we construct what is on someone's mind by trying to put ourselves in their shoes, as it were. We ask ourselves: what would it mean if I were to act or say these things?

"Years ago I had a curious conversation with my son. He had just turned four and, as I tucked him into bed for the night, I said that he was old enough now so that in a few months he would be able to start at the Park School, where I was a teacher. After a lengthy pause, he told me that he liked being four. Somewhat

taken aback, I said I was happy he enjoyed the prospect of being four and I was sure he would like being five and six and so on.

"Something was up, but I would not figure it out until several months later when Pete spent a day at Park. We picked him up at the end of the day and he had this big grin on his face. 'They have little kids!' he exclaimed. You see, I taught in the high school, and Pete must have assumed that when I said he could go to Park that I meant he would go to the high school. A little concerned about his father's judgement, he had offered the simple observation that he liked being four. Unfortunately, I had no idea the problem this observation was addressing and poor Pete had to suffer my lack of understanding for some time."

"Aha—so the point is that we are always archaeologists, à la Collingwood, trying to reconstruct intent and purpose from what is presented to us. Even when they are giving us answers, we are faced with the problem of figuring out the questions they are answers to . . . problems at the beginning of the chapter."

"Right, only we are going to make this process more explicit. To do this we need to find something that is tantalizing, something that is almost there, something that students thought they understood—like Meno. Then we turn a corner. We ask a question and pull the rug out from beneath their feet. We aren't starting with something completely new; instead we're taking a new look at something they already knew. By starting this way, with a problem, we acknowledge that the material is an answer to questions that people have been asking for a long time, and so we give the material the context it deserves. The key is that the lesson is not organized around an answer, or a demonstration, or an interesting phenomenon, or some activity that is meant to show how everyone should think about a topic. Instead it centers on a problem. It centers on a problem because what we really are after is for students to explore, examine, and come to make sense of things. What we really are after is that they can explain things. What we really are after is talk."

"But isn't there any value to the other sort of question that comes at the end of the chapter?"

"Yes, Sancho, but we need to be careful. We want a lot of those questions to be open. The problem is that too often they are short answer questions that don't require students to understand what's going on. You want to make sure there are questions that push the material, using what was in the chapter as a platform to move on to something else that connects but is new."

"What about here, D.Q., with this text?"

"Yes, we will work to bring things together and there will be questions, but not the sort that 'covers' the chapter . . . nothing like 'What is a Camarasaurus?' or 'Who wrote Motel of the Mysteries?' *Instead we will have a kind of afterword for each chapter.*

"The main body of this book is a sequence of eight chapters. Between chapters are interludes. These are not offered as amusing diversions. They use the chapter as a platform. Things do not speak for themselves. That is as true of classrooms as it is of dinosaur vertebrae. And classrooms and the enterprise of teaching science

are every bit as complicated with as elaborate an anatomy as the great beasts of the Mesozoic. We pause with an interlude because some quality of the things themselves would be lost if we didn't stop right there and consider it.

"I would often explain to students that teachers lie all the time. It's what we do. So that a student's job is not simply to take what is presented as 'gospel,' but instead to poke it to see if it works, and if it doesn't then raise a question. When they would ask why teachers don't simply tell the truth, I would ask them to try something. 'I want you to imagine a fourteen-sided object,' I would say. 'It has six faces that are octagons and eight that are triangles.' Can you picture that, Sancho?"

"No, I have no idea what that might be, D.Q."

"O.K., can you imagine a cube, like a die from a pair of dice?"

"Sure."

"Well, what happens if you cut across a corner of the cube?"

". . . you get a triangle."

"How many faces are there in a cube?"

". . . 6."

"And how many corners?"

". . . 8."

"And if you cut all the corners off, what's the shape of the old face of the cube?"

"I get it, an octagon. And so you would have six octagons and eight triangles, a fourteen-sided object."

"Yes. The truth, Sancho, is a many-sided object. To get students to appreciate this complexity, we always start with a cube . . . something simple. If we do our job well, we show students how the cube doesn't really work, and that we need to cut a corner here and there to make it work. All too often, however, we give students the impression that what we offer them is the whole truth. 'These are the facts.' But that's all wrong. There's always someone who knows more. For them what we have is just the beginning, a cube that needs to have its corners cut. That's what scholarship is all about . . . working out the many-sidedness of things.

"Our interludes are corner cuttings. They take a core notion and play with it a bit, connect it to the classroom, to activities, to assessments, and show where the complexities lay. In this first chapter we began with the notion that a puzzle is more important than the right answer. Perplexity provokes, it pushes. This might have struck you as reasonable, but not very realistic. After all, we are charged to teach the material and our textbooks overflow with elaborate concepts, analytical strategies, and hosts of algorithms. On top of which, it seems all of our students are below the national average. There is so much to do and they need so much help, there can't be enough time to talk about what these things really mean or engage in Socratic-like dialogues.

"For sure, time is an issue. But we also pay a price when we don't take the time. That's what this first interlude gets at . . ."

Interlude
A Note on City Schools

Schools are a central institution in the lives of children, and even though there are no classes on apathy, alienation, and disempowerment, it is clear that our children are learning these all too well. We can administer tests and determine that the average student entering high school in Baltimore reads at the fifth grade level. If this were the only issue, it would mean nothing more than the routine challenges confronting the typical sixth grade teacher. But this is not the case. What is packed into such statistics is a far more complicated set of realities.

The atmosphere of a school and the classroom is a critical piece in the alienation of students. Instruction is not simply a matter of texts, tests, and teaching techniques. It sets the table. It gets at the fundamental business of the place of the student—of their voice and their concerns. Instruction needs to connect with the mind of the student in order for significant learning to take place. It also needs to connect with students in order to make real the respect that the teacher and the community have for them.

An intriguing study by Clarissa Hayward examines the role and character of instructional atmosphere. Dr. Hayward compared an inner city elementary school and a suburban school. She found several key differences in what we might think of as the "politics" of these schools. Consider the broad area of student management: at the urban school, rules were made and enforced by the adults, and students were required to obey without questioning. When rules were presented to students, reference was rarely made to the purpose of the rule—you do what you are told to avoid being punished. In contrast, at the suburban school, students participated in creating and enforcing rules. Teachers, for example, frequently explained how particular rules promoted student welfare in creating a place conducive to learning (Hayward, 1999; see also P. Eckert, 1989).

Dr. Hayward offers instances of these approaches in her paper, but I would rather point to two experiences of my own that seem exactly right here. In one, an urban high school, I was talking to a colleague one morning several minutes before the start of the school day when a student came up to ask a question. Without saying: "Hello, Anthony. How are you this morning?" or "What's up, Anthony? Is there anything I can do for you?" or some such greeting—the colleague started in with the fact that he was not in proper uniform. The infraction of the rule was the first thing she saw, and in the name of the value of the rules it was necessary that the rule be adhered to. As a result, the day for both started in an adversarial way, kids versus adults, and the sort of alienation that is all too common in our schools got another boost. In contrast, not long ago I was talking to an administrator at a suburban high school. The conversation turned to discipline, and he remarked that he liked cafeteria duty because it gave him the chance to talk to kids about why it was important to behave in a reasonable way . . . that too often teachers are distracted by the fact that kids misbehave. Such moments are opportunities to talk to kids and remind them of the values that lie beneath "rules" and responsible behavior.

The differences here are crucial. We can count on kids being kids. They will misbehave. The issue is how we respond. Will we see their behavior as an act of defiance, testing our authority? Or will we see it as a chance to teach, to strengthen the student's appreciation of responsible behavior? By choosing the latter we help to set a positive atmosphere based upon respect for children.

Matters of discipline are fundamental to the tone of school-life and they are complex. I do not wish to suggest that disciplinary issues will fade away if only we are nice. Students need honest relationships with adults and that will include our disappointment. Yet, if we can hold back on seeing their behavior as deliberately out to test us, we are much more likely to catch the innocence within.[1]

Dr. Hayward found the same sort of political difference when it comes to what we teach. At the urban school, knowledge consisted of discrete matters of fact and the teacher was the keeper of this knowledge. The good student mastered this material and was not encouraged to question or inquire further about it. At the suburban school, things were very different. Learning was a matter of analyzing concepts and statements, and of devising problem-solving strategies. Questioning the material and the purpose of study was encouraged.

How should we understand these differences? They reach across a whole host of matters. Consider, for example, the not uncommon observation that students today have shorter and shorter attention spans. For some, with their eye on the mastery of discrete matters of fact and the application of algorithms, this has signaled a call to carve what we offer students into smaller and smaller bits or pursue the development of computer games to grab student attention. For

---

1   To jump to the far greater challenges of juvenile detention centers, I was heartened to read of the success of programs in Missouri. A *Baltimore Sun* article recently reported on their "homey" approach to things: "There are no handcuffs, no razor-wire fences, no uniforms, no cells . . . At the maximum-security lockup in St. Joseph, two cats, Midnight and Tigger, curl up on laps as the state's toughest teenage offenders explore the roots of their anger, weep over the acts of abusive parents and swap strategies for breaking free of gangs." The program is enormously successful (Fesperman, 2004, 5B). If prisons do not need to be like prisons, why should our schools?

others, with their eye on judgement and critical thinking, this has meant a still greater focus on classroom discussion and projects that engage students as a way to extend those attention spans.

Intriguingly, Hayward suggests these differences have a common source; that teachers and administrators at both urban and suburban schools are doing the *same* thing—responding to the pressures and perceptions of the immediate environment. In both settings teachers are working toward habits of mind they see as crucial for success: in the city it is doing what you are told, being managed; and in the suburbs it is acting independently, being a manager. However subtle this distinction might seem, it is not lost on ten-year-olds. When sharing Dr. Hayward's research with a group of elementary teachers from Baltimore City, one, a fifth grade teacher, explained that she asked her students at the beginning of the year whether they wanted to sweep floors when they grew up, or would they rather be the boss who tells others to sweep up? They all agreed they would rather be the boss. But that takes more work, she would explain. Are you willing to tackle more difficult problems? They all agreed they would, and for the rest of the year any time they were not working as hard as they ought, all she needed to do was bring out the broom.

Dr. Hayward's thesis is both plausible and harsh. It is plausible in that it is easy to see how teachers would teach what they see as central to their children's lives. It is harsh because it points to the overwhelming complexities in teaching all of our children to grow into independent, thoughtful, and productive adults.

The atmosphere and practice of a school is a function of the play of many social, historical, political and economic factors, and there are limits to what one may conclude from just a few instances. Nevertheless, Dr. Hayward's account resonates. How we regard students, the purpose of schooling, and the character of knowledge all matter. That is the real burden of this book. It matters how we talk to children.

Chapter 2

On the Shift from Answers to Arguments

It was some time ago now when my son came home from school and reported around the dinner table that he had learned something new, something that was neat. The moon did not shine by its own light. Instead, it reflected the light of the sun. "Ah," I sighed to myself, "it has started already." You see, I knew he didn't really understand it. It was just an isolated fact. Something he had been given and made to feel proud about having. That's why, after we had talked about things for a while, I asked him: "But, Pete, if that's so, how can we see the moon at night, when the sun isn't even there?"

He hadn't thought about that, and before long we were upstairs. I stood in the hall with a mirror and he was in the bathroom, looking at the reflection of a bedroom light he could not see directly. This set-up suggested that if the moon reflected the sun's light at night, the moon was so far away it could see the sun even though we couldn't. Here, for a five-year old, was the difference between a fact and an argument, a difference that made the heavens something you could play around with—something you could understand.

Why did this happen? Why hadn't Pete's teacher explored what it meant to see the moon as a reflecting body? It certainly was not that he didn't understand the relative positions of the sun and the moon. This was not really a content issue. It was what we may think of as a pedagogical content issue, an issue about what is involved when we teach material (see Gess-Newsome and Lederman, 2001). What does it mean to look at the world this way? What puzzles does it raise? What prior notions does it draw upon? What further notions does it suggest? These are critical questions for a teacher. They prepare us to offer understanding rather than knowledge. That is, when Pete and I put that mirror down, when we left that conversation, he did not "know" more. He understood. It was still the case that the moon reflected the light of the sun. This he had "known" already. But now, he could appreciate what this distinction meant.

"D.Q.?"

"Yes."

"You know, I never thought about it before, but why do we think the moon isn't a star?"

"That's a good question, Sancho. Do you have any ideas?"

"Is it because it's colder at night, even when the moon is out?"

"That's a good idea, but couldn't the moon radiate light without radiating heat?"

"I guess . . . I just never heard of cold light."

"Well, you might try an experiment. All it takes is a thermometer. We know that on a hot summer's day, it is cooler in the shade. Test it. See what the difference in temperature is in the shade and out in the light. Then do this at night. See if there is a difference between the glow of a full moon and a moon shadow. That would be a start anyway."

"Come to think of it, if the moon is reflecting sunlight, why wouldn't it be warm? Don't they have camp stoves that cook with reflected light?"

"Another good question. Things open up pretty quickly, once you start looking carefully. But let's go back to your first question: why do we think the moon is a mirror and not a lamp, reflecting light rather than its own source of light? Can you think of any central differences between the sun and the moon as we see them?"

"Other than temperature . . . I don't know. The moon has phases."

"That's right, Sancho, and that's all you need. If the moon were a star, even a 'cold' star, then it would always present a full face the way the sun does."

"So the idea that 'the moon is a mirror' isn't really a separate fact, it follows from the basic notion that it goes through the cycle from new moon to full moon and back again."

"You bet, and there's another important difference between answers and arguments. Arguments tend to connect up all sorts of facts into a bundle. That's why it is so much easier to remember stuff that you understand. Instead of a list of discrete items, everything seems to tie together."

The difference between answers and arguments was emphasized by the National Research Council (NRC, 1996) in its report on science education. The NRC is a prestigious body of master scientists, and they regularly examine issues and present their findings to the federal government. This important study examined the elements of pedagogy in the sciences and laid out content standards for the full sweep from kindergarten to twelfth grade. In the introductory essay on science teaching we are told there should be:

i.   less emphasis on discrete knowledge and more on scientific understanding and reasoning (100);

ii. less emphasis on demonstrating and verifying content and more on investigating and analyzing scientific questions (113);

iii. less emphasis on exploration and experiment and more on argument and explanation (113).

These are welcome statements. They rest education upon a natural foundation where the child learns science through the power of reason. This is a decided change at the deepest levels of the aims and practices of science teaching, and it presents a radical challenge to our work. At least it should. There is a profound difference between right answers and right reasoning. The sciences are a long haul from common sense, and the hallmark theories of modern science are stridently counterintuitive. Ordinary language everywhere calls a sunrise "sunrise" not "earth-spin." Atoms are real objects, but we cannot experience them; fire can be experienced, but is not a real thing. And evolution? The overwhelming experience of us all is that nature reproduces its own kind. Cats have kittens, dogs have puppies, and acorns give us oak trees. In these and a myriad of other examples, the problem is the same. There is a well-formed answer, but the way to get there is tough, especially for young students; and the careful exercise of reason may well lead them to very different places.

"D.Q., are you saying that right answers aren't important? You say the most outrageous things. It can't all be arbitrary. Don't we want our students to build an effective understanding of modern science? Don't they need to start with a solid foundation and then put things together? How could right answers not be important?"

"Whoa. That's quite a battery of questions, but the answer is 'yes.' 'Right answers' are not important; we 'do' want students to gain an understanding of the sciences, and a 'good start' is important. But, let me offer a different building metaphor, instead of foundations.

"Do you remember the story of the three little pigs? One pig builds a house of straw; but when it is challenged by the wolf, the straw gives way. Another pig builds a house of sticks. This is a better house. Sticks are stronger than straw. Nevertheless, the demands on it are too great, and the house collapses. There is yet another pig who builds a house of bricks, and bricks are stronger still. So strong that, so far, they have met the challenge. This rebuilding metaphor is a better way to think about education than foundations.

"Consider for a moment, the way we teach our students to become good readers. When we teach a child to read, we may have in mind that he or she will be reading Dickens, Shakespeare, Faulkner, and Ellison by the time they reach high school or college. But we don't get them there by teaching them the vocabulary they will need then. Can you imagine that? Instead, we offer them good stories, and over time these stories grow richer and more complex. We may start with Leo Leonni or Ezra Jack Keats. And as they give way to Beverly Cleary, and Beverly Cleary to Jill Paton Walsh or Walter Dean Myers, we move children toward more demanding work. That is what we should be doing in the sciences. Each level should tell its own story, taking on the deepest issues, pushing matters as hard as they can. This amounts to a natural philosophy. Kids should be building an understanding of their world, not preparing themselves so that later they may receive one."

"It makes sense when you lay it out this way, but it sure is wild to think that the best way to get to understand science doesn't involve making sure kids are securing right answers."

"We're going to work on this some more, Sancho, but the key idea is to build the best house you can at each level."

On Understanding

Let's play out the differences between knowing and understanding a bit. I can recall a conversation with a second-grade teacher, my wife as it happens, about water study. It seemed her students could understand evaporation but had a lot more trouble with condensation. That didn't make a lot of sense to me. The two are so closely bound that to know one was to know the other, and I suspected that her students had simply seen evaporation as a kind of magic: a word signifying that water disappears. After all, evaporation is really a pretty strange thing. We all know if I spill a glass of water it falls to the floor. Water is a heavy body. What would ever make it go up? Certainly, if I dropped my keys to the floor, we would not expect them to end up in the clouds.

Condensation is exactly what you would need to convince yourself that the water had not simply disappeared. But think how complex and delightful a set of questions it raises . . . You could start with a story. You had gone to a junk shop and found a special glass. It was old and magical. Like other glasses, you could pour water into it and it would hold the water, but at the same time, it would also let water pass right through! Then proceed to pour cold water into a glass. As condensation forms you announce: See the water has passed right through the glass. Here is a lovely perplexity, a direct and testable proposition that is likely to provoke protest.

How could you show that the water did not go through the glass? What if we used Kool-Aid? Would the water on the outside now be grape-flavored? If not, could the glass have acted as a filter, purifying the water as it had passed? What is a filter? How does it work? If I have a fine filter, could I filter out the sugar from the Kool-Aid? Or the color? How small can the holes in a filter get?

There's an interesting aside here. Back towards the end of the nineteenth century, researchers had developed filters that could catch bacteria. Now bacteria are very small, as small as 10^{-5}m. A typical meter stick or ruler will divide centimeters into little markings a millimeter apart. That is 10^{-3}m. Bacteria would be about one-hundredth the size of those little spaces. It turns out bacteria can be seen in microscopes, but they are right at the limit. You can't see things smaller than bacteria. Light doesn't bounce off of them in a coherent fashion. It's a little like riding your bike across a field. You can work your way by small objects and only bounce off of larger ones. In order to "see" objects smaller than bacteria, you would have to use more sensitive light—that is, light with smaller wavelengths. In the 1950s Watson and Crick were able to work out the structure of DNA, even though DNA is much smaller than bacteria, because they used X-rays and the wavelengths of X-rays are much smaller than those of visible light. Anyway, in the 1890s researchers were able to show that some disease-causing agents could pass through very fine filters. They were so small you could not see them. We know them as viruses today. These filters that could catch bacteria, but not viruses, were made of porcelain and the liquid would have to be forced through. The water wouldn't flow through on its own.

Here, indeed, was a magic container that could hold water, but could also be made to let it pass.

To get back to the main question, we have all been taught that the water on the glass actually comes from the air. What if someone suggested this was the case, how could you show it? After all, we can't see the water in the air. What if we took the air away, putting the glass with cold water in a vacuum, would the glass still become wet?

The point here is that evaporation and condensation, like so many notions in the sciences, can be reduced to a deceptively simple schema. We have all seen that diagram with the big arrow sweeping from a lake up to the clouds. But we do so at a great cost. Students end up being confident about notions that really make no sense to them. Things need to be batted around and taken seriously, just like with Jesse and Pete. As this happens, the real practice of scientific reasoning is displayed and exercised and becomes the real carrier of the learning. The "medium becomes the message," and so what children really learn is that characteristic critical thinking, that rule of reason so important to the sciences, and that's well worth having in your pocket.

This sketch of how evaporation and condensation might be explored is not offered in the spirit of a series of hands-on demonstrations. It is rather a scenario of how a class exploration might unfold. Teaching is interactive. As we talk to our students we are carrying on a dialogue with a host of voices. Whether we are talking about masses, molecules, or mammals, we aren't simply laying the material out. We are ferreting out the sensibilities of the many minds in the classroom and trying to connect with them. Some will respond and let us know where they are and what they think. Others will remain silent and so we often have to guess what they are doing with what we say. That's where the constructs come in, our projections of what kinds of things kids might be thinking, and our job is to address those constructs as we talk about the material.

This task is intimidating, and the more you think about the host of ways kids will be responding to what you say, the more incredible it becomes. The classroom is an elaborate conversation, a dialogue with dozens of voices. To really engage all these voices means finding a way to harness them all to the same set of issues. To do this, we need to present with some clarity a real problem, something that is perplexing. Student voices now can be seen essentially as conjectures about how best to explain the problem. As these voices are expressed they need to be attended to, shaped, linked to experiences, and translated into experiments. This is the key formative judgement of the teacher: how best to frame the ideas raised in a collective examination of a problem. It is the collective examination—the problem the class is addressing—that provides the meaning of class activities and experiments. To run through such activities without this context is to present an idle exercise that leaves the student guessing what the aim is.

The importance of context was emphasized in a set of studies put together by Roger Osborne and Peter Freyberg, *Learning in Science* (1985). They carefully traced the limitations of what is commonly referred to as "hands-on" inquiry. They interviewed students as they were engaged in various "hands-on" experiments. The explanations students offered about these activities and what they show are stunning. Students often don't know what they are doing or why. In one chapter, "Facing Mismatches in the Classroom," Ross Tasker and Peter Freyberg examined sixteen classroom lessons, interviewing students at length, and found that frequently pupils did not appreciate the purpose or the meaning of the lesson intended by the teacher. Similarly, students frequently saw lessons as isolated events where teachers had seen them as clearly linked by a scientific concept or principle. Such disconnects erode the value of these activities, and in many cases students become so alienated from the purpose of the activity that they cope by doing and writing what they think the teacher wants, without any serious effort actually to understand what's going on (Osborne and Freyberg, 1985, pp. 66–77). In such cases, what is clear is that the phenomena do not speak for themselves.

Having documented the lack of clarity in the classroom, Tasker and Freyberg closed their study with several suggestions about how to ensure that hands-on lessons would be meaningful—that the purpose would be clear and the character of the argument and of the activity equally clear. They offer a host of strategies. Students may be broken into groups, for example, where they would jointly examine the issues being addressed and the design features of the lab activity; or individual instructions for the activity may be placed on cards and scrambled, so that students must arrange them and explain why their chosen sequence makes the most sense. Checklists are offered, with a host of items for the teacher and students to consider. All in all, the strategies offered have the essential goal of ensuring that students will be engaging in activities where the issues and arguments are clear (Osborne and Freyberg, 1985, pp. 77–80).

However, I am sceptical of such tactics. Clarity is hard earned. It's not just a matter of getting the protocol right. We are not baking brownies. Any activity or experiment, to be effective, has to grow out of the common space of the classroom. It's not enough that we would turn the page of a text and so now find ourselves doing exercise 8.6, or whatever. Somehow a sense of purpose has to emerge out of the collective examination of an issue. That is why perplexity is so important. A puzzle is an engine. This is what John Dewey meant when he wrote: "Demand for the solution of a perplexity is the steadying and guiding factor in the entire process of reflection" (1997, p. 11). This is not only true for individual reflection. It is also true for the collective. Puzzles generate motion—different points of view, different ideas. Given a good puzzle, the real job is to direct and nurture the flow of issues and ideas. If we go back to evaporation, I've had discussions where students have offered any number of ideas about how water could rise. Some have seen evaporation as water turning into air. Others, drawing upon the language of the sciences, have spoken of chemical changes, as water molecules break into hydrogen and oxygen. Still others have seen it as a physical change. Liquid water becomes a gas, and then, drawing on the hypothesis that all gases would float, the now gaseous water rises into the sky. All of these notions lend themselves to a host of different experiments and conversations.

In such a setting, experiments are not activities that exhibit or display the right answer. They are not ways of getting students to label experience with the myriad of technical terms of the sciences: "This is the nucleus of the cell," "This is an igneous rock," or "This is a precipitate." Instead, experiments become ways to resolve conjectures. They are natural expressions of the examination of a problem. This takes us right back to the role of wonder in the sciences. What is so extraordinary about evaporation and condensation is not what you can see. It is, instead, the play of your imagination; what your mind's eye can "see" as it is led by reason. We need to spend less time giving our students' hands something to do and a lot more time giving their minds something to play with.

"Could you 'play' this out for me just a bit, D.Q.?"

"Certainly, Sancho. Let's take the notion that when water evaporates it is separating into hydrogen and oxygen, and then these rise because they are gases. Think about how things hold onto one another. Do you think the bonds that hold oxygen and hydrogen together in a water molecule are stronger or weaker than the bonds that act between molecules?"

"I know that water molecules are pretty sticky. I remember being amazed by how high you can get water to rise above the level of a glass, if you add it carefully. And I've seen people get needles to sit on top of water, though I'm not very good at doing that myself."

"But you're a lot heavier than a needle, Sancho!"

"I meant . . . never mind. The point is, I still don't know how this compares to the bonds between oxygen and hydrogen."

"Right. How do we get a handle on those chemical bonds that hold individual water molecules together? What happens when you put your hand into a bowl of water? If the bonds that hold a molecule together are stronger than those between molecules, then you would be breaking the link between the sticky molecules. But if the inter-molecular bonds were stronger, then you would be breaking up the link between oxygen and hydrogen within the molecule. What do you think?"

"Well, I can put my hand through water pretty easily. If I were breaking up water molecules and releasing oxygen and hydrogen, wouldn't I see bubbles?"

"Sounds good. What could we do to test your idea?"

"We could just stir water and see if we get a lot of bubbles. Or, we could get two glasses of water. One we would leave alone, and the other we'd keep stirring and see if it evaporates quicker."

"Those are good. Do you know any way to test more directly to see if oxygen and hydrogen are being released?"

"No . . . wait, don't they talk about hydrogen as a fuel?"

"You bet, Sancho. Hydrogen is highly flammable. So you could test for it by holding a match above a glass of water as you stir it around, and see if it explodes."

"Neat."

"The point is, Sancho, that as you begin to explore collectively the phenomena all around you, there are all sorts of experiments that make sense to do, and that is the best way to guarantee that students will appreciate the purpose of their work. Here, by the way, is the relevance of the three little pigs. You can explore this question with the whole range of students, from the youngest to the oldest. At each level, there would be a reasonable answer to the question raised, independent of whether you had arrived at the definitive answer of modern science. But let's get back to the text."

How can you assess students at the end of this sort of exploration? What do you test them on? What are they supposed to be learning? Whatever the flow of discussion, ideas, and experiments in any particular class, there is a strikingly natural way to frame what students are supposed to be doing: their job is to reconstruct the flow of the argument. What was the initial puzzle? What experiences and experiments were used to support inferences and common understandings? What issues were encountered? How did problems shift? In this way, students learn to argue staying close to the phenomena. You are holding students accountable for how they and the class had made sense of things. This, in turn, lays the weight of assessment on expository essays, on talk, as opposed to definitions, identifications and other more particular aspects of the material.

To summarize, I am proposing that the first step in the classroom be the puzzle that preceded the answer. As teachers, this means we need to take a fresh look at the world of science that we teach and rediscover the puzzles and profound issues within it. We need to raise questions, explore interesting phenomena, and examine with our students the kinds of ideas and arguments involved in how we understand a candle burning, a pendulum swinging, a ball rolling down a ramp, or milk being drawn up a straw, etc. As we do this, we need to be mindful that we must listen to children, to tap into their natural curiosity about these things.

We also need to push.

On Pushing

As the focus of teaching shifts from answers to arguments and the student's ability to make sense of things, so the ability to fashion an argument becomes increasingly central. In a lovely work, *The Origins of Scientific Thought*, Giorgio de Santillana explains that the Latin root of "nature" and the Greek root of "physics" were both agricultural terms. They referred to the internal *push* of plants, as they broke through the soil and asserted their place in the scheme of things. To seek the nature of things was thus to seek their internal push— that agency that made them what they were (de Santillana, 1961, p. 27). We preserve this vital sense of agency when, for example, we explain someone's behavior by attributing it to his or her nature. It is just this organic push that we seek to cultivate in our students: a growing sense of the critical processes of scientific analysis, of where notions come from and of how they connect, and an increasing sophistication in their sense of play and experimentation.

However, the elements, the qualities of "pushing" are hard earned. How can we cultivate this sense of agency, the independent, well-argued criticism that characterizes the sciences? One thing we can do is take advantage of the history of the sciences. I do not mean here an interesting story about Isaac Newton's childhood or how many metals Edison tested for the light bulb. The history of science affords us a wealth of instances of the push of reason. Everywhere you turn, every idea in the sciences is the result of a whole chain of problems, conjectures, experiments, agreement on new theories and then new problems, new conjectures, and new theories. The motivating force in all of this has been Jesse's "I wonder what it is." Not a wonder at nature's might and complexity, but at the human imagination's might and complexity. This is the same shift embedded in the urging of the National Research Council that there should be "less emphasis on exploration and experiment and more on argument and explanation" (NRC, 1996, p. 113). The real objects of study are the arguments.

Aristotle did not believe the world was made of atoms. Ptolemy did not think the Earth was a planet. Cuvier did not think life had evolved. Laplace did not think heat was a form of energy. The list goes on and on. Each of these important figures in the history of the sciences had well-formed reasons for holding views we later rejected, and rejecting views we now hold. Their arguments are a wonderful resource as we try to unearth what it means to look at the world the way we do. Such "archaeological" excavations are not idle pursuits of the curious. They are the scaffolding that leads to the present understanding. They reveal both what the modern understanding really means and what science and scientific explanation are really about.

This use of the history of science is so critical that we should push matters by sketching an example. Suppose we want students to understand evolution. We have not done an especially good job with this, given that the many efforts to take evolution out of the curricula or match it with creationist and biblically minded understandings have been peopled by folk who presumably had biology when they were in high school. So let's consider how the history of science would inform our approach.

On Cuvier and Darwin

Evolution is not a "fact." I mean this in a pedagogical sense. For our students to understand what we offer them, we need to give them a sense for where it comes from—what arguments carry it—and what issues it raises when we look at the world this way. If we go back to virtually the first science texts, the writings of Aristotle, we find an intriguing feature. Aristotle would give two introductions to a topic. He would start with what others had had to say about things—Thales, Democritus, Empedocles, or Plato (see, for example, the discussion of the shape of the Earth in Book II of *On the Heavens*, part 13). He would comment as he went along, pointing out issues and failings, using this opportunity to define what he saw as the central problems. Then he would offer his own answer, which he would offer from first principles. Aristotle's sensibilities here are exactly right, and the use of both an "historical" or "genetic" account and a "formal" account addresses an important aspect of any "answer." The formal system on its own is a fragment. It needs a context to be understood. By offering us that context, Aristotle can get us to see what he has been thinking about. That he chose to present his context in an historical fashion is also telling; for the views and issues of those who came before him constitute the fullest context for his work. It is the question his system addresses.

In giving evolution the context it deserves, I am looking to get students to consider the arguments beneath the facts. The tack I propose is an historical one, emphasizing the interaction between alternative understandings. Today the study of evolution examines the workings of molecules such as nucleotides and transfer-RNA. But how can the dance of such minute particles be the key to the sweep of life's history, a sweep that includes the rise and fall of those great beasts of the Jurassic, as well as the differences between humans and monkeys? How did we come to locate the processes of evolutionary change in genetic processes within cells?

To answer this question we need to shift back to Darwin's work of more than a century ago. But even as we take this step, it is clear that it is not yet the context we require; for what we need is the context for Darwin's work. And so we push even further back to the master work of the great French scientist, Georges Cuvier.

Cuvier and Design

Though accomplished in several domains, Cuvier was, above all, a biologist. It was his mastery of the workings of life that enabled him to transform the study of the fossil record—so much so that he was able to establish a new science, vertebrate paleontology. I have already described my own encounter with this science and my wonder at Bakker's ability to see dinosaur vertebrae in those two rocks. Cuvier was the original master of this science, and we may appreciate the drama of his ability to breathe life into lifeless rocks by turning to the writings of Honore Balzac, the great French novelist of the early nineteenth century. In a passage from *The Wild Ass' Skin*, written in 1831, Balzac speaks of the immensity of time and space as you read the geological writings of Cuvier and of how you hang as if suspended by a magician's wand over the illimitable abyss of the past. Cuvier, wrote Balzac,

> has reconstructed past worlds from a few bleached bones; has rebuilt cities, like Cadmus, with monsters' teeth; has animated forests with all the secrets

of zoology gleaned from a piece of coal; has discovered a giant population from the footprints of a mammoth.

(Balzac, 1906, p. 19)

This enthusiasm for the magic of resurrecting the many lost worlds of life's past would soon translate into great halls at museums filled with the skeletons of lumbering beasts of a size and form beyond the common imagination. But we must ask how Cuvier was able to do this, and our answer takes us to his general approach to life and design.

The young Cuvier, like other naturalists for over 2,000 years, would have been introduced to the study of life through the writings of Aristotle. Aristotle had defined the essential character of life, laying out those basic categories so familiar to all of us, and the grounds for understanding them. There were mammals, birds, reptiles, fish, and worms—natural groups that rested upon clusters of properties. A mammal, for example, is distinguished by several leading characteristics. It is warm-blooded; its skin is covered by hair or fur; its young are born alive and are nurtured by their mother. On these grounds, Aristotle argued that dolphins and bats are mammals, despite their evident similarities to fish and birds. He was a most astute and perceptive thinker.

Cuvier took a dramatically different approach to these matters. With the eye of an architect, he classified animals on structural principles. Symmetry was a key element here. Some animals have a radial symmetry, such as starfish. Others have a cylindrical symmetry, such as round worms. Still others, like humans, have a bilateral symmetry, where opposite sides correspond to one another. These principles of symmetry get at how the animal is organized, what its *system* is, how its organs are distributed, and how the major activities of life— such as movement, breathing, digestion, and reproduction—are accomplished. We see here in Cuvier's work the beginnings of that profound shift from the science of natural history to the science of biology, a shift from feature to mechanism (Cuvier, 1813; see also, W. Coleman, 1964).

It had been decided before Cuvier's day, that is, before the start of the nineteenth century, that fossils were broken monuments of ancient life, but it was the genius of Cuvier that gave them that life. He could do so because, like Sherlock Holmes, he could make a fragment speak to the whole. As Holmes could see the health, history, and habits of a man in his hat, so could Cuvier see the corresponding history and habits of an ancient beast in fossilized teeth and bits of bone.

Cuvier's new science rested upon a theory of the coordination of parts. Each anatomical part of an animal pointed to the whole. A tooth implied a diet, a diet a set of habits and related dispositions that were supported by coordinated adaptations in jaws, shoulders, backbone, means of locomotion, etc. From any of these, inference could be made to another, and so on to the whole. Each fragment was representative. Such inferences rested upon Cuvier's mastery of comparative anatomy, and his intuitions for the rules of nature's architecture and the limited ways in which structure could satisfy function.

"D.Q.?"

"Yes—"

"I think I get 'nature's architecture,' but could you trace an example?"

"Sure thing, Sancho. There are a host of general notions that just make a lot of sense. Grazing animals have hooves; broad, flat teeth for crushing plants; and sturdy backbones to hold up their large frames; while hunting animals such as lions and tigers and bears have clawed feet, sharp teeth for ripping flesh, and flexible backbones to allow for leaping, pouncing, and the like. But here's a better instance, a lovely tale Cuvier himself tells of examining the fossilized remains of a small mammal, where only part of the skull could be seen. He announced that it was an ancient marsupial, much to the surprise of those assembled. It had been thought that the only structural differences between marsupial and placental mammals were the pelvic bones, and you could not see them in this fossil. Cuvier then cut away the surrounding matrix rock and sure enough, the pelvic bones were those of a marsupial.

"Here's where you can see Cuvier's genius. A critical difference between marsupial and placental mammals is the whole birthing process. In a marsupial, the young are born 'early' and are so small their passage through the birth canal does not present a problem to the mother. Adult kangaroos, for example, are about our size, but their new-born are as small as a little finger. Things are very different for placental mammals. Their ability to keep the fetus until it is more fully developed makes passing through the birth canal a truly pressing problem, especially because of the head. If the skull of the fetus were somehow collapsible, birth would be much easier on the mother. And this is exactly the case. The skulls of placental mammals are divided into several plates that only tightly knit together after birth. That's why you have to be so careful with the 'soft spot' of a new-born. The same sort of thing happens with placental cheekbones. They are shaped so that one part is able to slide over another. Thus the skull is less rigid and can squeeze through the birth canal" (Rudwick, 1972, p. 113).

"I get it. Cuvier knew this and could see that the tiny fossil skull lacked these sorts of features. So it was a marsupial."

"That's right, Sancho. Pretty neat, eh?"

At the heart of Cuvier's work lies the brute perception that life is "high-tech." The system of an organism is so complex, the coordination of its parts so intricate that there is no room for play. Just as, in contemporary terms, you could not put the fuel-injector from a PT Cruiser into a Volkswagen Beetle, so the various parts and their arrangement in different species are unique. To modify any one part would require changes in each adjoining part, and so on throughout the entire organism. Hence, any theory of evolution suggesting that organisms have slowly modified over time must be wrong. You cannot tinker. For life to succeed, all of its parts must be "in synch," and this was a most complex and subtle matter. There was no room for the odd alteration; for to modify any part significantly was to set into motion a whole chorus of adjustments and so, in effect, to instance an entirely new design. Hence, for Cuvier, the "motion" from simple to complex evidenced in the fossil record could not have been a movie; it was a sequence of "stills."

History by Stages

Instead of a theory of gradual development where life forms would evolve from one type into another, Cuvier saw the history of life as a series of epochs where sets of animals flourished and then were replaced by successive types. The key to this theory was the problem of extinction. Before Cuvier, the fossilized remains of exotic beasts had been seen as unlikely forms that had more or less naturally failed. But Cuvier's reconstructions of these animals had shown them to have been perfectly viable, since they were built according to the same principles of anatomy that characterized existing life. If ancient grazing animals had been built the right way, with large molars for grinding plants and vertebrae that interlocked to support their heavy torsos; if prehistoric predators had claws and sharp teeth for ripping flesh, why then were they no longer around? The answer was catastrophic violence. These ancient beasts had been caught off guard by events of cataclysmic proportion—mountains raised and seas violently displaced. This violence brought an end to one epoch, and wiped the slate clean for the next (Cuvier, 1813, p. 24).

Darwin and the Process of Change

This was the broad context for Darwin's work, a context that highlights several features of his approach to the history of life. First and foremost is Darwin's dramatic denial of Cuvierian catastrophes. Instead of a succession of steps, punctuated by dramatic violence, Darwin offers changes so gradual they are literally indiscernible. Further, nowhere in the *Origin of Species* does Darwin examine the fossil record. Though we are accustomed to find the "Hall of Evolution" at a natural history museum filled with the sweep of life from trilobites to the great beasts of the Jurassic and on to the prototypes of the modern lions, tigers, and bears, that is not the "Hall" Darwin gives us. Instead, we find in the house of Darwin a menagerie of short-legged sheep, pigeons, and of course, the finches and tortoises of the Galapagos Islands (Darwin, 1859).

Cuvier is the reason for this.

Right at the beginning, it is important to recognize how completely evolution flies in the face of ordinary experience. Nature *is* enormously regular. Carrot seeds do, with extraordinary regularity, grow into carrots. How are we to understand this fact alongside the notion that life has evolved? If carrots produce carrots, if every dog we know of has given birth to puppies and cats to kittens, then how is it possible that life has evolved?

In *On the Origin of Species* Darwin did not deny "plant a carrot, get a carrot." He could not. It is the overwhelming experience of us all. What he did was examine with great care just what it means to be a carrot—or a frog, or a dog—not by examining the physiology or comparative anatomy of these forms, but by questioning membership in the set. Are all carrots identical? Of course not. But just how much room is there, Darwin asked, between the not identical but still very much like the others?

This is what makes the fossil record so misleading. It everywhere shows "stills" rather than moving pictures. We find the remains of various animals or plants. They are either so similar as to be the same species or they are not. We could never find so rich a succession of intermediate forms as to actually *see* evolution. "Plant a carrot, get a carrot" guarantees that we *cannot* see it. The changes are too gradual.

So instead of fossils, Darwin turned to short-legged sheep.

For Darwin, the fact of domestic breeding establishes the pliability of life. How has it been possible for farmers and breeders over the years to produce such distinctive varieties of animals, he asked? Whether it was sheep, horses, pigeons, cattle, corn, or carrots, Darwin saw in domestic breeding a wedge between the clarity of "plant a carrot, get a carrot" and the play of generations. Here were clear instances of the modification of a population.

In this way, Darwin shifted the problem, moving the discussion from the fossil record, on the one hand, and the physiology of life, on the other, to heredity. He was intrigued by the complex way one generation is connected to the next. Inheritable traits are a kind of toolkit living things have with which to cope with life's demands. This shift is precisely why the work surrounding DNA and molecular biology has been so closely connected to evolution and the broadest sweep of the history of life. Darwin's approach to the history of life was as a process of change.

Darwin saw the evolution of life in the wild as analogous to the modification of domestic species. He called it "natural selection." Nature selects by virtue of a struggle for survival, which drastically trims a population to those few most fit. They breed the next generation. Natural selection is thus able to modify a population's profile in a subtle but steady fashion, much as farmers are able to modify their stock. This aspect of Darwin's argument is widely known and appreciated. Here, in the words of the poet, Alfred Tennyson is "nature red in tooth and claw" ("In Memoriam", 1850, canto lvi). Nature is tight, and the struggle for survival is so intense that only a hearty few live long enough to produce young. The same two elements apply as were central in domestic selection. Each generation begins with a broad range of varieties. "Life" then trims this population, selecting the few who will breed the next generation.

A Problem and an Initial Solution

Thus, Darwin's argument rests on the proposition that there is a naturally occurring variation in wild populations. Yet, when we look we don't see it. In fact, it is not evidently there. The robins in your backyard, the squirrels in the park, the great host of plants and animals "out there" are all remarkably true to type. Both Cuvier and Darwin knew this. Cuvier explained it by suggesting that those species that had been domesticated had been unusually variable in their "superficial" characteristics . . . color, shape, size, etc. That is why wolves could be domesticated into the extraordinary range of dog breeds—from toy poodles to St. Bernard's—but zebra and deer and foxes never were. Darwin had to take an altogether different tack. Having devised a general argument that allowed for the steady evolution of life from pond scum to people by loosening up the absolute fixity of "plant a carrot, get a carrot," he came to a basic obstacle. If there is no evident variation "out there" for Nature to act upon, the analogy between domestic and natural selection breaks down.

Darwin solved this problem by saying the variation is there, we just can't see it! All the animals that differed from their parents had not been fit for the environment in which their parents had been successful, and so they had died. In Darwin's world, it's not a good idea to be weird. So, naturally, since all the weird ones have died, we can't see them.

"Wait a minute, D.Q. Isn't this cheating a bit? Natural selection can only work if there is variation to act upon. To say that we cannot see this range because nature has already eliminated it, is hardly satisfying. Or do we simply posit that individuals will differ because that's the way things are?"

"No, you are quite right Sancho. There is a sleight of hand here, at least as things stand now. Let's look at things from the perspective of a good Cuvierian. A Cuvierian would hold that all the members of a species in the wild are essentially identical, and that some survived and others were killed, not because they differed in some critical respect, but because of the play of fortune. It was just bad luck. Whoever survives would have the same species traits and so carry on the species in good form. No evolution."

"So it's not just that individuals within species differ from one another; for evolution to work their differences must somehow be deep and directly connected to their survival."

"That's right, Sancho. Think of a deck of cards. Have you ever tried flicking them one at a time into a hat?"

"Yeah, but I'm not very good at it."

"No, neither am I. Only a small number of cards actually land in the hat. The others fly off, one way or another. You wouldn't be tempted to conclude that the ones that successfully landed on the target had been fundamentally different from the others. One card is essentially like any other. The difference in success was just a matter of luck, the play of this and that. Our good Cuvierian would offer that this is equally the case with robins and mice, or lions, tigers, and bears."

"So, how could Darwin show that there were individual differences and that they were both deep and really counted for survival?"

"That's where the finches of the Galapagos Islands come in. They lent Darwin's analogy between domestic breeding and life in the wild some direct empirical content. It wasn't all just a card trick."

A Stronger Solution

In 1831, having completed his undergraduate work at Cambridge, the young Darwin secured a position as naturalist aboard the H.M.S. *Beagle*, a ship of the Royal Navy. He was, in a sense, a Mr. Spock—resident scientist for an exploratory voyage. The *Beagle* would take Darwin around the world, though the bulk of the 5 years would be spent mapping South American coastal waters and inland resources. The Galapagos archipelago was simply a stop on their way home across the Pacific. What Darwin found there was an extraordinary array of unusual animals: cormorants that could not fly, iguanas that fed on seaweed, tortoises of great bulk, and a surprising number of unique varieties of finch (Darwin, 1845, Chapter xvii; see also A. Moorehead, *Darwin and the Beagle*, 1970).

The finch is a remarkably successful class of bird. Continents are loaded with varieties. Sparrows, for example, are finches; as are cardinals, canaries, and the purple finch, which is a delightful variety here in Baltimore. To have met with finches is by itself not at all surprising. It is among the single-most successful kind of bird. What was surprising was that there were so many *weird* ones.

Generally speaking, finches are seed-eating birds, with small conical beaks. The twenty or so varieties Darwin found on the Galapagos, however, included some outrageous beaks and associated diets and habits—outrageous, that is, for a finch. Some, for example, were woodpecker-like! On a small set of not very hospitable volcanic islands about 600 miles off the Ecuadorian coast, Darwin had found a greater variety of finch than was known across the major continents of the world. How come?

One possibility was that finches had simply been distributed that way, with this small, intense pocket of finch eccentricity tucked away on the islands. Darwin set this aside as artificially cutting off an interesting question. Instead he sought some account of how this might have come to be. Perhaps, he conjectured, an original pair of finches—an Adam and Eve equivalent—had somehow been blown out to sea; finches would not be likely to look for islands— they are not long-distance fliers and ocean waters are not filled with the promise of seed. But caught in a storm and tossed about, they may have taken a wrong turn toward home and found themselves, instead, lucky to make it to these islands. Finches were the only birds on the islands—not counting the curious walking cormorants. But how could that single, "ordinary" pair have become such an interesting variety of varieties?

When he first wrote up an account of his voyage, he offered no answer. The finches of the Galapagos were an interesting observation (Darwin, 1845). Fifteen years later, however, in *On the Origin of Species*, Darwin knew precisely what these birds represented. They were the weird ones that had not died.

In the absence of competing types of bird, there was nothing to dampen exploration. In fact, it would soon have become an advantage to migrate from the mean. There was an abundance of food on the islands, a great untapped reservoir of seeds and other varieties of foods, with no struggle to complicate things. By hypothesis, wild populations are like domestic species, and each generation begins with a variety of characteristics. Weird finches would have been at the fringes, but they too would have survived. In time, as numbers grew, the center would have felt a competitive pressure. But the fringes would have been spared. As the number of seed-eaters pressed against the limits the islands could support, it would be to your advantage to be able to exploit other resources—that is, to be weird. The relative number of woodpecker-like finches, for example, would rise, as they were subject to much less in-species competition and *no* outside-of-species competition. There are no woodpeckers on the islands, so an amateur woodpecker-like finch could get along just fine even without all of the finely honed trappings of a real woodpecker. When Darwin visited the islands, this process had advanced to the point where a single pair had given rise to twenty distinct types of finch. The absence of competition had taken the lid off. Varieties had established themselves. Thus Darwin had been able to see what ordinarily could not be seen, the varieties of finch that had everywhere died on the mainland. Note: this account differs sharply from the not uncommon view that somehow Darwin had seen evolution in the Galapagos —an especially curious notion since he only spent about two weeks there.

In Conclusion

This brief sketch of Darwin's theory—really just a small part of his theory—has, I think, made clear the importance of Cuvier's work as a context. Far from a simple fact, evolution is connected to experience by a subtly woven fabric of inferences. Darwin had found a way to unravel the tight fabric of Cuvier's brilliant work by shifting the analysis from the fossil record to an array of features of the present order of things—whether it was the breeding of short-legged sheep or the curious birds of the Galapagos. Today, a century and a half later and with all of the advances in our understanding of genetic mechanisms, the issues Darwin traced are still directly relevant. Evolution is not simply the result of mutations, of changes in nucleotide sequences. Such changes have to translate into differences in structure or behavior and have to pass through the filter of life in the wild and accumulate, all within the parameters set by Cuvier's powerful analysis of the conditions for existence.

Stepping back to evaluate this context we have set for the study of evolution, we may ask if we have weakened its authority by tracing Cuvier's alternative understanding and the arguments that Darwin employed, instead of simply laying out the modern understanding as matters of fact? This is an important question. I am convinced the answer is straightforward: Not at all. By examining the reasoning that carries the argument that life has evolved, by setting evolution upon a foundation that makes sense, we heighten its authority. When evolution is more than a fact, when it becomes an argument based on a variety of considerations and a solution to otherwise puzzling phenomena, then it has a texture students can take a hold of.

"D.Q., at the close of the first chapter you explained the purpose of the interludes as a good model for more open questioning at the end of a chapter. But isn't there a place for a more direct kind of summary as well, so that people can pull things together?"

"That would be fine, Sancho, but I think you asking me questions is a better format. You might share how you see things; how you have pulled things together, and whether anything has struck you as incomplete or confusing. Right now, for instance. What would you say about this chapter?"

"First off, there's so much in the work of Cuvier and Darwin. I'd like more examples of how living things work and how we figure out what dinosaurs were like. And there's the whole thing about catastrophes, which are always neat, but then you said Darwin rejected them. He seems to have been, I don't know, kind of radical. He offered a history of life that presumably went from the first cells all the way to humans, over millions of years, and you say he didn't use fossils. I always assumed fossils showed you that life had evolved. I guess it's like you said: the material doesn't speak for itself."

"Your comments point to how intriguing this whole set of issues is. I should point out that this sketch of how one might approach teaching evolution is misleading in its brevity. To lay this host of issues out from Cuvier's masterwork and Darwin's would routinely take two months in a course I taught to ninth graders. The point here is that you can draw from the development of the sciences key arguments and issues that continue to have vitality. We would have lots of discussions, for example, about design in nature and whether it was reasonable to think that something as intricate as an eye could have evolved in a piecemeal fashion over hundreds and thousands of generations. We would have debates with sets of students defending a Cuvierian or a Darwinian perspective. And the many political and cultural issues surrounding the teaching of evolution now come to have a rich and valuable context, most especially with regard to design.

"Anything else, Sancho?"

"You talked about a lot of things, like whether right answers are important and how the story of the three little pigs is a better way to think about how our understanding grows. This set the stage for the history of science, like teaching Cuvier before doing Darwin."

"Making sense of things is hard work, Sancho. Both Cuvier and Darwin were brilliant scientists, and following their work is both demanding and exhilarating. They each were superb naturalists and drew upon a commanding mastery of facts. But what is most telling here is the play of ideas. We may remind ourselves of the recommendations of the National Research Council in its important study of science teaching. There should be less emphasis on discrete knowledge and more on scientific understanding and reasoning (NRC, 1999, p. 100). There should be less emphasis on exploration and experiment and more on argument and explanation (p. 113). This is exactly what our study of Cuvier and Darwin accomplishes. It shifts the lens of the class from the facts to the figuring out, from

answers to arguments. It does this not by setting the facts aside, but by highlighting their setting, the arguments that gave them place.

"This was a good way to pull things together, Sancho. We can return to the text now."

There are several issues that present themselves here. Most especially, what does class look like every day? What is the flow of class discussion? And what am I doing, as a teacher, as my role shifts from presenting facts to setting up the evaluation of arguments and the call to make sense of things? In short, how do I make sense of being a teacher now?

Interlude

On the Differences Between "What?" and "So What?"

One of the questions raised by the shift from answers to arguments is the question of assessment. Rather than focusing on what students have come to know, we want to engage what they have come to understand. This distinction is broadly reflected in the differences between the two questions: "What?" and "So what?" So whether we are talking about atoms, forces, evolution, or whatever, it is always on our minds that there were particular items in the nature of things that we needed to appreciate and there are also theoretical frameworks that gave these items place or are challenged by them. The distinctive variety of finch on the Galapagos Islands is a nice case in point. Suppose we asked, "What?" Students could describe what Darwin saw and how this variety was so surprising. If we asked further, "So what?", they could discuss the analogy between domestic breeding and natural selection and the importance for Darwin's argument of establishing variation in the wild. These are two very different matters, and I have found that while most students routinely rise to the challenge of the "what" question, that is not so with the "so what" question. This is my concern.

We must first acknowledge the significant distance between "what" and "so what." There are various schemas for understanding cognitive analysis. Bloom's taxonomy is perhaps the most widely recognized (Bloom, 1984). He distinguishes six levels from knowledge to evaluation, and our simple "what" and "so what" correlate with his end-points. The challenge, therefore, is significant. How do you nurture growth from comfort with the one to comfort as well with the other?

I recently taught a ninth grade science class in an urban high school. The material I taught was drawn from the same material I have taught ninth graders at Park, an independent school, for over 20 years. Many of the issues we engaged and the sorts of considerations we discussed were identical. Yet, there was a significant difference on just this matter of "what" and "so what" questions.

The call in a "So what?" question is a difficult tone to catch, as I found out when I asked students early in the school year to write an essay on the difference between a rock and dinosaur vertebrae. We had talked about the story of my having discovered dinosaur vertebrae but having to leave before I could really see that that was what they were, and it was in the material I had given them to read. Not one student in my class of twenty-two answered by taking the question to the story. Instead, they each discussed rocks and then discussed dinosaurs. Here is an example or two:

> A rock is not smooth its hard and lumpy. But a dinosaur bone is made to be smooth and looked like it its hand crafted. But a rock is made to come out any kind of way. But a bone has to be a specific way for it to aline with the other bones. And rocks just come from dirt sometime. And that's the difference between a rock and a dinosaur bone.

> The difference between a rock and a dinosaur is dinosaurs are bigger than most rocks except baby dinosaurs. Plus most rocks are older than dinosaurs. Any rock can be up to a gazillion years old, like the rock Dr. Lou showed us in class. Dinosaurs can moved around. The only way a rock can move is if you move it. That's the difference between a dinosaur and a rock.

> A dinosaur vertebra use to be a part of a living organism. A rock is just mineral and different molecules combined to make a solid rock. A dinosaur bone is organic. A dinosaur bone was created from another organic being. A rock was created from the earth. A rock was never alive.

It was clear that these were earnest students, but they had not caught the real question. This was still pretty much the case a bit later with an exam following our study of Darwin. When asked to discuss short-legged sheep and their significance, they were comfortable describing the sheep, the farmer's preference for lower stone walls, and how they had gone about breeding shorter legs. But many did not know what to say about their role in Darwin's argument or why we had discussed them.

Let me underline the phrase, "what to say." It is hard to gauge the distance between what students may appreciate as they listen and what they can reconfigure into an explanation. There is many a proverbial slip between the cup and the lip. Small distances can allow for lots to be lost. It is my sense that their difficulties reflected a discomfort with the nature of the question. If we assume that their schooling had—for the most part, if not entirely—been a matter of "knowing that" rather than coming to an understanding, then they may well not have developed that habit of mind that links items to their place in an over-all analytical framework. This is certainly what Clarissa Hayward's study (1999) would lead us to suspect.

What makes this so disconcerting is that we may assume that we are not, by and large, talking about the native ability of these children. We are talking, instead, about the consequences of not developing particular habits of mind. The ability to listen not only for "what," but also for "so what" is learned, but only if it is taught. But how do you teach this ability?

Often, it seems, people translate cognitive hierarchies into a succession of developmental plateaus. From this perspective, if a student is not yet at a given point, it is pointless to ask them to perform at this plateau. I associate this sense with Piaget, where there seems much less interest in the transition from one phase to another than with the integrity of a given phase. But there is a fundamental flaw with this approach, a flaw each of us may relate to as it rests in the experiences we each have confronted; for we have each grappled to gain mastery of language. Stop and think about the challenge facing an infant as he or she would first forge language. We are born without a mother tongue, without a predilection to speak any given language. Whatever language we first learn, we must first decide that there is some significance to the array of sounds and gestures that others are making around us. Then we must construct what that significance is. Never again do we rise to a challenge more daunting or more abstract. Here is the topmost of every cognitive developmental schema, and it is there at the earliest ages. We create the "what" through attending to some sounds and gestures and not others. We then must create the "so what" by inventing the categories that capture the "what" (see Steven Pinker, *The Language Instinct*, 1994, for a rich examination of initial language learning).

Years ago, while traveling, I found myself in the living room of a bed and breakfast for evening tea along with a family of four. Dad and the two kids were evidently playing a game, calling out three digit numbers and getting phrases like "one cow" or "two cows, one bull" in reply. After a while, I asked what they were playing, and the father suggested I try to figure it out myself. This was a trivially modest imitation of children figuring out language. I wrote things down, looked for patterns, and ultimately figured out the game they were playing. While mastering language is far more complicated, there is a basic similarity in this challenge: the role of rules. I couldn't have figured out the game simply by imitating the numbers or phrases in reply. Nor is that the way we learn language. Language learning is inventive, not imitative. This was made clear to me as a father, when my son first said "go-ed" instead of went. My younger daughter would make this same error, by the way. Neither had ever heard the past tense of go as "go-ed;" yet both offered it as the natural consequence of applying "-ed" to form the past tense. Such rule-making and related intellectual play is the very essence of the most abstract and sophisticated cognitive work. It cannot be that we only reach this summit after years of wallowing in more "concrete" valleys of reasoning. We were there at the start.

Where does this leave us? As children, we have the ability to perform a whole range of critical thinking. Certainly we lack experience and we lack the language to characterize what we are doing. But we can see things and infer from them relations, patterns, and rules. That so many would come to have difficulties with analysis and critical thinking suggests that these facilities have not been nurtured. We may go further; they have been turned off. We routinely underestimate what children can see and what they are doing as they make sense of things. Remember Jesse's glass ceiling in the sky. (Another parental aside:

watching *Sesame Street* on a day when the magic number was six, my daug watched a slalom skier whip past six flags on a ski slope. When the program went on to some other activity, she called out that she wanted more. She was ready for more, but the program hadn't trusted the attention span of children and quickly jumped to another snippet.) We have been offering our students too limited a diet. We need to feed the fuller range. We need to open things up, provide stimulating challenges, and nurture facilities and capacities that are already there. And we need to keep at it.

Analogies are crucial here, and they formed a steady part of how I framed our study. Analogies work because they do the same thing that theories do; they provide a context, a lens that gives things their place. It is not enough to say that critical thinking is important; we have to find a way to nurture it. Often students who are struggling try to memorize everything they think they are supposed to learn. This is often a daunting task. Too often teachers will try to help students deal with the mass of material students "have" to memorize by giving them little rules or tricks that are essentially arbitrary . . . such as the acronym "FOIL."

"I don't know that one, D.Q."

"It's a way to remember the steps in multiplying algebraic expressions such as (x + 5)(x + 3). Let me see, x × x is First; then x × 3 is the Outside case, 5 × x is Inside, and 5 × 3 is Last . . . FOIL."

"That's cute and it works. Isn't that good?"

"Good for what? If your goal is to have students do routine problems like this when you ask them, it might be O.K. But it doesn't foster any understanding. It's just a set of steps in keeping with the pattern set by an unrelated word."

"What would be a better way?"

"Wouldn't it be far more effective to set things up so that students figure such things out for themselves? They will know that 6 × 4 = 24. Suggest to them that 6 could be written as (1 + 5) and 4 as (1 + 3). How would they multiply (1 + 5)(1 + 3) so that they got 24? Through this they are likely to see you have to multiply each element (1 × 1) + (1 × 3) + (5 × 1) + (5 × 3). You can then substitute x for the 1's and you've figured it out. Now instead of an arbitrary rule, you've underlined how sensible mathematics is."

"O.K. I'm sure that this would work better, and I can see that making sense of things is better than simply trying to remember them."

The idea, then, is to use analogies not so much because they are easy to remember, but because they have a kind of internal logic. In the course of discussing a central concept you are likely to touch upon an array of items. Our little sketch of Darwin's work touched on imperceptible changes that accumulate over generations, as witnessed in the ability of farmers to breed short-legged sheep. In moving off of the farm and into the wild, we saw that there was an issue with variation, and this led us to the Galapagos Islands and on to the idea of "weird ones" and the tension between variation and competition. Each of these topics might involve considerable discussion and examples.

Instead of leaving the students with this array as a kind of jumble at the bottom of a purse, analogies and theories draw lines that link items, give them place, and provide a kind of flow from one to the next.

For example, we would follow our study of Darwin with a look at the sweep of the history of life, pausing to make sense of the differences between cold-blooded and warm-blooded animals and to consider whether dinosaurs were cold-blooded like reptiles or warm-blooded like birds. The exam we had at the end of this study keyed on these analogies, precisely because of the way they frame items. Among the questions on the exam were: What's the connection between cold-blooded animals and tents? What's the connection between wet sponges and bird's eggs? Why did we talk about going to the beach in the summer and the way the water feels as opposed to the sand, when we talked about fish becoming frogs?

It's interesting to see what growth there had been over the approximately 5 months of school between that first question about rocks and dinosaurs and this exam. Here are some observations from their replies to the question about cold-blooded animals and tents:

> When a cold-blooded animal go inside a tent it is cold.

> Both of them are cold because of no heat.

> Cold blooded animals and tents are the same degrees as outside.

> I guess cold blooded animals change through the weather in different times.

> Just like warm blooded are like houses, cold blooded are like tents. Whenever a temperature is at a certain degree then cold blooded creature changes to that temperature.

The only answer in the class that failed to get to the underlying commonality within the analogy is the first one above. The other four items reflect a certain confidence with this type of question, emblematic of the class as a whole. The second answer mistakenly sees cold-blooded animals as cold and the phrase "I guess" in the fourth reply suggests a spontaneity; as though they just realized how the analogy would work. The last reply nicely extended the analogy, underlining how comfortable they were with such matters.

There clearly had been growth.

A fuller instance of this growth comes from a class still later in the year. We had been talking about two different approaches to understanding what it means to be human. One way looks at what we are, our chemical machinery from brain waves and neurotransmitters to hormones and the like. Another way sees humans in historical terms. Just as we see the modern world as the outcome of historical events and movements, so humans can be understood as the outcome of what we have been and how ancestral forms coped with their settings, such as early primate adaptations to life in the trees. In exploring the chemical machinery perspective, we talked about the differences between positing that there is both a mind and a brain, and that there is only the brain. At one point, I began to talk about schizophrenia because it is wholly remarkable that a disorder that challenges our most intimate and fundamental sense of self can often be controlled by medication—that is, dissolve the right ions in the blood stream and a more coherent sense of self appears.

A student then asked how you can get schizophrenia. I paused for a moment and replied by asking her how a television breaks. Lots of students joined in the conversation, talking about the different sorts of things that had happened to televisions in their homes. After a bit, I summarized the conversation, noting that televisions can break through abuse or because they had had some defect in the first place. I then suggested that the same thing applied to schizophrenia; that we might have some traumatic experience or we might have had some genetic fault that makes us more susceptible.

I'd liked this analogy and was rather pleased with the way things had unfolded. The analogy helped to set a confident tone to the discussion. Then a student raised her hand and suggested that another way a television can break is if you leave it on too long. Perhaps it was a "be there" moment, but I was stunned. Her observation was so out of place, and by this time I was confident that the class was handling such analogies. The role of the discussion about televisions was simply as a metaphor, a way to appreciate the two factors of trauma and genetic make-up. Yet for her, there had been two distinct conversations, one about schizophrenia and the other about TVs. I acknowledged her observation and summarized the discussion, underlining the purpose of the conversation about televisions as an analogy and that we had really been talking about schizophrenia the whole time.

This is, I believe, a fundamental strategy in teaching analytical awareness. If you can talk about schizophrenia and televisions and kids can see that they are the same conversation, then you have shifted their interaction with the material to a new plane. They are not really in the conversation about televisions. Instead they are "above" it, looking down at it with their eyes on possible relationships between televisions and schizophrenia.

You, the reader, are doing precisely the same thing as you read this discussion about schizophrenia and televisions. You are looking at possible relationships between this material and the fundamental matter of the shift from answers to arguments and how you can nurture growth and comfort with analytic sensibilities. It is a very different thing to teach critical thinking than to present information, and very often analogies play a crucial role.

Nearly two centuries ago, Samuel Taylor Coleridge reflected on just what was involved as a reader settled into a work of literature. The author has to provide, Coleridge wrote, "a semblance of truth sufficient to procure for these shadows of imagination that willing suspension of disbelief for the moment, which constitutes poetic faith" (Coleridge, 1817, Chapter 14). This gives us a natural opposition. On the one hand, there is fiction, which requires a suspension of skepticism on our part. We put disbelief on hold and go with the flow. On the other hand, there is non-fiction. Here we have de Santillana's *push*, our independent assertion. We are agents. It is an agency reflected in our skepticism, our disbelief.

The heart of what is going on with critical thinking is a kind of distance from the material, so that you are routinely gauging things. That is what happens with analogies. Students are invited to stand back from the material and find some sort of structure within it that connects the two domains: in this case, televisions and schizophrenia.

Over all, one thing would seem to be clear: a science class ought not to ask students to "buy" something they did not understand. To do so would be self-contradictory. It would be asking students to treat the material being studied as if it were fiction. Yet, all too often, this is standard operating procedure in our classrooms and in our textbooks. We present the material, but lose sight that it does not speak for itself. Moreover, that is not enough. We want students to become comfortable with both "what" and "so what" questions. That is the mark that they have been agents. To get there we need to consciously nurture critical thinking.

"D.Q., you said the interludes were about cutting corners. What corners did you just cut?"

"Well Sancho, the heart of this chapter was the shift from answers to arguments, a shift that calls for a profound re-imagining of what teaching is all about. We have seen four aspects of this re-imagining:

- *The importance of problems and perplexity as the motor that drives inquiry. This was our opening discussion about wonder and the richness of reason as a guide.*
- *Changing labs from witnessing the right answer to more open investigations . . . which involves worrying less about the procedures for a given activity and more about the problem that students will investigate. In this way labs become more minds-on than hands-on.*
- *There's the rethinking of the role of the history and philosophy of science, which becomes less a matter of heroic anecdotes or making the sciences present a more human face and more a matter of laying out alternative understandings and constructs so that students can earn the modern understanding. We saw this in the brief sketch of the work of Cuvier as a key context for understanding Darwin's work.*
- *And finally, there is a basic shift in what we hold students responsible for. The standard practice in our schools today is holding students responsible for right answers. With the shift to arguments comes the shift to showing or ˙ving an idea by using phenomena to make your case. We saw this in the ˙ɔn of evaporation and condensation and in the lengthier discussion ˙ life.*

"But your question, Sancho, was about the interlude. In the interlude we picked up on this last matter of rethinking student responsibility. The difference between 'what' and 'so what' nicely captures the shift called for by emphasizing arguments over answers. But there is an issue here. It takes work to get students to engage material with a 'so what' sensibility. It is not enough to decide that we should be asking students to explain the material. We need to help them see what is involved in such explanations."

"That's why you told the story about televisions. You see analogies as critical here."

"You bet, Sancho, but not just analogies. I am convinced 'so what' thinking is not a late-stage phenomenon. That's what the conversation about language learning and rule conjecturing was about. The full cognitive package is there at the beginning, but we're not tapping into it well-enough. Analogies are important, but so is scepticism. Telling a group of seven-year-olds that you've got a magic glass that holds water but also lets it pass right through is bound to provoke all sorts of good critical thinking."

"And that's where the Coleridge passage fits in. We have to decide whether we are going to invite students to exercise their critical faculties or if we just want them to take it all down. Being a dutiful student in this sense is very much like reading fiction. The corner cutting is really a warning of sorts. It will take a lot of work to pull off this shift in teaching. We are going to need to consciously nurture critical thinking."

"That's right, Sancho. A key step in trying to make sense of the practice of good science teaching is to seek the heart of non-fiction—that is, the application of disbelief. Let's play with this some more. What would it look like? We may begin by thinking about conversation and the logic of the classroom. And that's the next chapter."

Chapter 3

On the Logic of the Classroom

There is a critical gap between knowing and understanding, as in the difference between my son's knowing that the moon reflected the light of the sun and understanding how this might be the case at night when the sun is not—ostensibly—there. We met this same gap when I stood looking at two dark rocks in the bleached out hillside in Western Colorado, unable to *see* the vertebrae I knew were there.

How can we avoid this gap?

The first thing we ought to do is recognize that students are always in the middle of things. Teaching is not a matter of writing the day's lesson out carefully upon the clean slate of a child's mind. It's an interaction. They come into our classrooms with minds crowded with all sorts of notions variously associated, and just taking in what we say is a complicated dialogue in many voices. Returning for a moment to Osborne and Freyberg's work, their many interviews with children illustrated, they believe, that: "From a young age, and prior to any teaching and learning of formal science, children develop meanings for many words used in science teaching and views of the world which relate to ideas taught in science" (Osborne and Freyberg, 1985, p. 12). These prior notions become the context for the interpretation of what is presented in their schooling and so play a critical role in how the material is understood. As one thoughtful child put it: "You know, teachers have got all that knowledge but we are thinking about it differently because there are so many ways you take something in" (Osborne and Freyberg, 1985, p. 5).

There are certainly lots of ways to take something in. Consider, for example, a remarkable study that was done in remote regions of the Soviet Union in the late 1920s. A young psychologist, Alexander Luria, realized that the first of Stalin's five-year plans, which called for the collectivization of farms and an educational program that would bring schooling to regions where there had never been schools, was going to transform communities and whole ways of life. He quickly assembled a team of researchers and devised a small set of tests to try to capture the depths of this transformation as it was taking place. His study paints an extraordinary portrait of the deep differences in the character of language and logic across the divide between those who can read and those who cannot (Luria, 1974).

In one task, a great many skeins of wool were dyed different shades of color. When asked to label them, adults who could not read, which had been the case for virtually everyone in these pre-literate societies, named some few skeins with standard color names such as red or yellow, but most were described metaphorically as the color of a cardinal's wing, of rusting wheat, or the lake at mid-day, etc. Moreover, when asked to cluster the skeins, they complained that one really could not.

"D.Q.? What do you mean they couldn't cluster the colors?"

"Well, Sancho, a skein wasn't red like a cardinal's wing, it was the color of a cardinal's wing, and that kept it from belonging with the brownish-red of rusting wheat. Wheat and a bird's wing are completely different."

"Whoa. That's incredible. You mean things that would strike us as broadly red wouldn't be seen that way? I never would have thought that anything would affect what you see, let alone simply how you named things. How did the ones who could read respond?"

"They answered the way we would, Sancho. They answered entirely in terms of the standard colors. Skeins were red or yellow, or some variation thereof . . . they were reddish, light red, dark red, etc. Even if they had only been in school for six months, the villagers no longer saw things metaphorically, but in terms of categories.

"A different task pointed to the same divide. Adults were asked to choose which three items of a group of four items made the most natural cluster. The answers of the pre-literate were strikingly different from the clusters you would make Sancho. For example, given a saw, an axe, a log, and a hammer, what three items belong together?"

"A saw, an axe, a log and a hammer? I would pull the three tools together and leave out the log."

"Exactly, but those who had not been schooled, who could not read, resisted forming a cluster of tools. It made no sense to remove the log from the axe or saw because they were only useful together. The hammer really belonged there as well, but it was less essentially bound to the log. Luria's study is fascinating. I point to it simply to remind ourselves that the reasoning within the material is not itself an obvious matter of fact. Children engage things. They seek out meaning. The material does not speak for itself."

"That's incredible, D.Q. I would never have guessed that learning how to read could so completely change the way the mind worked. Who knows what other kinds of lenses we wear."

Teaching, like communication, is interactive, and the key to examining the practice of teaching is to keep our eyes somehow focused upon that interaction—that space between the material and the mind of the child. It is not simply that teachers should listen more, though of course we should. Rather, we need to keep always in mind that what constitutes coherence is not the logic of the material but the logic of that space—the complex exchange between the material and the mind of the child. After all, they may be making connections that seem natural but that are not the same the textbook takes for granted.

The logic of the exchange as opposed to the logic of the material is almost always overlooked. For example, such authoritative publications as *Benchmarks for Science Literacy* (1993) by the American Association for the Advancement of Science and the *National Science Education Standards* (1999) by the National Research Council include a bewildering array of expectations about what students ought to have studied. These expectations trespass, I believe, way beyond what these students could plausibly be expected to understand.

As this claim is vitally important to the practice of science teaching, let's dwell here for a moment and trace an example or two.

"Still, she moves."

This lovely line where Galileo murmurs his allegiance to the Copernican hypothesis despite the injunction of the Church is dramatic. Yet, even Galileo's authority cannot transform the proposition that the Earth is a planet into a *fact*. In the chapter of the *Standards* on the middle grades, 5 through 8, content standard D says all students should develop an understanding of the Earth in the solar system. More particularly, it says: "Direct observation and satellite data allow students to conclude that earth is a moving, spherical planet, having unique features that distinguish it from other planets in the solar system" (NRC, 1999, p. 159; see also AAAS, 1993, pp. 62–63). But is this so?

"D.Q., of course it's a fact. Isn't it?"

"Well, Sancho, let's look at this for a bit. There would seem to be three possible lines of argument that the Earth is moving: we can feel it move; we can see it move, or we can infer that it is moving by watching other bodies move. So what do you think?"

"I must say, I've never felt the Earth move. I've never thought about that. Should I?"

"Given the proportions of the Earth's motion suggested by modern science, perhaps it should make you wonder. We are supposed to be moving at a quite staggering rate. The Earth is hurtling through space at approximately 70,000 mph, and at the same time it is spinning on its axis at as much as 1,000 mph. How remarkable that we cannot sense such motion. This is significant, because it takes a goodly measure of careful thought before we can see why, even if the Earth were moving, we would not be able to feel it. But this does not thereby imply we are moving, only that we might be."

"O.K., I can't feel it move, but we know it is moving. If we could get off of the Earth, then we'd see it move."

"I'm not so sure, Sancho. Suppose you were on the international space station in orbit around the Earth. We see it moving in the night sky, so presumably you would see the Earth moving in return. That works, but what about the ideal

communication satellite? Such a satellite would orbit the Earth in such a way that it appears to hang in just one spot in the sky. That way we can use it as a relay station, sending signals out to it that then bounce back to various sites, far beyond the horizon of the original site."

"I get it. It's like a mirror floating up in the heavens. But what does it have to do with whether the Earth is a planet?"

"Sancho, the passage in the Standards *suggests that satellites somehow enable us to see the Earth move and so solve the problem directly. But this won't work. Our ideal communication satellite would not see the Earth move."*

"But we are moving. The only reason the satellite doesn't see us move is that it is moving."

"Yes, but if you were on the satellite, how would you know whether you were moving? And if you cannot tell, then if you see the Earth is standing still, well then maybe it is."

"Aha, and that means that even if I could see the Earth move, I wouldn't know if it didn't just look that way because I was moving. Very clever. So then, how did they figure it out?"

"The idea that the Earth is a planet is not a fact we can experience. It is something we figured out. It is an inference drawn from watching other bodies move. Yet, we could always choose to see the apparent motions of the heavenly bodies as the real thing. That is, we see the sun rise, move across the sky, and set. We may understand this as a consequence of the Earth spinning, but we may also choose the more direct notion that the sun is actually moving when we see it move. That is precisely what thoughtful people like Aristotle and Ptolemy did across classical antiquity. Moreover, when Copernicus made the first well-formed argument that the Earth is a planet, there were no direct observations that clinched the matter (Kuhn, 1957). Like so much else in the sciences, even major notions such as the motion of the Earth are not direct matters of fact, but theoretical constructs deeply embedded in argument and analysis."

The real issue D.Q. and Sancho have examined is not whether the Earth is a planet. It is whether the point of study in the sciences is to secure the "right" answers. If we are to emphasize a student's ability to construct arguments and so practice science by practicing its rule of reason, which is the heart of what the National Research Council was urging in its *Standards*, we need to consider what students can constructively arrive at through argument and analysis, instead of what they can witness and appreciate when we tell them.

Consider the difference between two claims about the Earth: that it is roughly spherical in shape, and that it is a planet. I taught a course on the historical sciences to high school students for more than 25 years, and I would always begin the year with a discussion of the Earth that would focus on these two propositions. These notions are each pretty far removed from everyday experience. Yet, there is a key difference between them. Students could regularly come up with good arguments to justify the belief that the Earth is round. They would point to photographs from outer space, or the voyages of

European explorers, such as Magellan, who sailed around the world. Pushing the conversation a bit, I would ask them if they could imagine some direct experience that would convince them the Earth was round. When they couldn't, I would point out that Aristotle said it was common knowledge that the Earth was a sphere (Aristotle, *On the Heavens*, Book II, part 14). What sort of arguments might ancient Greeks have been able to come up with? This changes the focus and after some discussion, they can see that how objects, such as ships coming into port, come up over the horizon suggests the Earth is round. Aristotle, in fact, used this argument and several others, such as the Earth's shadow against the moon during an eclipse; but interestingly, he did not think the Earth was a planet. He did not think the Earth moved.

So, then I would ask: Can they prove the Earth moves? They couldn't—at least, they never did. Indeed, the difference between these two propositions and the ways they are understood would stand for us across the year as signposts, as markers of the qualities of knowing. There are those things we know because we can explain them and why we think they are the case. And there are those things we know simply because others have told us that that's the way things are. Our job was to be aware of this distinction and to move as many things as we could from "simply because" to "I can explain."

What are we to do with notions, however "big" or "basic," that students cannot reach? Are we to give them up? This is not just a matter of basic astronomy. It is a global issue. As we have observed, the sciences are a long haul from common sense, and their hallmark theories are stridently counterintuitive. The shift from right answers to good arguments is critical, but there is a tension here. There are answers that students can witness, like "the Earth is a planet," but that may well lie outside the reach of constructive analysis for students with a given background. This tension between good arguments and right answers is the key problem-shift embraced in principle by the *Standards* and by *Benchmarks*, and it is exactly the right shift—the shift that offers the greatest promise of strengthening the character of science instruction. Yet, it is a shift that both the *Standards* and *Benchmarks* back away from, in that they each enumerate a host of concepts and items as content standards that, as we have seen, are not transparent. What a shame that they did not more fully embrace their own pedagogy and urge that we rethink most profoundly the content we examine in our schools.

On Shifting the Problem from Answers to Reasons

The shift from facts to arguments is more than a shift from answers to reasons. It is a shift from the formal exposition of the material to the naïve inquiry of the child. As I have suggested, questions are important in this regard, but not all questions can carry the weight of genuine inquiry. It is not enough to ask: "Is the Earth a planet?" or "Is its crust broken into a dozen or so major plates?"

Such questions lie too close to the answer. The value of a good question is not to set up a quick hop, step, and jump to the right answer. It is, instead, the basic matter of moving toward the open mind of the child. The content of our teaching should emerge, therefore, from engaging students in puzzles that are real to them. It has to address, to make contact with, their notions on the matter. That is, it has to step forward from their understanding of the world, which is a very different matter from stepping backward from the right answer. This is the real difference in my approach and the real challenge.

To get a better handle on this difference, we can consider what happens when we teach the youngest students. For example, seeds are often used in experiments to demonstrate that plants need water and light to grow (NRC, 1996; see the K–4 content standards in the life sciences). But there are two very different alternatives here. To explain to children that we have seeds and that we are going to use them to see what they need to grow is one sort of inquiry. But imagine if you were to start with a different sort of question, such as: "Where do plants come from?" How very different this is, as you tease out from children their own ideas about these things and proceed to take these seriously and evaluate them. In several conversations with young children about where plants come from, I have been able to glean several intriguing notions: that new trees grow from leaves, and that's why they fall off in the autumn; that trees grow from twigs or from roots; and further that since nobody plants the grasses in the wild, it must be that the ground is alive and plants grow like hair out from heads. These are the notions that should be investigated. Such investigations might well discover the importance of seeds, though they might not get to that. More importantly, they will have involved students in the practice of science, not only because they involved experiments, but also because they used what we have called the rule of reason, through which the sciences arrive at explanations (Popper, 1963). And so the focus rightly shifts from a familiarity with answers to the ability of a student to argue for himself or herself that a given theory solves a problem or explains a puzzle. This is the key distinction between the logic of the material, and the logic of the classroom exchange.

We have come, therefore, to a working notion of a particular approach to inquiry: inquiry should be drawn from student understanding. In terms of the practice of science teaching, therefore, the first imperative would seem to be this: to make certain that our questions really make contact with the open mind of the child, and thus that we will build forward from student understandings.

Carry Over

There is a difference between the logic of the exchange and the logic of the material. Gauging by the sorts of expectations laid out in *Project 2061* and the *National Standards*, we can see that the logic of the material has prevailed over the logic of the exchange. We are setting standards and expectations that essentially call for an appreciation of a body of material rather than invite a more open and genuine inquiry where students build an understanding of their world through the practice of the rule of reason. What does the research say about this state of things? Are there items established through the careful measure of science teaching and learning that shed still more light on the differences between the logic of the material and the logic of the exchange?

There are.

For example, there is an intriguing body of research that concerns "carry over," that general sense of the material learned that is useful from one year of schooling to the next. In terms of the banking model of education, carry over is the learning available in your savings account that can be drawn upon in a subsequent course of study. More colloquially, it is what you have in your pocket as you leave a course.

The research on carry over has had several different goals. Colleges and universities are routinely presented with the problem of placement. They need to assign students to different levels of introductory courses in physics, chemistry, and biology. How do you make such decisions? How well a student has done in a corresponding high school course would seem to be very relevant. Perhaps also, how demanding the text had been? Grades they earned in other science courses? Math courses? Then there is testing. How well had they done on the achievement tests, the SAT II's? Or even on the general SATs or ACTs? Lastly, there's over-all grade point average. This is just the sort of research question where large spreadsheets and statistical schemas come into their own.

Others doing research on carry over have had other problems in mind, but the range of data is similar. Some, for example, have been interested in evaluating different textbooks, trying to gauge, for example, the impact of particular physics texts. Still others have had a far broader project. They have sought to decipher just what our students are learning—what they are interested in—and what they find relevant or compelling.

All in all, these studies affirm that there is a measurable carry over—there is some value to prior study, but it is woefully meager and the measures are offered in a pretty qualified manner. This result is so surprising that it would be worth our while to look at one or two of these studies more closely.

Perhaps the most stunning study correlated achievement in an introductory college physics course with high school background (Finger, Dillon, and Corbin, 1965). The students in their sample were divided into three groups: those who had used the new PSSC physics text, those who had a conventional text, and those who had not taken physics in high school. Not only were there no appreciable differences between the two groups who had high school physics, but they shared no significant advantage over those students who had not taken physics! What a remarkable condemnation of the state of affairs that there would be so little carried over from one year of study to the next.

In another study, Bolte looked at almost 1,000 students in an introductory physics course over a period of 5 years (Bolte, 1966). This time the question was a bit broader: what background factors correlated with success. Bolte looked not only at whether students had studied physics, but he carefully examined math background, study in chemistry, and over-all grade point average. Of the few factors that correlated with success, the single most significant factor was grade point average. Bolte summarized his results this way: "High school physics has predictive value in determining a student's probable success in college physics although the factor of native intelligence as measured by the high school grade point average is of much more value" (Bolte, 1966).

From such studies, it would seem that what it takes to do well in a college science course has less to do with what a student would have carried over from his or her high school science courses than over-all academic strengths—the ability to learn French vocabulary, to solve simultaneous equations, or to write a short essay with a good thesis statement (See also Tai, R. *et al.*, 2006; Sadler, P. *et al.*, 2001; and Hart and Cottle, 1993.)

What a remarkable situation. How can "carry over" be so small, so modest? These are good students. The studies cited are at the college level. These kids have dealt well with the material, and yet by the time they get to the next course, it's as if they hadn't even taken it. It's a kind of intellectual Teflon effect: too little is really sticking.

If we ask ourselves what's going on here, we can point to a number of factors. A large part of the story, I suspect, was caught by the TIMSS Report (*Third International Mathematics and Science Study*, 1996), which leveled an important charge against our K–12 science and mathematics teaching. We are leading our students across too many topics, and spending too little time on each. As one leading researcher, William Schmidt, put it, the U.S. approach is "unfocused, repetitive, and undemanding" (Schmidt, 2005, p. 532). We have opted, as a nation, to expose our students to the wonders of nature and the technical language of the sciences, rather than lead them to examine and reconstruct the arguments they rest upon.

This suspicion has recently been confirmed by an intriguing piece of research. More than 8,000 students were considered in a recent study that sought to gauge the carry over from high school science courses to science courses at the college and university level. It was found that those who had spent one month or more studying one major topic in depth in high school earned higher grades than their peers whose study had been spread across more topics. While the over-all carry over is modest, the impact of depth over breadth is striking. For example, studying a small number of core topics for a year is statistically equivalent to a year and a half of study without that depth (Schwartz *et al.*, 2009, p. 814).

"Is it really that we are teaching too much, D.Q., or are the sciences just too hard?"

"Certainly making sense of the world around us is demanding, Sancho, but we aren't really taking up that challenge. This was highlighted by a delightful piece of research by Robert Yager. Yager took a careful look at our science textbooks, focusing on the imposing array of technical terms these books employ. Drawing

upon the judgement and expertise of another language intensive activity, Yager compared the number of new terms introduced in science books with the amount of vocabulary introduced in foreign language study. The comparison proved to be illuminating.

"Foreign language texts typically introduce approximately 1,250 words to a middle-school-aged child in a year. This rises to twice that in high school, and up to 3,000 words per year in college courses.

"How do our science texts compare?

"Examining two major elementary school text series, one published by Harcourt, Brace and the other by Silver Burdett, Yager counted the highlighted words, the terms in the glossaries, the ones defined and often spelled phonetically. What he found was extraordinary. He found, for example, that in the third grade one text introduced 1,275 technical terms and the other more than 2,300. By fifth grade, both series had upped the ante to over 2,700 words, and in high school the technical vocabulary had climbed commonly to over 10,000 words—way beyond the standard set by foreign language study (Yager, 1983).

"If we remind ourselves that it is not just a matter of identifying that 'haricots verts' are green beans, but that students have to figure out what is going on conceptually with terms like 'mitosis,' 'metamorphic,' 'proton,' or 'kinetic energy,' we can readily appreciate how absurd things have become. Can it be that such texts are really inviting our students to understand these concepts, to examine them critically and respond to the arguments within the material? I think not. We aren't even getting students to the point where the material is 'too hard.'"

"But why has this happened, D.Q.? It seems so obvious that you should teach toward understanding and not just memorizing a set of technical terms you don't really understand."

"In the end, Sancho, it's a question of politics. If we stop and think about the classroom, one of its central realities is that students are essentially powerless and vulnerable. That is, they are if they buy into the set-up. Some don't, perhaps many don't; but when they do, it is clear that the teacher holds all of the cards. Given this state of affairs, it is likely that any time students can influence the course of things, it would plausibly be to increase their own control. We can see this in such questions as: 'What do we need to know?' or 'Will this be on the test?' Such questions echo across our schools. Their purpose is to reduce ambiguity and so increase a general sense of security. They know what is expected of them and can go on about their business.

"Curiously, there is a certain harmony of interests here; as reducing student ambiguities also reduces the teacher's anxieties. 'How can I foster the under-standing?' is gently transformed into 'How should I present the information?' and the profound differences between 'understanding' and 'knowing that' are lost in the shuffle of worksheets, homework, and standardized tests. This is independent of any external pressures from politicians, school boards, or administrators. There is a built-in set of mechanisms ready to collapse the search for understanding to a mastery of information.

"*Let me tell you a story* . . . *The extent of the push toward reducing classes to 'knowing that,' was impressed upon me a long time ago. My first teaching job out of college was at a high school for the deaf. It was the first year of the school, and for several months there were no students and no building. As most of the teachers had no experience with the deaf, we spent a lot of time talking about the deaf and learning the sign language. This was no problem for me, since I'd had deaf parents. I focused my energies on pedagogy. Most schools for the deaf in those days had seen the use of the sign language as a mark of failure. Success meant students could read lips and speak so that hearing people could understand. In that way, the handicap would be surmounted.*

"*Many argued that this focus on speech was a mistake, that the sign language was a natural language and an effective means of easy and exact communication, and that the young deaf child deserved a substantive education—deserved a chance to develop a 'voice.' This new school, I thought, would be a delightful opportunity for students to come together and talk/sign about things. Our central responsibility would be to nurture their voices, to challenge their views, and to stimulate their imaginations.*

"*To my utter dismay, several of my colleagues wanted to replace 'class' with a series of individualized workbooks. Invoking an educational terminology that seemed more like book-keeping, they spoke of behavioral objectives, pre-tests, and learning packets. The more I urged the need for students to talk, and most especially deaf students who had likely been deprived of the chance to discuss things in school, the more isolated I became from these colleagues.*

"*At first I couldn't understand why. Then it hit me. They were new to the sign language. Student discussions would be very difficult. Everything I said went straight toward their weakness. They saw a way out of the thicket by reducing class to the manipulation of information.*

"*Here was the complement to the students' push toward 'knowing that' instead of understanding. Teachers, too, may take comfort in the elimination of ambiguity. The complexities of discussions, the nurturing of student voice, and the unfolding of material in a way that fosters understanding—these are difficult for any teacher in any classroom. My experiences with these teachers of the deaf only highlighted the dynamic. The result, unfortunately, is not happy. The price we pay for collapsing understanding into 'knowing that' is reflected in the striking lack of carry over in our students . . . what I have called the Teflon effect. It is reflected in the criticisms of the TIMSS report and Yager's study that we have been teaching material a mile wide and an inch deep. And it also spills over into a sense of purposelessness, such as we saw in the Osborne and Freyberg studies when students had too little confidence in what a lesson was all about.*"

"*I guess the moral is: when everyone takes the path of least resistance you just keep going downhill.*"

"*That's pretty depressing, Sancho. But happily not everyone takes the easy path . . . the 'knowing that' path. Let me share a recent experience. My work often takes me into different classrooms, and I have come to know a young teacher we may* call T.J. When I last saw him, he explained that he'd been going on about his business last semester, but he wasn't very happy. He felt he was leaning on the textbook too much. He and his students had come to focus on the information so much that they didn't really talk things through and they weren't really getting into the good questions and the most powerful ideas. This semester, to make sure that didn't happen, he gave out the textbooks on the first day and told the students to take them home. He didn't want to see them in class or even in the hallways. And though the new semester was only a few days old, T.J. was already delighted by the differences.

"He went on to explain what class was like now. They sit in a circle and they talk. The students have their notebooks in their laps with their notes from their readings and previous classes, and they talk. He emphasized how he had to trust his students now, because if they hadn't done the readings and thought about things, then class discussion would be flat. But so far, that hadn't been a problem. In fact, quite the opposite. Conversations had been exactly what he had hoped for . . . even better, and for the first time in his short teaching career. This is T.J.'s second year as a history teacher. For the first time, he'd had a student challenge what he had offered. It is a measure of just how thoughtful T.J. is that not only did he come to see the issue with his teaching and how to go about changing things, but he was delighted that a student had disagreed with him. Here, Sancho, is the logic of the classroom as opposed to the logic of the material writ large."

"I see. This gets back to that conversation about pushing. You want to present things in a way that provokes a response, one that nurtures their capacity to challenge what's been said. When they are doing that, then clearly they are reasoning their way through things and not just witnessing someone else's ideas."

"Exactly, Sancho. And that means that the way T.J. prepares for class is going to be different. Before, he might well have worked out the clearest way to present the material; but now he wants to engage students in a conversation that gets down to the most fundamental matters. This takes us back to our first chapter. He needs to find something that is perplexing.

"As it happens, this is exactly what we talked about after I had sat in on one of his 'new' classes. He had asked students to read a section of the text on geography, where it laid out that there were five core aspects to this discipline. T.J. was discussing these with the students and found himself slowing down across two in particular: location and place. Why was that, you think, Sancho?"

"Because location and place mean the same thing?"

"You bet. Why would you have two different categories both about what seems to be the same idea? He was right to dwell here, but he had overlooked a sweet opportunity to have the students uncover what was going on. What if he had started this conversation by saying something along these lines: Have any of you heard this expression . . . 'A house is not a home.'? I can remember first hearing that and thinking adults sure are strange. Why would they say something so curious? I mean, not all homes are houses, some could be apartments or teepees for that matter, but why say it this way?"

"*I get it, D.Q. You get students thinking about why a house is not a home as a warm-up for the differences between location and place. They will see the difference between a house as an object and a home as a set of qualities, and when you turn to geography, they will see location and place and, 'bang,' they'll make the connection. It's like televisions and schizophrenia.*"

"*Right. 'A house is not a home' is clearly not a matter of geography. It is so far out in left-field, it announces itself as an analogy and alerts the students that something is up that is going to be like this pair. You're announcing there's a puzzle of a certain flavor right around the corner. And so instead of being careful to explain the distinction, you have empowered students to see that there is an issue here and suggested how they might think about it.*"

"*Very nice, D.Q. Shall we get back to the text?*"

"*You bet.*"

Assessment and the Logic of the Classroom

In our new classroom, where the logic of the exchange prevails over the logic of the material, assessment takes on a different character. The logic of the material disposes us to hold students accountable for elements of the material. Hence we are led to the facts, to definitions of terms, and to solving problems in terms of algorithms and formulas. This is what we do. We ask students to label diagrams: the parts of a cell, the parts of the solar system, the parts of the atom. We ask them what seeds need to survive, what are the defining characteristics of life, and how old the Earth is. We also ask them about the difference between ionic and covalent bonds, about the three basic rock types, or to define an air mass, inertia, an Ohm or a volt . . . and when we have had enough to do with words and definitions, we ask them to balance chemical equations or to calculate the time it takes for a rock to fall 5 meters or, for that matter, the number of kilometers in 5 miles. This is what we ask students to think about, and it is not the wonder as Jesse thought about what holds the water up. It is not the wonder of Playfair looking into the abyss of time. It is no wonder at all. No wonder, so many of our students find that the sciences are not for them.

The logic of the exchange pushes us in a very different direction. It disposes us to hold students accountable not for the material, but for the way we came to understand it. That is, we hold them accountable for giving an account. The real work of the class has been to make sense of puzzles and issues the teacher has seen within the material. Since this effort invariably involves alternative views and experiences or experiments that help to decide between these alternatives, the natural assessment is to ask students to reflect and reconstruct these explorations and explanations. So, instead of having students plant seeds under various conditions and then asking them what seeds need to grow, in the new classroom there would be a discussion of broader, more "naïve" questions, such as "Where do plants come from?" In the course of this discussion a student might offer that the ground is alive and that plants spring out of the ground the way hair grows on your head. To test this idea he or she might suggest collecting some dirt from the lawn and putting it in a cup on the window sill, then taking care of it to see if anything grows. Another student might suggest that they should get dirt from other places, too, because some dirt might be alive and other dirt might be dead. Still another student might ask how they should take care of the dirt. Should they add water? Or fertilizer? Why on the window sill? Soon there are all sorts of experiments. And as plants grow in some cups and not others, there would be all sorts of ideas and conclusions.

What does assessment mean here? We might ask students to pick an experiment, perhaps the one they did, and explain what issue or question led to this experiment and then to explain what happened and what they think this means. What we will get from them is a kind of story, and if told well it would explain the reasoning that supports why they did what they did and why they have drawn the conclusions they have drawn. It might well be the case that they don't get the "right" answer. They might find, for example, that you don't need a seed in order to get a plant to grow. But mindful of the shift from answers to arguments, the "right" answer here is much less important than the character of their reasoning. It is not that anything goes, by the way. Recall Jesse and what is holding the water up. I was impressed by his theory, and I "tested" it. We need to take what they think seriously and push it. This is how we show them respect. But our push need not end with the answers of the modern under-standing. What counts is the growth, growth in the complexity of their views, growth in their analytical sophistication, growth in their capacity to engage issues and value working things out.

Assessment should always raise this issue of answers *and* reasoning because our teaching should always operate in both of these arenas. This was highlighted by Gerald Goldin in a fine essay, "Toward an Assessment Framework for School Mathematics." He urged that assessment was not about determining a student's competence with various types of problems. It was about the cognitive skills one uses in solving those problems. Too often, however, we collapse our teaching to the mechanics of problem-solving and no one has their eyes on the prize; neither the students, nor the teachers. This has only been made that much more complicated by the heightened importance of standardized testing. Teachers, administrators, school boards—everyone has been reluctant to devote class time to conceptual understanding or exploratory activities because they see them as "untested and irrelevant" to the test scores that are the bottom line. "In the long run, of course, the damage shows up in many forms, including low scores even on the standard test items, because students have not developed adequate conceptual foundations" (Goldin, 1992, p. 66; I am also pleased to note my debt to hours of conversation with Dr. Marshall Gordon on these matters).

Usually, we take how a student performs on a test as a measure of their competence and the basis for their grade. But when we have our eyes on these underlying habits of mind and cognitive skills, how a student performs on various test problems becomes a diagnostic challenge for the teacher, who has to read from the test back to the cognitive skills of the student. The assessment instrument is not the goal, but rather the way we gather information about the real goals of mathematical education.

"*Excuse me, D.Q., but wasn't the ability to do the multiplication problems I had on quizzes when I was in grade school exactly what my teachers were teaching me? I don't see two different sets of goals here.*"

"*Yes and no, Sancho. Let's step back a bit and look at this notion of conflating two different things. When you study biology you are learning how we talk about living things. It is an analytical discourse about a patch of nature. Similarly, astronomy is about heavenly bodies and geology about the Earth. But look at history. It refers to both the full set of past events and to the discipline that examines these events. That is, we could say: History is about history. Goldin is suggesting that we have a similar situation with mathematics assessment. The problems we give students to assess their understanding of mathematics have been confused with the mathematics we are teaching, but really what we should be teaching are much deeper ideas than the mechanics of solving a linear equation or determining the area of a triangle.*"

"*So what should I have been really learning as I worked on my multiplication tables?*"

"*Goldin doesn't lay out all of the cognitive skills relevant to learning and teaching mathematics, but he does list a few, some of which are attitudinal, such as a willingness to try different procedures or to cooperate in group work, and others are more a matter of strategies, such as being systematic, and still others are more epistemological, as in thinking about why something has worked in one case and whether it would always work.*"

"*These seem important, but they are pretty vague aren't they?*"

"*Yes and no, Sancho. They certainly are less explicit than the definition of some technical term such as 'mitosis,' or some item along the lines of 'Paris is the capital of France,' but they are tangible qualities. Students often will say they understand the material, but they can't do the word problems. What's missing are just these habits and cognitive skills. That's what carries you beyond the mechanics of the algorithm.*"

"*You mean these are the things that would be important if you were really solving a problem, rather than just following some routine.*"

"*Uh-huh . . . you know, Sancho, this discussion has reminded me of something that happened a long time ago. It was, perhaps, the most intense moment of my many years of schooling. As an undergraduate I took an independent study in physics with a wonderful teacher, Dr. Faber, who met with me every day for an hour. We studied modern physics, and I worked as hard as I could because it was so extraordinary that he would give me so much time. Come the end of the semester, he asked me about a final exam. I had hoped things wouldn't come to that . . . we hadn't had any tests and I hoped he would just give me a 'gentleman's B' . . . but he thought a test would be a good idea. So again, I really gave it my* all, postponing the exam to the end of exam week so I could study an extra day after all my other exams were over.

"I can still conjure up the lab room where I sat alone that afternoon, reading through the five problems of the exam. I couldn't answer any of them. I was mortified. Here he had given me all that time and I had nothing to show for it. It was awful. I can still feel the anxiety I felt then . . . just talking about it. I decided there must be something I knew that fit in with one of these problems; so I took a blank piece of paper and started writing everything I had learned . . . sketching different topics, experiments, derivations, problems we had worked on . . . everything. Then I went back to the test and compared it to what I had written, asking myself whether this question could be about that or that one about this. It was pretty conjectural at first, but things started to fall into place and I worked up answers for each of the problems.

"I don't know if Goldin's list of cognitive skills covers what I went through, Sancho, though I suspect it does; but there was a lot being exercised that afternoon other than quantum mechanics and relativity."

As we are considering Goldin's paper, one of the more intriguing conclusions he draws from the importance of these cognitive skills has to do with the limited value of "harder" problems. His argument goes something like this:

- The methods currently used to assess mathematical achievement are having a negative impact on learning.
- It is often assumed that if we replaced tests that focused on low-level skills, algorithms, and routine problems with tests that featured more sophisticated, non-routine problems, then student performance would reflect student understanding.
- However, no matter how sophisticated the problems, there are always ways to teach "practical, rule-based, noninsightful procedures for solving them" (Goldin, pp. 63–67).

This argument takes us back to Barry Sanders' discussion of talk and the idea that student voice is more important than answers. We need to keep our eyes on underlying habits of mind, rather than definitions, algorithms, and the mechanics of routine problems. We need to engage students in puzzles. Puzzles trigger scepticism . . . something has to give . . . something we have always taken for granted must be wrong. Triggering scepticism taps into underlying habits of mind crucial to the sciences. Puzzles also shift the politics of discourse in the classroom. Puzzles invite students to participate actively. We have done our job not by presenting information, which students are then to soak up like sponges; but by framing a challenging question that connects with their sensibilities, their background . . . how they have made sense of things.

Pushing this notion of challenging work, within the context set by the logic of the material, there is a temptation to race across things, especially with the more "able" student. Students who don't get it are "slow." A good class is one where you can cover things quickly. Advanced work is linked to pace. Accelerated courses are thus taken to be more rigorous, but is that really the case?

Over the years there has been a steadily growing push for AP courses as proof that high schools and high school students are doing a good job (NRC, 2002, pp. 52, 65, and 185). This push has become such a significant issue that the National Research Council examined programs for advanced study in mathematics and the sciences, notably AP and IB programs. Their findings were sharply critical, as when they wrote that these programs:

> . . . do not yet effectively utilize what is known about how people learn. In many instances, they insufficiently emphasize conceptual learning that uses inquiry-based methods, nor do they adequately take into account the importance of prior knowledge (including student preparation in earlier courses).
>
> (NRC, 2002, p. 174)

These programs are driven by the logic of the material. The standards they commit to involve mastering bodies of information and problem-solving techniques. The results have been disappointing. For example, after noting that teaching to the test is the norm in AP and IB programs, the NRC found:

> In sum, teaching to AP and IB tests for the purpose of raising test scores can lead to superficial coverage of a broad base of content knowledge, to teachers ignoring the importance of meaningful inquiry-based and laboratory experiences (AP only), and to students feeling that what they are learning in school has little application to the real world.
>
> (NRC, 2002, p. 187)

If AP and IB programs are off-base, what, then, is the character of advanced work? Of rigor? And what are legitimate goals for students? The real goal at every level is that students find purpose and meaning in their studies within an environment that nurtures their voice. It is important to underline the character of rigor in such an environment. Rigor is a course of study grounded in reason that is transparent to the student. Things make sense not as the flow of ideas on some chart, but in the unfolding of the material in a given classroom with a given cluster of students with the mix of their backgrounds and prior knowledge. In their recommendations, the NRC emphasizes depth of conceptual understanding over familiarity with factual content and that instruction "should engage students in inquiry by providing opportunities to experiment, analyze information critically, make conjectures and argue about their validity, and solve problems both individually and in groups" (NRC, 2002, p. 200). Here we see the thrust of the logic of the exchange as opposed to the logic of the material.

Let's pursue this briefly by considering an instance of rigor. Consider the rule that when you divide by a fraction, you invert and multiply; e.g., $6 \div \frac{1}{5} = 6 \times 5 = 30$. This seeming sleight of hand is not as arbitrary as it seems. It is grounded in mathematical reasoning. Dividing by a fraction is awkward. It would be much easier to divide by 2 or, better still, by 1. Is there anything we can do to change this problem so that we are dividing by an easier number? Yes, there is. We know we can multiply any quantity by 1 and not change its value. We also know that any number divided by itself equals 1. Putting these two together, we choose to multiply the fraction $6 \div \frac{1}{5}$ by $\frac{5}{5}$. This doesn't change the value of the fraction, but it certainly simplifies things because it reduces the ugly fraction in the denominator to 1 . . . because $\frac{1}{5} \times 5 = 1$. That leaves us with 6×5 in the numerator and so we end up with $\frac{30}{1}$ or just 30. To take students through this reasoning and to both trace an instance and suggest its extension is what rigor means in mathematics.

Rigor is knowing what you know and being able to explain how it is so. How else might we understand it? Would we capture the value of rigor by noting that some student was able to do what thirteen-year-olds commonly do when she was only twelve or eleven? Surely not. It is not the race across the material that we are interested in. It is the quality of understanding.

We have been using examples from mathematics, but the case is very much the same in the sciences. To consider assessment in the sciences, we may take advantage of our discussion of Cuvier's work in the previous chapter. In a given class, we might have examined the contours of the zygomatic arch and the bones that make up the cheek as part of a discussion of anatomy and the coordination of parts. Is it important that the boundary between two of these bones is slanted in placental mammals? Yes, but only in the broader context set by the issue of the size of the head when placental mammals give birth. And this is important in the still broader context set by Cuvier's appreciation of the degree of "designfulness" in all animal life, a principle of design that led him to reject the possibility that there could be piecemeal changes in organisms over generations. Life could not have evolved. It is too high-tech, too intricately dependent on coordinated nuances. And this substantial objection to evolution is important as the challenging context for Darwin's own work on the history of life. To know that the boundary is slanted, but not appreciate its significance is to have missed the heart of the lesson. But even a mastery of this hierarchy of contexts is less important than the still deeper rule of reason that operates within the sciences. An effective assessment would ask the student to display an unfolding of the material where there is a steady interaction between issues and evidence, so that the story that is really being told is an argument. You could do this by simply asking students a "what and so what" question: discuss the contours of the zygomatic arch and its significance for Cuvier's approach to life and whether animals had evolved.

Another important aspect of Cuvier's work was his extension of anatomical rules from living things to fossils. His realization that extinct animals could be reconstructed following the same rules that govern living animals set the stage for the problem of extinction: if these animals had been built right, why were they no longer around? His answer was that they must have been hit by a catastrophe so far out of the ordinary that the species was wiped out. Hence, he understood the history of life to be episodic, with stages of life punctuated by catastrophes. Again, an effective question might simply ask students: how did Cuvier establish the problem of extinction and how was his solution in keeping with his views on evolution?

These two questions open the door to a certain kind of rendering of Cuvier's work. They are less a matter of the facts, of definitions and particular items, than of how such material was understood by Cuvier. The students are being invited to tell a story, and to do it well requires both an appreciation of the data and the context Cuvier gave it. This is hard work, and though routinely many students saw what was being asked of them . . . others did not. I found a couple of things were helpful with these students. We would talk about the essays in class the day after the test, while the questions were still fresh in their minds. When I returned the tests, I encouraged students to read the essays others had written. Often, they would say things like . . . "Oh, I knew that, but I didn't realize I should talk about it in this question." And finally there was my feedback, the comments I had made on their essays.

Assessment as feedback highlights another key aspect of the differences between the logic of the material and the logic of the exchange. Broadly speaking, within the context set by the logic of the material, tests give students the opportunity to demonstrate competence. The good student knows what the teacher has told him or her. Doing a good job means knowing a lot of the answers; whether it is math facts, the names of the presidents, or what happened in Chapter three of *To Kill a Mockingbird*. A good test rewards those who have paid attention, who took notes, who did their homework, and who studied. For the others, the test catches them at what they do not know. Feedback is straightforward. "How many did you miss?" is the question of the day.

However, there is another way to go about things, a way set by the logic of the exchange. Here, instead of looking to see what they don't know, ask questions that go straight to the heart of the study to see how they have pulled the material together. This is where feedback is so crucial. We are gauging the cognitive skills beneath their work. I would look to see, for example:

- how coherent their essay was;
- how well they used examples and evidence;
- if they were clear about the reasoning that warranted an inference;
- if they saw the full sweep of the issue;
- how complete their discussion was;
- how well they appreciated alternative understandings of the same data.

This is hard work for both teacher and students, but it is right at the center of what it means to come to an understanding. There is no question of its relevance, nor of its importance.

Assessment is fundamentally teleological, giving the teacher the opportunity to see how well students are achieving desired ends. There is a certain similarity here with the notion of "backward design" in the work of Wiggins and McTighe (1998), but there is also a difference. It is important to connect what you assess to what you have taught, and what you have taught with what you think is important. Further Wiggins and McTighe rightly emphasize that what is important has more to do with content than with engaging students in pleasant activities, and they urge that teachers come to what is important through the "enduring ideas" within the material. This I share with their work. We diverge with my emphasis on the logic of the exchange.

Directing the thoughtfulness of a teacher toward enduring ideas is a crucial shift toward powerful teaching. For a teacher to know the material well is important, but not because it is important to know lots of technical language. Knowing the material well is about being able to be thoughtful about core notions and concepts. But there is more. We have to be thoughtful in ways that allow us to see, to imagine a naïve encounter with the material. That is, effective teaching goes beyond a thoughtful "feel" for the material. It requires that we find a way to frame a puzzle, a perplexity the engagement with which, the unraveling of which, leads to a direct encounter with enduring ideas.

"D.Q., I'm not sure I am getting this."

"O.K. Go back to one of our bits of science . . . such as the discussion of seeds. One might reasonably assume that to teach this well, you would need a background in botany and so are aware of the many mechanisms plants use to produce seeds and guarantee fertilization and dispersion. Right?"

"Sure."

"There is a wealth of information here about flowering plants, stamens and pistils, and the delightful wonders used to lure insects. And so we are quickly off to the races. But not so fast. As we have seen, students already have a wealth of ideas about where plants come from, especially when it comes to plants out in the wild where no one is planting seeds. Beneath this array of botanical mechanics is a simple question: where do plants come from? We get there because we have thought about things with an eye toward a naïve encounter with stamens and pistils, etc. We get there because we want to engage students in a puzzle. If plants come from seeds, who planted the forest?"

"O.K., I can see that. The idea is that knowing the material well isn't necessarily about knowing a lot of detail. You want to have thought about what it really means."

"I have no problem with knowing a lot of science, Sancho, but for effective teaching it has to translate into what are the deepest and most naïve questions the material is addressing. And these then become the first step forward.

"As for enduring ideas, if we have them in mind as we teach and frame issues for a class to examine, then we are in a good place. Wiggins and McTighe offer a lovely example . . . if you are going to teach about the American Revolution and so want students to push their thinking about independence, then start with

a discussion about their own growth toward independence as adolescents. It is easy to imagine a conversation about issues, tensions, factors as children grow and become more independent. But Wiggins and McTighe also link a study of the Magna Carta to the enduring idea of the rule of law, limits to a government's power, and the rights of individuals (1998, pp. 10–11). Here the enduring idea has become a more profound answer. This is certainly better than teaching names and dates, but Goldin has already alerted us to the danger of taking solace in more difficult math problems. There is always a routine, what he calls a 'noninsightful procedure.' Students are very adept at 'learning' slogans and definitions without really appreciating what they mean."

"So what you are getting at is that enduring ideas can fall within the trap of the logic of the material. The challenge for the teacher is not simply to be thoughtful, but to somehow connect that thoughtfulness with the logic of the exchange."

"You bet, Sancho, in a nutshell. We want to underline that the puzzles at the heart of the material, our wonder at the mechanics of nature and the proportions of our understanding, these will carry a class far more effectively than profound insights, as valuable as they are themselves."

By linking assessment to the logic of the exchange, we find ourselves right in the middle of the notion of formative assessment. The shift from answers to arguments and from the logic of the material to the logic of the exchange has led us to the critical importance of extended feedback, both in class discussion and in evaluating written work. Our goal, like those who have urged formative assessment, has been to nurture voice, a student's capacity to come to an understanding and to explain the foundations of this understanding. This requires care and attention and well-formed feedback. And so we are not surprised to learn that when teachers come to place increasing emphasis on formative assessment—that is, they work to give feedback that will help a student to better understand the material—that students learn more and test scores rise (see Black, 2004, and also William, 2004). Once again—as with the research of Marc Schwartz *et al.* (2009) where teaching with suitable depth was shown to have lasting value—we find that if we teach to understanding, students learn more and it shows.

They learn more and it shows in ways beyond standardized testing and better grades in college. In the first interlude I touched on the broad reach of educational values as we discussed a paper by Clarissa Hayward (1999). The habits of mind, cognitive skills, and critical scepticism schools nurture will both reflect and reinforce a student's place in society and the differences between the managed and the managers.

Years ago I taught briefly at the University of Leeds. One of the professors there took me under his wing. We would often walk to the university together, and I can recall with clarity a conversation about a television program he had watched the night before. It was about the Westminster School, an old and very established private school in London. Much of it involved a reporter discussing issues of the day with students. My friend observed that he had two children of approximately the same age, both of whom had attended what we call public schools, government schools. What these Westminster students had said was not striking. His children had said as much. What was striking was the confidence and composure of the Westminster students, as if it were perfectly natural for adults to take an interest in what they had to say. His own children, he offered, would have been far more guarded and suspicious, and would probably have kept their real views to themselves. Is this not as crucial a quality as test scores? If we want our students to have a voice, we need to nurture it. We need to make it perfectly natural for adults to take an interest in how they see the world and what they think.

Unpacking the Proposition

We have been trying to take the measure of the Teflon effect, the rather remarkable way in which even for our successful students, too little is sticking. I have suggested that part of the problem is the approach we have taken to the material, reducing our aims, lowering our sights, from understanding to "knowing that." There is more to the problem.

What do students do with the reduced material we offer them?

Back when I was twelve or so, my mother started taking courses in a local community college. Early on, she had to take a non-credit math course that was often beyond her ken. I spent a lot of time helping her out as best I could, and I can remember trying to decipher for her such curious words as "sin," "cos," and "tan." I was pretty good in math and enjoyed the challenge of making sense of these terms—working out what they meant in a functional sort of way. I remember feeling pretty good about getting her to see how to solve various problems, even though I knew I didn't really know what I was talking about.

There is a lovely essay somewhere by Bertrand Russell where he proposes that mathematics is that discipline where you don't know what you are talking about. This, of course, is true in a certain way. There is a fundamental sense in which the truth of "3 + 4 = 7" is independent of whether you are talking about baubles, bangles, or bright, shiny beads. My experience figuring out the operations with "sin," "cos," and "tan" was not what Bertrand Russell had in mind. Several years later when I found myself studying trigonometry, "sin" quickly became the sine function. More importantly, "sin" gained a certain clarity and reasonableness. I understood the issues it addressed, the strategies it embraced, and where they came from. The operations linked to the trig functions had not changed, but the quality of my new understanding meant, for example, that I could now see the connection between the way the ratios of the sides changed, the wavy form of a sine curve, and the patterns generated by movement along a unit circle.

"D.Q., is it important that I understand what movement along a unit circle means?"

"*Of course it is, Sancho, but not especially for this conversation. We are examining the Teflon effect, and suggesting that whether students can or cannot give the material a context and make sense of things is critical. It is possible to make your way with a kind of operational context. It might be that the sine of an angle is the number you get when you press the appropriate buttons on your calculator, and this might be enough to get you through the problems you are given. Yet, such a shallow read of the material, really a calculus of operations, plausibly has a limited lifetime and little utility.*"

"*Why is that D.Q.? What difference does it make as long as you can get the right answer?*"

"*Let's see . . . stop and think about a common student psychology project that tests how well people do memorizing different kinds of words. The person doing the project would read off a list of, say, ten words and then the subject would try to say the words back. The person doing the project would keep score of how many trials it took before the subject could recite all ten words in order. One of the findings here is that people do better with words than with nonsense syllables.*"

"*That makes sense.*"

"*My mother did an interesting variation on this theme in some research she did as a psychology graduate student. She set up a visual perception and memory test. She would give the subject a card with four drawn images superimposed on one another. Then she would take it back and lay out say, ten cards that had individual images. The test was to see how good the subject was at picking which of the images had been in the mix. Got the idea?*"

"*Yes . . .*"

"*O.K. The key to the experiment was to compare how well three groups of subjects were at the task: deaf kids, hearing kids from middle class communities and hearing kids from impoverished communities. With household objects and geometric figures, the middle class hearing kids did far better than poor or deaf kids. But with abstract figures, swirls and such, all three groups fared about the same. What do you think?*"

"*The abstract figures were like nonsense syllables, right? They were harder to do. The middle class hearing kids had some sort of advantage with the other images . . .*"

"*That's right. My mom saw it in terms of language acquisition and general cultural deprivation. Both the deaf kids and the poor kids had weaker backgrounds to draw upon as a context to give images meaning; so household and geometric items were often essentially abstract for them. The broader context for this project was to get at whether the deaf suffered from some physiological reduced brain capacity, which had been suggested, or whether instead it was a matter of their experience and issues surrounding language acquisition.*

"*I went through this, Sancho, because I liked the project and because there is a straightforward connection to a contemporary issue in educational policy. With the marked rise in standardized testing, there is now a lot of data on how students perform. One of the patterns people have picked up on has to do with growth across the school year. It seems that everyone improves their testing scores at about the same rate across the school year. Where more successful students pull away from their struggling peers is over the summer. Roughly speaking, middle class, suburban students start the fall pretty much where they were the previous spring, while inner-city students fall back. Some educators have used this data to say the real problem is the summer break, and to turn things around they propose various summer programs. That makes some sense, but can you think of another way to read this pattern, Sancho?"*

"You are coming at this from the whole question of nonsense and meaningfulness, but I don't see . . ."

"That's a good start . . . maybe add a dose of Clarissa Hayward's research on the different notions of what it means to be a good student in the inner city and in the suburbs."

"Oh, is it that if we are not teaching kids to understand the material, then it stays at a certain remove and, like nonsense, is harder to remember? Over time, over a summer vacation, what they knew is lost really because it was never owned."

"That's how I see it, Sancho. The reason inner-city students are falling behind is not what happens during the summer, but what happens in school. This is also where the research we have seen fits in. Dwelling on material has a significant impact on the carry over problem precisely because students come to own it . . . that's the Schwartz team's research on the value of depth over breadth. And formative assessment has a significant impact because it fosters understanding over competence. Let's get back to the text."

Alongside this basic matter of how well students understand what they know, there is an extensive literature on misconceptions. Evidently, many of our students are not learning what we think we are teaching them. Thus, for example, in addition to Osborne *et al.*, there is a nice study by Berg and Brouwer (1991) that focuses on students who had taken physics courses. Student views were examined on a number of phenomena involving basic concepts. In one example, students were asked to predict the path of an object swung around in a circle and then let go. Less than one-fifth of the students selected the right answer, with over half saying the ball would continue to move in a circle. In a further task, students were asked to describe the forces acting on a ball tossed into the air, as it rises and falls. Only about one in twenty got this one right, with most students linking force directly to motion; that is, the force was understood as being upward as the ball rises, downward as it falls, and non-existent at the very top. It is worth noting that though college students did somewhat better, these sensibilities are essentially common to students in high school and college.

As they reflected on their study, Berg and Brouwer spoke about the need to confront student naïve conceptions directly; for, as they see it: "It is clear from this study and other research that students can be successful on knowledge-based questions or numerical problem solving without having integrated the desired scientific conception into their conceptual structure" (1991, p. 12).

We may add to such studies as these another interesting piece of research. In a study by Finley (1983), eleventh grade physics students were asked to read a thousand-word passage on energy. They were then asked what the passage had been about. Finley found there were several natural groups within the sample, clustered about various more or less concrete illustrations that had been used in the passages. This is a plausible result, reflecting the importance of anchoring abstractions in particular experiences. More intriguing, however, is the observation that most of the accounts of the passage included considerable material that was not explicitly there. Anywhere from one-third to half of the attributed propositions had been relevant but invented. Here, again, we see how richly learning is active and integrative. Students are not clean slates upon which the lesson of the day is written. They come into class with minds that are charged with all sorts of notions variously linked.

Misconceptions and inventions seem to characterize a good portion of what is happening in the classroom. We can add these to the criticisms of the TIMSS report and to Yager's measure of the extraordinary weight of technical vocabulary in our textbooks. The sum, from our perspective, underlines the profound differences between the logic of the material and the more essential logic of the classroom. We need to rethink our practice in light of these issues.

In an early essay, "Ethical Principles Underlying Education," John Dewey tells of a school in Chicago that purported to teach children how to swim without having them go into the water. Instead, they would be taken through a sort of ballet of motions: when to turn your head and when to breathe, etc. When asked how he had fared trying out this procedure, one student shrugged his shoulders and said, "Sunk." This is not surprising. If you are going to teach children to swim, there needs to be water in the classroom. Dewey was talking about thoughtful, reflective behavior. School cannot be a preparation for ethical social behavior without reproducing within itself the typical conditions of society (1964, p. 116). There needs to be water in the classroom. Extending this to the teaching of science, let me offer this remark by Richard Feynman about the character of scientific thinking, that "the first thing really is, before you begin you must not know the answer" (1999, p. 103). With our extraordinary emphasis on answers, we begin to suspect that, like that Chicago school, there is no water in our classrooms.

We have come, therefore, to a central challenge to the practice of science teaching. We have seen the need for water in the classroom, for engagement with substantive matters, but again we must remember that the material does not speak for itself. Recall the extraordinary work of Luria on the impact of learning how to read on the way we think about things. Recall, as well, the surprising lack of "carry over" as students move through courses. Too little is sticking; too little is making sense. To turn things around, we need to do five things:

- we need to talk and to listen, and so attend to the logic of the exchange;
- we need to dwell on material;
- we need to support student efforts to come to an understanding, using the right sort of assessment where students explain how they have put things together;
- with this we need to give them extended feedback that not only judges whether they got the facts right, but also how well they appreciated how the evidence supports inferences;
- we need to build this understanding from perplexities that tie to the essential questions at the heart of the material.

That is, in a fundamental way, students need to not know the answer. Inquiry needs to be genuine. In order for this sort of inquiry to succeed we need to do much more than we have. The problems posed need a far fuller context, one that draws out and stimulates student notions. And most fundamentally, we need to find a way to institute inquiry with an emphasis on argument and explanation over answers and activity.

Interlude
The History of Greece

Note: I offer here a conceit, an extended comparison. Presumably, such analogies have earned this name because there is a certain arrogance to playing things out at such length. Conceits are conceited. So, in advance, forgive me, but I find the differences between Mitford and Thirlwall, two classical historians, to be a wonderful analogue to the differences between the logic of the material and the logic of the exchange. Their differences are profound and the light they provide valuable.

William Mitford's *History of Greece* was one of the first analytical histories on the whole of the classical Greek experience. It was an exceptionally successful work from its first publication in 1784. Much of its success derived from its outspoken politics. Mitford, a gentleman Tory, sought to undo the myth of the great Grecian democracies. And certainly the times were right—for his history was published across an era marked by the fear of the mob, be it Robespierre's, Napoleon's, or Thomas Paine's.

The immediacy of ancient Greece for Mitford was more than a matter of political parallels. Mitford wrote confidently of an age that was not so far distant in time or aspect. The passage of time had not clouded history's vision, and Mitford drew directly from the "judicious" commentaries of the ancients a rational account of major political and cultural events.

One key to Mitford's interpretation of ancient mythology with its weave of fact and fancy was the poet. As the poet had practiced a creative license, so the task of the historian was to undo this creativity and regain the authentic patterns of historical fact. Take, for example, the adventures of Jason and the Argonauts. Placing these exploits in a coarse age that honored piracy, Mitford sees them as focused on the ambition to secure the princess Medea and the riches of her kingdom. The magical Golden Fleece sought by Jason and his crew was not, Mitford assures us, a magical skin of gold. Rather, the fleece was a symbol of wealth, a symbol derived from the ancient practice of using fleece to "pan" gold from streams, the tight fibers of the wool catching the tiny flecks of gold as they passed by (1808, pp. 30–1).

Similarly, Mitford sorted the many tales of the great hero, Hercules, into two classes. There was the vagabond whose only covering was a lion's skin, whose only weapon was a club, and whose strength was equal to that of hosts. This was a mythical fancy, the invention of poets built upon the real exploits of a great hero. The real Hercules had been a prince, the commander of an army who had wielded the sword of justice in an age when governments were too weak to wield it for themselves (1808, pp. 25–26).

Mitford understood historical agency to be finite and discrete. There was no development to history; rather a series of particular individuals—heroes, colonizers, law-givers—and particular events. The task before the historian was to arrange these into a chronological sequence and to practice a critical scrutiny reducing the outrageous proportions of ancient legend to a more prosaic measure.

Things are very different in Thirlwall's *History of Greece*. Written in the 1830s, Thirlwall continually shifts the resolution of his lens from events and records of the past to views and arguments of the present. The result is a certain distance between the reader and antiquity. With Mitford we had been drawn into the world of mythology, heroic deeds, and events of great proportion. With Thirlwall that world is farther away. We are drawn, instead, to wonder at the range and creativity of scholarly judgement: an echo of the differences we noted between science as the wonders of nature and as the wonders of the human imagination.

Thirlwall denied the authority of the ancients by reading them within a context set by their own understanding. Their accounts represented how they had seen the world, not how it had been. This shift from fact to perception profoundly changed the task before history. Myths were no longer the poetic inventions of the ancient bard, built upon annals and recollections. They were the intellectual and existential resources of early humankind. As these needs had changed, so had the forms of ancient legend.

Consider Thirlwall's account of Hercules. There are two orders of hero, he suggests. The one

> . . . carries us back into the infancy of society, when it is engaged in its first struggles with nature for existence and security: we see him cleaving rocks, turning the course of rivers, opening or stopping subterraneous outlets of lakes, clearing the earth of noxious animals, and, in a word, by his single arm effecting works which properly belong to the united labours of a young community.
>
> (1855, p. 142)

Here we see Hercules enabling the settlement of the first villages, clearing fields of beasts and boulders, even changing the course of rivers to better advantage.

In contrast to the earliest stage of a young community, another order of Herculean deeds reflects another order of society. Here we find

> . . . a state of things comparatively settled and mature, when the first victory has been gained, and the contest is now between one tribe and another,

for possession or dominion; we see him maintaining the cause of the weak against the strong, of the innocent against the oppressor, punishing wrong, and robbery, and sacrilege, subduing tyrants, exterminating his enemies, and bestowing kingdoms on his friends.

(ibid.)

Here is a more advanced state of society where other questions have become pressing. It is less a matter of explaining how community had been established than of determining the limits of power and the nature of one's obligation to those above and below your station.

Hercules was a conceptual device. At first he had been a form of cosmogony, describing how the world had come to be the way it was: fields had been cleared, boulders cleaved, rivers channeled to their present beds, all by the mighty arm of Hercules. The later Hercules brought the imagination forward to the threshold of civilization, to the day when society sought justice and order and propriety.

Like Mitford, Thirlwall has distinguished two sets of legends, but he did not see one as more probable than the other. Instead, he saw two stages of society. He has not reduced myth to rational proportions, nor arranged discrete events in a chronological sequence. He has unfolded a developmental history of the ancient imagination, where conceptual devices are played and replayed against changing conditions.

What does this brief excursion into classical history have to do with our discussion thus far? In Mitford's approach we can see the logic of the material, and in Thirlwall's the logic of the exchange. Mitford examines the myths themselves, finding within them clues to various historical events. Thirlwall moves the conversation from the myth itself to the mind of the myth-maker. By focusing on what myth meant to the story-teller, he invites the reader to see the material from within. Instead of events, the tale is about how the ancients understood their world. Myths framed explanations; they made sense of things. Moreover, there was an organic, ecological quality to Thirlwall's reading. As time passed and societies changed, so too would the problems change that myth addressed. In this new soil, myths would be retold, and mythological figures would change accordingly. Conceptual devices would be refashioned to meet new demands.

What would it mean to present the sciences in the same way? It would mean modeling the effort to make sense of things. That is Thirlwallian pedagogy. It presents the material in the context of issues, puzzles, and perplexities that provoke the understanding. The material does not speak for itself. It does not stand on its own, as it did for Mitford. The student is led to step back from the phenomena. And so he or she gains a certain distance from things themselves, and comes to appreciate the range and creativity of judgement, of theory, and of understanding. Moreover, a corresponding ecology emerges. As time passes, as we learn new things, understandings and theories—conceptual devices—are reworked.

Chapter 4

Inquiry as Reconstruction

For some time now inquiry has been front and center in our science classrooms, but there are telling issues. And to these we must now add significant pressures arising from the growing emphasis in our schools on high-stakes testing. In the face of these pressures there is a tendency to see "inquiry" as inefficient and time-consuming, as was clear in a California State School Board decision in 2004 to cut the percentage of time given to inquiry in the science curriculum.

Bruce Alberts, President of the National Academy of Sciences and the head of the group that prepared the NRC report on science education, replied vigorously to the California board. In a letter to the board, he urged them not to undermine the efforts of "the thousands of scientists, administrators, and teachers who are working to incorporate effective hands-on inquiry strategies and related instructional materials into classrooms nationwide" (Alberts, 2004).

Let us then examine what inquiry has to offer; for there is a gem at the heart of inquiry, but we have to work to uncover it.

On the Wisdom of Walking Backwards

We may begin with a traditional Sufi tale that seems most relevant. It is about a teacher, the Mullah Nasrudin, and his students. The mullah is an interesting character. A mix of sage and ingénue, he is a rich source of insight. In one story he enters an inn announcing that the moon is more important than the sun because it shines at night, when you need it. In another he discovers the wisdom of Nature in the difference between the watermelon vine and the apple tree. Struck by the irony of the magnificent apple tree with its puny fruit and the scraggly watermelon vine with its magnificent fruit, he is brought around to Nature's wisdom when an apple falls and strikes him on the head and he realizes how different it would have been had he been hit by a watermelon! In yet another tale, my favorite, the mullah is invited to dine with a prince. When he arrives, the doorman says he is not properly attired. Without any protest, the mullah returns to his home and changes into his finest clothing. Now when he arrives at the prince's estate, the doorman welcomes him and the mullah proceeds to his place at dinner. Soon he is served soup and the mullah begins to ladle his soup onto his vest! The prince is puzzled by this behavior and asks the mullah why he would do such a thing? He replies that evidently it was his clothes that were invited to dine and not his person (Shah, 1973, p. 42). Enough—on to the story connected to our study.

In this story the mullah finds the distinct advantage of not looking where you are going. He is reflecting on the relationship he can have with his students. He may walk ahead of them, but then he turns his back on them as he does so, and though he may lead them, he cannot engage them on their journey. It is also possible for his students to walk before their teacher. But now, though they have the comfort of his presence, he does not lead them and they may readily go astray. What is a teacher to do? Then it occurs to him . . . there is a third possibility. The teacher may walk ahead of his students, but walk backwards as he does so (Shah, 1973, p. 84). I think that this is supposed to be one of those foolish stories, like the one about the moon being more important than the sun, but I think the mullah is exactly right. What is most important about our work with children is that we engage students, and for that we need to look them in the eye. We need to talk to them and prod and poke until we know we have taken things to the edge of their understanding. But we cannot do this if we have our eye on the landscape in front of them. Our mastery of the material, of that landscape, is not the point. It's our mastery of teaching and the logic of the exchange that is to be called upon, our read of the children and our ability to connect them to issues.

Let us take advantage of the mullah's insight, and use it to consider inquiry in our classrooms. The first two of the mullah's three ways reflect the two leading options in inquiry-centered science teaching that have been followed: teacher-led inquiry and student–led inquiry. The third way may be compared to our own suggestion of inquiry as reconstruction.

On Teacher-Led Inquiry

We have already offered important criticisms of the first of the mullah's cases. Too often, inquiry in the classroom leaves the student behind. The work of Osborne and Freyberg is an excellent case in point. By talking to students both in and out of class, they and their team of researchers found that most of the time most students did not understand the purpose or meaning of the activities or labs in their science classes; at least, not in the way that text and teacher presumed.

I am reminded of those lovely Abbott and Costello routines, where we are treated to the rich ambiguity of conversation. Many are familiar with "Who's on First," but Abbott and Costello had many other routines. One of my favorites has the straight man, Abbott, returning to announce that unlike the lazy Costello, he has a job. "I'm a loafer," he says. Costello, who has spent the day lounging about, replies, "Me, too." "No you're not," says Abbott, "you're just lazy. I knead dough." Again Costello says, "Me, too." Only to find Abbott saying he can't because he hasn't joined the union. This leaves Costello dumbfounded and by the end of the routine he asks Abbott: "What makes a balloon go up?" "Hot air," Abbott replies. "What's keeping you down?" rejoins a fully exasperated Costello (Abbott and Costello, 1952).

The echo of such routines can be found in our classrooms. Osborne and Freyberg uncovered a host of them in their conversations with students. Imagine the simple confusion, for example, when students are told in an ecology unit about consumers and producers. Just what would it mean, by way of explanation, that plants make their food? Doesn't it take hands to make things? How are lions, tigers, or bears consumers? What stores would they go to? (Bell and Freyberg, in Osborne and Freyberg, 1985, pp. 35–6).

In fact, let's look at a more extended example of the way teacher-led inquiry can fail to work out. Again, this is taken from Osborne and Freyberg, in an essay by Tasker and Osborne, "Science Teaching and Science Learning". Two thirteen-year-old students are doing an experiment called "breaking up a compound." It involves batteries connected to electrodes in a water bath where copper chloride has been dissolved. Evidently the students expect both electrodes to generate bubbles. When only one does, they assume something is wrong and start to tinker with the set-up. They flip the connections to the batteries and now get bubbles with the other electrode. We then get this snippet of interview between the researcher and John, one of the students:

Observer:	When you swapped the connections over . . . you did that because it wasn't working too well?
John:	Yes, it was working at one (electrode) but not the other. One of the batteries was too weak.
Observer:	You had a weak battery?
John:	Yes, when we swapped the terminals over the good battery made the other terminal work.
Observer:	If all the batteries were good would both of the terminals work at the same time?
John:	Yes.
Observer:	Would there be an electric current in the liquid?
John:	Um . . . no . . . the electrodes are apart . . . there is no connection through there (the liquid).

(p. 19)

This episode is curiously like the "duality" of an Abbott and Costello routine, in that there seems to be a pretty extended alternative student interpretation of what is going on with this experiment. It becomes even more interesting if it is complemented by a discussion of a common student interpretation of electrical circuits. Students often see electricity as flowing from both terminals of a battery to an appliance—say, a light bulb—rather than seeing the flow of electricity as around a loop (p. 23). In this case we can readily imagine that the two students felt that electricity was only being delivered to one of the electrodes, whichever one was attached to the good terminal. Bubbles were a sign of the presence of electricity, and there was no need for any electricity to pass through the liquid. This is a quite reasonable interpretation, and it is clear that these students have engaged the material. But there is a problem here.

I have already suggested that I don't think we should be consumed by "right answer" anxiety. So what is the problem? It's a matter of what happens next. This is a "Jesse" moment. John has a theory. It needs to be engaged. Student accounts of the material need to be shared and there should be opportunities to push things further and test the adequacy of different interpretations. That would be lovely. There is an important collective, public moment after labs where the teacher needs to step forward and examine what has been learned. If something of that sort does not happen, then students like John are likely to be left unclear about why they were wrong. This is how we convince students they are not cut out for science.

The central lesson here is that activity does not speak for itself. Without talk, without the active engagement of the teacher, students may run through the activity as if they were baking brownies, replacing judgement by routine; or, they may grapple with the material, but without the kind of support that would enable them to get clear of the thicket. In either case, it's not what ought to happen.

The issue then is this: if we would lead our students by walking ahead of them we need somehow to make sure they are with us.

On Student-led Inquiry

The second of the mullah's options was recently examined in a paper by Piet Lijnse, "Didactics of Science" in *Improving Science Education* (2000). Lijnse offers an important critique of student-led inquiry. He argues that though it may well be engaging, it isn't enough. Students are not getting to the core of genuine scientific concepts.

Take, for example, the structure of matter, the idea of atoms and molecules. Are students arriving at a scientifically acceptable understanding? Lijnse thinks not. Students are merely wrapping acceptable words, like "atoms," around naïve and unscientific notions. Students see atoms as tiny bits of the whole. An atom of silver, for example, is seen as a tiny bit of silver, metallic and shiny, and silver in color. But this is not the scientific conception. Moreover, Lijnse is convinced that there is no way to get there from here via students' own inquiry. Children's ideas will not lead to a proper understanding of the scientific concept (Lijnse, 2000, pp. 315–17).

This is a serious criticism, and it is not limited to the particular case of the atomic nature of matter. As we have emphasized, scientific concepts are a long haul from common sense, and the hallmark theories of the sciences are stridently counterintuitive. Ordinary language everywhere calls a sunrise—"sunrise"—not "earth-spin". Atoms are real objects, but we cannot experience them, while fire can be experienced, but is not, itself, a thing. In these and a myriad of other examples, the problem is the same. Ordinary experience and ordinary reasoning do not ordinarily lead to scientific notions.

In the case of the particle theory of matter, there is a conceptual leap in the way we understand the world beneath experience. Magnifying lenses and microscopes show us worlds vastly more intricate and delicate than we might have imagined, but they are worlds we can recognize. The world of the atom is very different. It is a world constructed by reason and only faintly touches the world of experience.

Often we use models to represent the world beneath experience, but it is important to recognize that such models are not images. They are traces in the mind's eye, satisfying theoretical demands. Consider, for example, the complex structure of the DNA molecule. This myriad of atoms arrayed in a twisted double helix is often presented in an abbreviated fashion using A's, T's, C's, and G's to stand for the nucleotides that connect the two legs of the double spiral. I know I often had to talk about just what these A's and T's, etc., represented, so that my students would not walk away from these representations assuming that if you had a good enough microscope you would actually see something like alphabet soup, with little A's and T's, etc.

When we are talking about atoms, the difference between the model and the scientific conception takes on a heightened significance; for with the atom, the qualities of ordinary experience don't apply. This was at the heart of the original conception of the atom in antiquity. Galen, a physician who lived in the second century AD, said of the atomists:

> All these people presuppose that the primary element is quality-less, having no natural whiteness or blackness or any other colour whatever, and no sweetness or bitterness or heat or cold or in general any other quality whatever. For, says Democritus, "by convention colour, by convention bitter, by convention sweet, in reality atoms and the void".
>
> (in Barnes, 1987, p. 255; see also Lucretius, Book II)

This is the cutting edge of the atomist hypothesis. The whole range of the ordinary properties of matter is reduced to a narrow set of primary qualities—the size, shape, and motion of an otherwise quality-less matter.

"D.Q., I was holding on by the skin of my teeth, but that passage from Democritus really threw me. What did he mean when he said 'by convention' whatever?"

"Generally speaking, Sancho, 'by convention' means by common agreement . . . like a set of rules for playing a game of touch football. In this case, the early atomists were forging language that would capture the differences between the way things are and the way they appear. 'By convention' doesn't mean we all sat down and agreed to see things as colored in one fashion or another, but that color *and other qualities such as taste and texture are not actually located in the objects themselves, but are the product of the way we sense them. They aren't really there, but rather they're in our heads, and so they are of a different order, more like rules we have made up."*

"Can you do this a bit more?"

"Sure. Have you heard that old riddle: if a tree falls in the forest and no one is there to hear it, does it still make a sound? Most people don't see what it's getting at. Regardless of whether someone is in the forest, the tree is going to do exactly the same thing. It falls and in slamming onto the forest floor it sets up all sorts of vibrations. These are carried by the air. If someone is there, then the vibrating air enters the ear canal, strikes against the membrane of the eardrum, and a chain of events leads to electrical pulses moving down the auditory nerve to the brain, which then generates the sensation we recognize as sound."

"Wait a minute. Are you saying that all the tree does is make a kind of shock wave? We, in turn, take that shock and turn it into sound?"

"That's right, Sancho. By convention, a noise. In reality, nothing but air particles doing a dance. In the same way, gold atoms are not tiny bits of gold. That is, they are not tiny metallic bits of gold colored stuff. There is something there, but the qualities that make it appear as gold, are the result of our sensing apparatus."

"Why?"

"Because it doesn't work if the colors are really in the objects. Carbon is a good example. A lump of coal is virtually pure carbon and it is black. At the same time, a diamond is also virtually pure carbon and it is essentially colorless, as is the carbon dioxide we breathe."

"Of course . . . I always wondered about that. But how can that be? Most things have colors. Where does the color come from, if atoms are colorless?"

"That's a great question. Do you see how you have stood things on their heads and that's exactly right? That atoms must be colorless is now reasonable, so the question becomes: Where does color come from? Here, as with so many other central ideas in the sciences, the move to really understand is very demanding, far beyond familiar experiences or simple schema. Lijnse was right to call the question. If we turn things over to our students and let them set the agenda, do we have any reason to believe they will work their way to a legitimate end, one that is fairly deemed scientific? Lijnse doesn't think so, and I don't either."

"Then, how do you get there?"

"You go a long way, Sancho, with what we may think of as a naïve response to the world and to the answers our textbooks offer kids. The world is a curious place, but not as curious as the ideas we are led to as we try to explain things.

"Do you remember the example of spilling some water and dropping my keys (in Chapter two)? Both are heavy bodies and both naturally fall to the floor. So now let me ask you the question: How long before my keys end up in the clouds?"

"But the keys would never end up in the clouds. They're heavy and you would have to lift them and somehow put them in the clouds."

"So what about the water? The water is heavy. What is lifting it up?"

"I don't know, D.Q. I remember your discussion of evaporation and condensation with the magic glass, but I don't remember anything about how the water would go up."

"O.K. What is critical here is that everyone learns about the water cycle. We all know about evaporation and condensation, but we are rarely led to stop and ask what it really means. What must the world be like, if these things take place? This is how you put wonder back in the classroom . . . a wonder at how things work. This is how you shift from answers to arguments. You simply ask: Why would they say that? That is what inquiry as reconstruction is about. In effect, it starts in the middle of things, with that swirl of answers and incomplete understandings that each of us carries. It then turns this upside down in an effort to get at why we would think these things in the first place and what these things tell us about the world.

"Let's go back to the text and consider the atom as we might if we taught the third way, the mullah's way."

The Third Way: Inquiry as Reconstruction

The task before us is to develop a sophisticated concept of the atom in an interactive way, responsive to the ideas and understandings of students. As we do so, I am reminded of that disclaimer on videos about the tape being reformatted to fit your screen. This narrative represents one side of a conversation with students on a given day or two: what I would say. Their various replies, comments, and questions would, of course, significantly effect the unfolding of these ideas. Yet we lack this format, and so the narrative has been altered to fit our screen. In what follows, the issues raised with students are in **bold** print. Student comments and questions are left to your imagination, while my editorial comments, appropriate for you, the reader, will be in regular type.

The atom is not large enough to trip over. It cannot be picked up and looked at. It can't be placed on a scale and weighed. How then was it discovered? . . . It wasn't. It was invented. A product of our imagination, it first appeared on the horizon of intellectual discourse some 2,000 years ago—2,000 years, that is, before it hovered over the horizon at Hiroshima.

We may assume that students of virtually every age have heard of atoms. A natural start to the conversation is to explore the rational grounds for belief. Why does the scientific community buy the idea of atoms? And so we are led to an exploration of those things the mind invents.

The ancients did not discover the atom. They could not have. It cannot be experienced. It was invented. There is an intriguing tension between those things the mind discovers and those it invents. Consider, for example, the path or orbit of a planet. Many ancient peoples discovered the planets as distinctive heavenly bodies, stars that wandered against the background of

the fixed stars. Only in ancient Greece, however, did the gaze shift from the planets themselves to the path the planets took as they wandered. It would, in fact, be the problem of how we understand the shape of these paths or orbits that would dominate astronomy and play an absolutely central role in the development of the sciences from Plato and Aristotle through Copernicus, Kepler, Galileo and Newton, and Einstein as well. But what is an orbit? It is certainly not an ordinary thing that may be tripped over or weighed. It is a product of our imagination, a trace in the mind's eye and not in nature, at least not in an ordinary sense.

Both orbits and atoms were theoretical entities, underlying structures, conceptual devices (like Hercules). They were what they needed to be in order to form a more perfect explanation. Even though we cannot experience them directly, these conceptual devices have evolved as different arguments have been offered about how best to "see" the relation between the world as it appears and the world as it might be structured.

Strikingly, the atom as a thing invented was somehow transformed into a "real" object. That is, to state it in its most dramatic terms, when the bomb bay doors of the Enola Gay opened as it flew over Japan in August of 1945, it was not a host of words and equations that tumbled out, but a device. The human imagination has invented a host of theoretical objects, from notions of loyalty, truth, and beauty, to gods and goddesses. The atom, however, is among a small number of such entities that have become actual objects; perhaps the only case. How striking that it would lead to a weapon of such destructive might.

What problem led to the invention of the atom? This is a difficult question to answer. We have been so carefully taught that the world is composed of atoms; it is hard to think in any other fashion. The atom is a truth that has been handed down to us with all the authority of teachers, Golden Books, television specials, and newspaper headlines. Yet, if we ask ourselves why we should believe in tiny, invisible spheres of utterly insignificant mass and measure, we are hard pressed to find an answer. Can you think of any argument that might lead to the idea of atoms?

We may expect students to come up with arguments for indiscernible particles, tiny bits of matter beneath experience. One of my favorite examples comes from Lucretius. Some 2,000 years ago, Lucretius, a Roman, wrote *On the Nature of Things*, a lengthy essay in poetic form about the atom! In it he tells of a statue that stood outside a gate to Rome. The outstretched hand of the statue had gradually been worn down by the repeated slaps of pilgrims and passers-by (Lucretius, 1968, Book I, lines 310–320). But is this what atoms are all about? Lijnse has emphasized that it is not enough to buy into tiny bits (2000, pp. 315–316). Students need to see that the qualities of experience do not obtain at the level of atoms. So we can ask the question, are the indiscernible bits of Lucretius' statue atoms? Are there atoms for each kind of thing? For water? Or chocolate? Or hot dogs? For some, it may be clear that this is not a satisfactory result, that it means there would be too many kinds of atoms. But for others, this may be reasonable; that is, there's no reason to object. You might then pose a question about how things can change or grow (shifting back to student talk) . . .

People are made of bones, sinew, and flesh. By the time you are in school, your bodies are much larger than when you were born. It seems reasonable that growth is related to the food you've eaten, but if hot dogs are made of hot dog atoms, then are there parts of me that are hot dog atoms? Wouldn't I be made of people atoms? Can an atom of one kind become an atom of another kind? Where did my atoms come from?

This sort of question was first raised long ago by Parmenides, a Greek who lived early in the fifth century BC. To understand why people believed in the existence of atoms long before there were any empirical grounds for this belief, we need to recognize that the atom was an answer to a question, a question that Parmenides had posed.

Parmenides examined the notion of change, of a given thing undergoing the process of becoming something new, and found that you couldn't make sense of it. He felt that it was magic to think that something could be one thing at one moment and then become something else the next. Furthermore, it was a cornerstone of Parmenides' thinking that if something didn't make sense, then it couldn't be true. The world was not arbitrary. Events unfolded in a rational manner. We might experience the appearance of such changes, but they must be only the outward suggestion of change. In reality there could be no change.

Parmenides offered an argument using three pretty straightforward ideas:

1. What is, is.
2. What is not, is not.
3. Nothing can come from nothing.

His idea was that whatever really exists, like hot dog atoms, really exists and so could not then be destroyed or created (de Santillana, 1961, pp. 88–102; see also Popper, 1963, pp. 66–96 and 136–165).

Let us break here, and try to make sense of what Parmenides was getting at. There are lots of instances we might explore, such as a leaf in autumn as it changes from green to a brilliant red. To begin with, no one stole the green leaf while our backs were turned and replaced it with the red one. That would be magic. There was a change, but it was a transformation. Nothing disappeared and nothing simply popped into being. Nothing passed away into nothingness, and nothing came into being from nothingness. What, then, happened? Where did the red come from? And what happened to the green?

This is a lovely question—where did the green go? I have explored it with kids of all ages and it is remarkable what notions we harbor. One of my favorites was the child who suggested that the green is drawn back into the tree and sits in a chamber beneath the ground throughout the winter cold! Let's go back to the classroom, picking up in the middle of a discussion of where the green went . . .

Science books tell us that the green of a leaf is located in chlorophyll. When chlorophyll "breaks down," other pigments define the overall appearance of the leaf. The key here is this business of breaking down. Chlorophyll is a complex substance composed of carbon, hydrogen, oxygen, and other materials. When it breaks down these materials don't disappear; they rearrange, and as a consequence no longer yield the same color. It's just the green that disappears.

This business of breaking down and rearranging sounds a lot like eating. Suppose hot dogs are not made of hot dog atoms. Whatever it is that is in a hot dog gets broken down into component parts and is rearranged into ourselves. It's much like the old Franklin press. You had a large wooden frame and a great many small steel bits with the letters of the alphabet raised on them, in different sizes, some lower case, some capitals. You would compose a page by placing the letters in order and spelling out the news of the day. You would then ink the whole array and by pressing paper down onto the frame print the newspaper. When you finished the run, you would put the letters back into their various compartments and get ready to compose the news of the next day.

There is an important shift here with both food and letters. The properties of the food and the meanings of the words are not a sum of the properties/meanings of the component parts. The properties of words emerge at a level beyond the letters. That is, the meaning of a word is not the sum of the meanings of the letters that spell it out. Consider the meanings of this growing series of letters. Begin with the familiar word "he." Now add an "r," so you have "her." Now add an "e" and get "here." Finally add a "t" and arrive at "there." Meanings changed pretty dramatically with every additional letter, and it wasn't the meaning of the letter itself that carried the change. That is, you can't get from "here" to "there" by adding the meaning of "t." Perhaps, it's the same story with the food we eat and with atoms.

In solving this problem, what have we done to the idea of the atom? We started off with atoms that were tiny, indiscernible bits of stuff. But now they've become curiously interchangeable. They can be parts of hot dogs or of ourselves, or whatever they get into. We can see the same inter-changeability in the broadest sweep of things. A log burns, becoming ashes and smoke. In such changes, the basic stuff remains the same; yet the way it looks is completely different. We do not look like the food we eat; nor does a log look like a mixture of ash, air, and smoke. Atoms are evidently significantly different from the way they might look in any given cluster. Somehow, the way things look is an effect, and not really the way things are at the bottommost level. To go back to an earlier observation about atoms being colorless: substances have the potential to be perceived in different colors by virtue of their association (just as letters have the potential to mean different things by virtue of their association). These elemental substances are real; the colors are not. That the green of the leaf would disappear is okay because "green-ness" is not a thing. It is only an effect, derived from an underlying structure. That structure is the real world— though, of course, we never see it directly. We reasoned our way to it.

We may stop our classroom piece here. By this point we have earned the distinction that is so critical to Lijnse's essay—the break between naïve and scientific understandings of the particulate theory of matter. There is a fundamental divide between appearances and reality. We have earned this distinction by posing problems and trying to make sense of the issues raised by Parmenides and examined by those who came after him, such as Anaxagoras and Democritus. We did not, that is, simply announce to kids what the character of the scientific understanding is. We earned it by going back to the original issues and arguments that attended the development of the concept.

"Can I jump in here to see if I got this right, D.Q.? There are two standard approaches to inquiry, teacher-led and student-led, and problems with both. In teacher-led, students tend not to have an adequate understanding of the issues, and consequently they don't really understand what they are doing. That's what the Osborne and Freyberg book is about. In student-led, they generate the questions, so they appreciate what is being asked, but they can't push the material very effectively, so they don't get to the fundamental matters."

"Excellent, Sancho. You can hardly expect students to match the great insights of the master thinkers across the ages on their own."

"But there is a third way, a form of inquiry that leans heavily on the history of science. It's the mullah's notion of walking backwards. Here inquiry is shaped by the interaction between teacher and students; so you avoid the ambiguities of teacher-led inquiry. And the history of science helps to direct study toward those issues and problems that were crucial in the development of our understanding; so you meet Lijnse's challenge of pushing beyond where students could get on their own."

"That's right, Sancho. In ancient story-telling, the aim of the story was often to explain how the world had come to be the way it is. The Tower of Babel is a nice instance. The first humans—that is, Adam and Eve—would have spoken one language. So where did we get all the many languages of the present? The Tower of Babel explains it. Walking backwards not only underlines the importance of engaging students, it also reminds us as teachers of the landscape of the past and how the modern understanding has come to be the way it is. The mullah was no fool."

Interlude
Peter Rabbit and Plato

Years ago my wife was teaching in an elementary school program for deaf children. She began to have the children read the Beatrix Potter classic, "The Tale of Peter Rabbit." Her colleagues wondered why she would choose such a difficult book, one the children would not understand; nor would they be able to relate to its remote setting or its quaint language. But my wife was convinced there was a fundamental "draw" to the story, its language and the illustrations, and that the children would become so absorbed they would work hard to make the story work.

And that is exactly what happened. The children loved the story, especially when poor Peter becomes entangled in gooseberry netting as he runs away from farmer McGregor. Here's the next line from the story: "Peter gave himself up for lost, and shed big tears; but his sobs were overheard by some friendly sparrows, who flew to him in great excitement, and implored him to exert himself" (Potter, 1995). That is quite a sentence, with a complexity and vocabulary far removed from their ordinary reading and their everyday speech. But the draw of the story was such that the children made this language work. They exerted themselves.

There's a moral here that has to do with relevance. For years, various programs and curricula have proposed to turn things around in our schools by tapping into material that is relevant. Just recently, for example, there was an extended flap over a new curriculum adopted by Baltimore City's public schools. Aimed at improving reading for middle-schoolers, it used popular magazines that target teenagers as reading material. The city soon dropped the program in dismay at the hue and cry let out over having students read articles about dating or how to kiss (Neufeld, 2006, p. 1B). The core idea behind this curriculum was straightforward. Too often our students are not doing their work. Teen magazines and the like would pique their interest and open the door to further reading. I have no real problem with this, but I think it sadly reduces the notion of relevance to popular culture. Dating and football, fashion and automobiles are but a shadow of what relevance is about. Recall John Dewey's story about water in the classroom: what makes something relevant is not that it smells like home, but that it addresses something we can connect to.

"Peter Rabbit" was relevant to that class of students, however remote the tale of a rabbit in a farm field . . . however remote its language. There is a draw in perplexity and in arguments that work to make sense of things in the face of these problems. There is, in this sense, a certain substantiality to the likes of Peter Rabbit, and it works to draw the reader in despite a seeming distance.

We can see this as well in Plato.

Plato's dialogue, *The Republic*, is a substantial work. Where most of the dialogues are, perhaps, thirty or forty pages long, *The Republic* is more than 200 pages long. Where most are marked by real exchanges and give and take, *The Republic* is marked by long discursive passages by Socrates. Plato is laying things out here. I read *The Republic* as an undergraduate. It is a standard in humanities courses, most especially political science classes where it is seen as the first political vision of a utopian society. I know many people who have read it once. I know very few who have read it more than once. That's what makes Huey Newton's story so remarkable.

Huey Newton was one of the founders of the Black Panther movement, a forceful group in the charged atmosphere of the late 1960s. The Black Panthers generated a number of effective community programs, seeking to meet the needs of the black community without having to depend on the larger white community. At the same time, many found their words and work threatening. How does this all connect to Plato's *Republic*?

Huey Newton was from Oakland, California, and when he graduated from high school he decided that he really couldn't read. He could read in a functional way, but not the way one might. Being Huey Newton, he decided that that was what society had wanted. So he took himself down to the library, and this story, which comes from his obituary in the *New York Times*, doesn't say how this next step took place, but when he left the library he left with *The Republic*. He read it. He knew he didn't understand it. He read it again. That is remarkable. Here is a streetwise kid, out of school, and he sits down to reread the *Republic* because he knew there was something in it he didn't get. He read it a third time, and a fourth. He read it five times. Five times (Hevesi, 1989). Huey Newton went on to earn a bachelor's degree and a doctorate, as well as create the Panthers with a small cadre of others. It is a remarkable story.

In his prescient novel, *Fahrenheit 451*, Ray Bradbury foresees a society where books are banned and life is played out in shallow distractions. There are but a few souls who still cherish learning. One of these, an English professor who lost his job when the last liberal arts college closed, explains why learning was so important: "I don't talk *things*, sir . . . I talk the *meaning* of things. I sit here and *know* I'm alive" (Bradbury, 1953, p. 75). To have read *The Republic* five times, Huey Newton must have felt that same vitality in the meaning of things. Who would have guessed that a streetwise eighteen-year-old would have found the musings of a long dead rich white man who wore a toga relevant? I think Dewey would have. There is plenty of water in Plato's classroom.

Note

For those of you who attend to such things, this is the mid-point of this book, a matter of some importance according to an old acquaintance. Years ago, when I was just starting high school, my family moved out from the Chicago area. My father had lost his job in the stockyards along with thousands of others, and we moved so that my mother could attend Gallaudet College in Washington, DC. She had a wonderful time as a student, and at the center of that good time was a literature professor, Dr. Leonard Siger. He was a well of unfathomable depths, with intriguing theories and observations, a sardonic take on life, and a ready wit. Even so many years later, I can recall many of his offerings, including a little dissertation on the structural decoding of literature. If one graphed the lengths of the chapters of Francis Parkinson's saga, *The Oregon Trail*, for example, it mirrored the topography of that trek across the plains and the Rockies. But middles were the real key. Good story-telling would pivot at the middle, revealing the heart of the tale. So, for example, at the mid-point of Cervantes' great novel, *Don Quixote*, the hero climbs a mountain and reaches the height of his madness.

Sadly, my artfulness is not up to the task. So allow me to simply insert at this mid-point the following telling tale . . .

Years ago a survey was taken, a Harris poll, a Gallup poll, what have you. Regardless, lots and lots of people were asked: What would you do to improve communication? Almost everyone answered the same way. They would think more carefully before they spoke and they would speak more clearly . . . a very reasonable reply. A small number, however, had a very different take. All of the American Indians in the survey, and only the American Indians, answered that to improve communication they would listen better.

Isn't that spectacular? Everyone else took communication to be about what they themselves had to say. But communication is an exchange, and it is crucial to listen well enough so that you will understand the person you are talking to and know what will be relevant and effective in explaining yourself.

I cannot cite this survey. I heard about it in a talk perhaps 20 years ago, and I haven't been able to track it down. But I am not sure it matters; for even as an apocryphal tale, it works. The image of the American Indian in our society reminds us of what we have lost as we have moved away from what is natural, what is simple and direct. Teaching is not just what we have to say. It's not just about being thoughtful and clear. If that were so, then textbooks would be far more effective. The learning we seek thrives on the connection between the material and the open mind of the student. That connection requires that we listen better. We all need to be Indians.

Chapter 5

What Do We Teach When We Don't Teach the Answer?

"Walking backwards" underlines that our real work is not getting students to some place on a map of facts, technical terms, and concepts. This is true for all of the analytical disciplines, not just the sciences . . . but it seems most especially true of the sciences. One of the first lessons that the history of science teaches is that science is not the steady accumulation of facts and truths. The growth of the sciences is far more complicated and organic than that, embracing revolutions and profound re-conceptualizations. Why then would we anchor science teaching in a particular body of answers? Why would we systematically hold students responsible for answers? It's not the answers that science is really about.

Though I have taught for more than 35 years, it is only over the last several years that I have spent a significant amount of time watching others teach. It is clear that most of these teachers have seen their job as facilitating a student's encounter with information. This is what they do, and they tend to believe it is what they have to do. Answers are the measure of a student. And telling is how teachers work to get students there. This is especially so because of the high-stakes testing environment we have established in most of our schools. But this issue is not a modern one. We have struggled for many years across this terrain, and still we are left with this simple question: What do we teach, when we don't teach answers?

Fifty Years Ago

We may begin with an article published in *Scientific American* in 1958. It was written by Walter Michels, president of the American Association of Physics Teachers. Michels wrote of the need for a deep reform of the nation's approach to physics in high school and undergraduate teaching. "In the public discussion that has followed the Russians' launching of their satellites," he began, "the word 'physics' has probably occurred almost as often as 'satellite,' 'rocket,' or 'missile'" (Michels, 1958, p. 57). And so the article immediately takes the modern reader to a world where school children learned to "run, duck, and cover" in case of nuclear explosion and the clock on the *Bulletin of Atomic Scientists*, a journal devoted to the geopolitical issues raised by atomic science, was just a few moments shy of detonation. Public anxiety over Sputnik was great, and Michels placed the reform of physics teaching right in the center of it. Russia had won the first round and who knew what kind of superiority this might foretell. Yet Michels was cautious. Before rushing into a program designed to persuade more students to take more physics, he asked—Are we teaching it the right way?

Michels was convinced we were not. Physics courses, he observed, had been "heavily influenced by the fact that a large proportion of the students taking them are preparing for engineering" (p. 58). This had led both courses and texts to emphasize technological applications, and this was the rub. From Michels' perspective, technology was not the proper aim of physics instruction, nor was the application of technology effective pedagogy:

> The future rests not so much on the number of engineers and scientists produced each year as it does on the intellectual and cultural climate in which they work, and this, in turn, will be determined by our success or failure in making physical science a significant part of general education.
>
> (pp. 57–58)

Thus, though Michels had linked the call for reform to the Cold War, the full-page illustration at the head of his article was not a mushroom cloud or a rocket rising from Cape Canaveral. It was, instead, a family tree tracing the lineage of the great ideas of physics through a pantheon of its most famous theorists, from Galileo to Einstein. The core aim of physics education was an understanding of the principles of physics and its methods.

Things have changed since Michels' critique. Our texts no longer "abound in pictures and diagrams of Diesel shovels, locomotives, gasoline engines and automobile transmissions" (p. 58). But if we look at what his real concerns were, we find that perhaps things have not changed quite so much.

In his call for reform, Michels drew a bead upon the "piecemeal" approach of most physics texts and lessons, an approach that leads students across the surface of the discipline. Instead of guiding students to powerful unifying principles, this fragmented approach too often involved "rote memorization of isolated facts and of formulas into which numbers can be substituted to achieve answers which often mean little to the student who has obtained them" (p. 58).

The "failure of the piecemeal approach" (p. 61) was the heart of Michels' paper. The point was to go beyond the manipulation of formulas and the reduction of the material to algorithms. What we really needed to do was to rid our texts and our lesson plans of their many distractions and to focus instead on the "ideas, methods and history of physics" (p. 62). We needed to put quality ahead of quantity, tackle the principles of physics directly, build a well-reasoned foundation for all its most central concepts, and to do this well.

Michels ended his article with optimism. Much was being done. Summer institutes and teacher training programs, new films and lab apparatus, and the promise of a fine new text from the Physical Science Study Committee (PSSC) of the Massachusetts Institute of Technology, sponsored by the National Science Foundation, all contributed to his hope that physics teaching was on the right track.

Fifty Years Later

The Russian space program is no longer the source of anxiety it once was. Things have changed. Physics texts are no longer dominated by engineering applications, and the PSSC physics text Michels looked forward to is now in its seventh edition. However, we are once again in the midst of an extensive review of science teaching in America and urgent calls for reform. The American Association for the Advancement of Science (AAAS) Project 2061 led to an important study, *Science for All Americans* (1989; see also *Benchmarks for Science Literacy*, 1993). More recently the National Research Council (NRC) published *The National Science Education Standards* (1996), and the International Association for the Evaluation of Education Achievement also released its *Third International Mathematics and Science Study* (TIMSS) in 1996. These studies echo across our classrooms, labs, and lecture halls. But where do we stand?

Strikingly, these recent studies repeat the central theme of Michels' article. The problem is still piecemeal instruction, where the quantity of topics and concepts considered overwhelms the student, who is left with an array of discrete items inadequately understood.

This point is made quantitatively in the TIMSS report. This extensive comparative survey of math and science instruction and curricula found that the US consistently led students across more distinct topics than most other nations in the world, suggesting that we had come to value exposure over understanding, familiarity over coherence, quantity over quality (International Association for the Evaluation of Education Achievement, 1996).

While both the *Benchmarks* and the *Standards* emphasize the need for depth of understanding over mere exposure in their more programmatic and methodological commentaries, neither retreats from a general regard for the full array in their content analyses. The leading concepts and content standards they outline cover an extraordinary sweep from atoms to zygotes.

Evidently the sciences are a hard text to edit. It is easy to imagine the difficulty. Even if everyone around the table should agree that there is too much, yet, to decide that the study of heat phenomena and thermodynamics should be cut from physics or that ecology should be cut from biology courses is evidently just too difficult.

We can see how difficult this paring down process is in the comments of James H. Shea, editor of the *Journal of Geoscience Education*. Shea was struck by the *Standards*' emphasis on arguments and understanding over knowing scientific facts and information, and he was led to ask: "Where was it ever demonstrated that school children could develop a deeper understanding of anything by knowing fewer facts?" (Shea, 1998). This is an interesting question. Understanding should be tethered in some way; somehow anchored in experiences. At the same time, an array of facts does not imply an understanding. Just think of a telephone book. Then there is the nuance in Shea's remark about depth of understanding. How does an understanding become richer or fuller? How does it gain depth? These are interesting questions, but this is not where Shea takes his query. Though he starts with the relationship between facts and understanding, in a twinkling he is talking about the usefulness of knowing the hardness of the 10 minerals of the Mohs scale. That is, he uses this question to warrant the attention to descriptive data, the facts. But what is it about the hardness of ten minerals that would lead to a deeper understanding? What, indeed, would it help us to understand at all? The burden of his remark is that we gain a deeper understanding with such facts, but he has not made his case here.

Shea, it seems, sees science as a body of information and the purpose of science education as the systematic exposure to this information. In terms of the efforts in Michels and the more recent work of the *Benchmarks*, the *Standards*, and the TIMSS report, Shea's concerns highlight the morass confronting reform. Eliminating "even" the Mohs scale of hardness provokes a sharp critique.

Shea goes on to cite another disturbing aspect of the *Standards*: teachers should put less emphasis on activities that demonstrate and verify scientific content and more on activities that analyze scientific questions. "The difference here is small," he goes on to say, "but important." Why should we not take advantage of what science has earned over the last three centuries?

> Of course, skepticism is an important value, but does it really make good educational sense to emphasize doubt regarding the atomic structure of matter, the structure and behavior of the solar system, the chemical formula of water, the shape and size of the earth, the relationship of frequency to pitch, the role of oxygen in combustion, or other topics students might investigate? This is nonsense, pure and simple.
>
> (Shea, 1998)

Now we get to the heart of the matter: Just what is science education all about? Should we actually be encouraging students to question central concepts earned through 300 years or even 2,000 years of careful scrutiny? Clearly not, for Shea. Here is the tension between right answers and right reasoning writ large.

"*D.Q., aren't there basic concepts at the bottom of things that we should lay out for kids?*"

"*I really don't think so, Sancho, for a number of reasons. In the first place, it seems clear to me that having students 'learn' what they do not understand is empty. Shea lays these various items out as if it were obvious what they are really about. But the material does not speak for itself—remember those two dark rocks.*

It is not obvious why we would think that the planets orbit the sun . . . for 2,000 years people thought the sun and planets orbited the Earth. For an even longer time, people thought water was an element and so wouldn't have had component parts, as suggested by the chemical formula H_2O. Each of the items Shea mentions raises good questions and are worthy of careful deliberation over why we would think about them the way we do.

"Shea sees scepticism here as nonsense, as if the point was to get students to doubt the truth. But that's not what's going on. At issue here is whether we teach students simply to recognize the truth. If we push beyond this to the goal of having students understand things, to make sense of them, then the role of scepticism is right there when they ask of themselves 'How do I know if this is so? What's the argument?'"

"As I see things so far, D.Q., your criticism of Shea and the whole tone of standard teaching in the sciences is that there's a lot more to it than the facts. That we need to break from emphasizing information—Shea's hardness scale and all the technical terms that Yager counted—and re-imagine teaching toward understanding, toward making sense of things. But don't you need facts for that, too?"

"Excellent, Sancho. Let's tackle your question with a specific example. In the last chapter we talked a bit about atoms. Suppose we had run though the standard picture of the atom, with electrons orbiting a nucleus composed of protons and neutrons. We can easily imagine questions about this model, such as: What are the component parts of an oxygen atom that has an atomic number of 8 and an atomic weight of 15? Is that pretty clear?"

"Yes, D.Q., I think I can remember. Atomic number is the number of protons and that would be the same as the number of electrons, so that's 8 apiece. Atomic weight is the number of protons plus neutrons in the nucleus, so that would be 8 and 7."

"You bet. Good job. To answer this question you had to have remembered the terms atomic number and weight. Now try this question: Why did we find ourselves talking about the difference between the meaning of the words 'here' and 'there' and the meaning of the letter 't'?"

"Well, D.Q., the idea was that the meaning of words like 'here' and 'there' is not directly related to the meanings of the letters they are composed of. In fact, letters don't mean anything. Words get their meanings in other ways. So, if we are talking about atoms, then this would have come up when we talked about things like salt or water and whether the atoms that compose them are salty or wet. It has been central to the idea of the atom ever since it was introduced in ancient Greece that atoms would not be either salty or wet, bitter or sweet. We know, for example, that atoms don't even have any color because carbon is black in coal but must be colorless in a diamond. So, the color of a substance isn't some sort of sum of the colors of its parts; just like the meaning of a word isn't the sum of the meanings of its letters. And this, in turn, means that the atom was something we must have imagined, because if it doesn't have color then you can't see it."

"Excellent, Sancho. Now tell me what you saw as the differences between these two questions."

"With the first question, I used the definitions I could remember and everything followed pretty straightforwardly. But with the second, I had to figure things out. It isn't that facts played no role in my account, but they played a different role. They weren't the end; they were evidence."

"I agree, Sancho. And that's the answer to your question. There will still be lots of facts and technical terms when we teach toward understanding, but they will have a very different place. They will be evidence. They will have place not because they are in our textbooks, but because we have used them as we argued toward an understanding."

Shea's remarks on the place of scepticism get at fundamental epistemological and pedagogical principles. What are we really teaching? Again, to cite Dewey, there is no doubt where he stands on the value of scepticism: "To maintain the state of doubt and to carry on systematic and protracted inquiry—these are the essentials of thinking" (Dewey, 1997, p. 13). What is important about what we know? What is useful? And how should we teach it? In a lovely essay, "The Bucket and the Searchlight: Two Theories of Knowledge," Karl Popper (1972) captures the essence of two very different views on the character of scientific knowledge. In one approach, science is an accumulation of data, careful observations that are somehow woven or pressed together into concepts and empirical laws. This is the bucket theory and it lends itself to a particular view of the practice of teaching: the teacher is a dispenser of information, carefully decanting science into the minds of his or her students. This would seem to be Shea's position.

The alternative construct, the searchlight theory, emphasizes the active role of the scientist, as opposed to the passivity of a bucket. For Popper, hypotheses always precede observations, shaping just what it is we are looking for. This is the great role theories play. They frame hypotheses that set expectations, which our observations either affirm or deny. Theory tells us the way nature should be. The scientist, as critic, then tests whether the fit between theory and phenomena is good. That is, science is a focused activity, hence the searchlight. It seeks problems or puzzles and how to resolve them. Scientific knowledge is not an accumulation of truths, but is rather an evolving body of theoretical understandings.

The natural approach to teaching linked to Popper's searchlight theory sees the teacher as one who focuses rather than decants. "How could we understand . . .?" is the question of the day, every day. Setting a problem that students can engage in is the critical first step—not, as the "bucket theory" might suggest, is it finding a way to access and verify aspects of the extraordinary body of scientific notions. And so we are brought back to the importance of wonder and perplexity. There is a difference between witnessing nature and trying to make sense of it. There is a difference between being told the sun and moon are different, and trying to figure out how the moon can reflect the light of the sun at night, when the sun isn't there. What children can learn in our classrooms is not simply the chemical formula for water or the role of oxygen in combustion, but more fully what it means to look at the world that way, and what reasons, what evidence supports this understanding. This is the unshaken heart of critical thinking.

Popper's searchlight theory underlines Michels' concern with piecemeal instruction. Teaching is not about delineating discrete items, bits and pieces of the received word. It is, instead, engaging students in the rigorous art of making sense of things. Even a cursory glance at our textbooks makes it clear that there is an overwhelming amount of stuff to teach. The problem, however, is not which answers to teach or how to teach all of them in some especially efficient manner. The real problem is quite different. The real problem is: What do you teach, when you don't teach the answer?

As far back as 1910, John Dewey criticized the science teaching of his day, emphasizing the need to focus upon the distinct character of scientific analysis rather than the content per se: ". . . science has been taught too much as an accumulation of ready-made material with which students are to be made familiar, not enough as a method of thinking, an attitude of mind, after the pattern of which mental habits are to be transformed" (Dewey, 1964, p. 183).

But how do you do it? Have Dewey, Michels, and the host of more recent authors sounded a noble theme upon a hollow reed? Is it inevitable that we will race across the full "accumulation," unable to pare it down? Certainly the reader of the *Benchmarks* or the *Standards* can hardly avoid being impressed by the sweep of the sciences the content of which is so elegantly parsed and parceled. Can we find some way to shift science instruction from content to method (Dewey and Popper), from isolated item to connected whole (Michels), and from discrete knowledge to understanding and reasoning (*Standards*)? I believe we can, if we are willing to shift our teaching from right answers to arguments.

On Alternative Views and the Value of Tree-Climbing

There are two tempting common beliefs in science teaching: that the sciences rest upon common sense, and that phenomena become intelligible simply by being displayed. Both of these are way off base. In fact, far more often than not— no, make that everywhere—the sciences are counterintuitive, if not completely outrageous. It is not just black holes or the incredible geometry of the images from electron micrographs of the parts of cells that are so fantastic. Ice ages, DNA, X-rays, fission, fusion . . . everywhere you turn in the sciences are notions that are more like science fiction than anything else. Goodness, just think that modern science envisions a time, not so long ago, when there was a sheet of ice more than one mile thick where Chicago stands today. That's spectacular. For us, as teachers, the implausibility of the sciences should be absolutely front-and-center. In the first place, it draws your attention like a barker at a carnival sideshow. But more significantly, it sets the right tone for analysis, that sceptical guardedness you would want for a good science lesson. As we have seen, given Coleridge's insight that fiction requires a willing suspension of dis-belief, surely a sound first step with non-fiction, and most especially with the critical rationalism of the sciences, is to have your dis-belief at the ready.

Let us consider some fundamental concepts in physics, the sort we touched upon in Chapter three (see the discussion of the research of Berg and Brouwer). We are not dealing here with anything quite as exotic as black holes, gravitational fields so strong they capture light, or 10,000 feet of ice covering much of North America. Yet, such concepts as inertial motion and the Newtonian approach to forces, which are taught in physics and physical science courses everywhere, are not obvious. The Aristotelian framework of natural and violent motions prevailed for close to 2,000 years. If it required the brilliance of Galileo, Descartes, and Newton to develop a well-formed alternative, then why should we be surprised that our students don't get it when we simply tell them about it?

When they don't get it, we tend to call what they have "misconceptions." There is an extensive literature on these misconceptions. Penner (2001) offers a nice account of this literature, seeing two major approaches:

i.   There are those who see the issue as getting students to restructure their understanding of things. This "radical" thesis leans heavily on Kuhn's (1962) notion of a paradigm and the importance of qualitative or gestalt-like changes in perception and understanding. The thrust of this approach is that the material is asking students to change the way they look at the world, and this change is not so much a rational or mechanical process as a flip in sensibilities. A nice example in physics is how students might see what is happening as a wooden block scoots across the floor and comes to a halt. At first they might see it as something like fatigue. When you gave the block a push, you gave it a commodity that wears down in the effort to move the block across the floor. It runs out of steam, as it were, out of the internal push you had given it. This is like the medieval impetus theory. Newton's approach was different. Forces work to change velocities. When you pushed the block, it gained a velocity as you pushed it. Friction in the floor then acts on the moving block to slow it down. There is no "thing" within the block that gets used up. In teaching, we need to be keen to pick up on these alternative constructs and work to have kids leap from internal impetus to the abstract quality of a change in state.

ii.   On the other hand, there are those who deny the discontinuity in the transformation from one understanding to another, seeing it as a more rational change than analogies with gestalt would suggest. This research highlights the importance of prior experience and how well organized it is, as students try to make sense of new phenomena or puzzles. Penner links this strand of research to constructivist thinking, which is a pretty comfortable connection, but the work of Imre Lakatos (1970) seems to me a fuller counterpoint to the influence of Kuhn. Lakatos emphasized broad continuity and the rational evaluation of experience in coming to judgements about alternative understandings.

But whether you see misconceptions from a more Kuhnian or Lakatosian perspective, what seems most important in terms of the practice of the teacher is to make the problem clear, to establish the perplexity. This is what happened when my son and I talked about the moon, and when Jesse and I talked about what held the rain up. "I wonder what it is" is the signature you seek.

But what would this look like for a class, as opposed to the odd conversation? How do you set up the study of some substantive chunk of material from a science lesson? And how do you make sure that the perplexity enables you to get at the substantive issues within the material? We have sketched two classroom conversations so far: the first seeking to show the value of teaching Cuvier before Darwin, the second examining the value of rationally reconstructing the basis for the concept of the atom. Let us now take up a third instance, exploring the question: Is the moon falling?

Most high school students have been in classes where they have studied gravity, and they know to link it both to weight and to why objects fall to the floor. They also have heard that gravity reaches across space and that the planets are held in orbit by the gravitational pull of the sun; just as the moon orbits the Earth because of its gravitational pull. But there is something perplexing here. Why would we think the moon was falling, if it's not getting any closer to the Earth?

This all becomes that much more confusing when we add the notion of weightlessness. The space station orbits about 300–400 miles above the Earth, while the moon is some 240,000 miles away. How can astronauts be weightless when they are relatively close, and yet gravity can work to pull on the moon, a far larger object at a far greater remove?

Such questions begin to forge a common context for study. Students can see that there is a problem. There are bits and pieces of things that they "know" are true, but they can't see how they all fit together.

What is the next step? If the class discussion has gone well, there is a collective sense that there is a problem. Kids will work to figure it out, trying to remember some key fact that must be there, but that they've forgotten. After all, they know the story is true. The Earth is a planet and the sun pulls all the planets around by the force of gravity. They've known that since they read the "Golden Book of the Big Planets." The moon is a local example of the same process. After a few moments, they will begin to say in one way or another, "O.K., we give up. What's the piece we've forgotten? What's the catch?" But there is no catch, no simple matter of fact that can be picked up or put aside or misplaced. There is, instead, an argument.

Once you have established the perplexity, the next step is to start walking backwards. In this case it makes sense to talk about Aristotle. Here's one way to understand the physics of the moon. Aristotle did *not* think the moon was falling. In the first place, the moon is evidently not getting any closer to the Earth, nor is it flying away. It is simply going around in circles. This was critical for Aristotle, because there were no apparent constraints on the moon. It was freely suspended, and yet it moved in a circle. Things on Earth didn't do that. When freely suspended, rocks and water and all sorts of things simply fell in straight lines. So, for Aristotle, the moon was made of something that was completely different. It was not the kind of thing that would fall.

"D.Q., I never thought about things this way."

"Well, Sancho, there are a lot of clever folk who have thought about things and have looked at them in completely different ways. By the way, I can remember visiting the National Air and Space Museum a long time ago and seeing a moon rock that had been brought back by astronauts who had actually walked on the moon. There were huge lines and we waited for a long time, but it was a treat finally to see a real piece of the moon. But then I realized that it must be a fake, because it was being held up from beneath, as if it were an ordinary rock, when it ought to be held in place by the side . . . since the moon falls sideways."

"You're kidding, right?"

"Yes, Sancho, just kidding."

"Natural motion" was a key concept for Aristotle. Consider the various major categories of things on Earth. When I drop a rock or some water they fall to the ground; that is, they fall toward the center of the Earth. Some things don't fall like this. A flame, for example, always points up no matter how we hold the candle, and the heat of the flame rises; it doesn't fall to the ground or push out sideways. It's hard to see what air is doing, but it is clear that it bubbles up to the surface when it is released under water.

A simple tally suggests, then, that earth and water move in a straight line, seeking the center of the Earth, and air and fire also move in a straight line, fleeing the center. We might conclude that earth and water were heavy objects, air and fire are light objects, and that heavy and light are categorically different properties. But Aristotle was very clever, and he suggested another possibility. Perhaps they are all heavy, but some are heavier than others. Hence, they would all be falling, but some don't fall as well as others. It's like the proverbial Christmas assembly. Everyone moves towards the doors when it's over, but the little kids move backwards as the big kids push their way ahead. This would explain how I can sometimes drop a piece of wood and it falls to the ground; but on other occasions I can let go and it rises—if I am standing in a lot of water. It isn't that the wood is absolutely heavy and then becomes absolutely light, but rather, whether it goes up or down is a matter of its surroundings. And so we can appreciate how Aristotle was led to see the moon as categorically different from earth, water, air, and fire; it went around sideways, not up, not down. It moved in circles.

Now, we can state the problem and the purpose of our study in relatively straightforward terms. In the late seventeenth century, Newton would argue that the heavenly bodies move in circles because the force of gravity is acting on them, the same force of gravity that causes rocks and water to fall straight down. Our job is to understand how this could be so, how could he have rationally convinced people that a circle was the same as a straight line?

Here again is the implausible face of the sciences, and it sets a striking task before Newton. Here also is the basic move to introduce material through a problem. In examining the issue, students draw upon their own sense of things, examine Aristotle, and come to see that there is plenty for them yet to figure out.

It is important to have students move from their initial perplexity to an alternative construct, rather than a quick jump to the right answer. By looking at Aristotle's framework they can see that this issue is not a simple matter of fact. Moreover, seeing Aristotle's concept of natural motion sets up a valuable comparison to inertial motion, and makes it easier to see what each was really about.

Aristotle's natural motion was what happened if you didn't do violence to an object. When, for example, you throw a ball into the air, you are doing violence to it. The ball responds and rises. When the violence is spent, then the natural motion takes over and the ball drops. For the Newtonian, inertial motion is similar. It is non-violent motion. It is what happens when *nothing* is pushing the ball around. The difference between the two notions is how they understood what doing violence is about. For Aristotle, a freely falling rock is natural, not violent; but for Newton it's a forced motion, not an inertial motion—the force of gravity is acting on the rock.

Now it turns out that students commonly misunderstand the concept of inertial motion (McCloskey, 1980; Osborne, 1982; and Berg and Brouwer, 1991). A discussion of Aristotle's natural motion, however, addresses these misunderstandings, because it presents an alternative understanding. Consider this story, traditionally associated with Giordano Bruno, an early supporter of Copernicus. Picture a tall-masted boat sailing under a high-arching bridge. In the crow's nest of the boat, at the top of the tallest mast, a man is holding out an orange. Just as the boat passes beneath the bridge another man, kneeling on the bridge, holds out another orange. Here are two virtually identical objects, the oranges, side by side, in virtually the same point in the whole of the universe, and at virtually the same instant they are both released. How do they fall, Bruno asked?

This is a good question, and we can start with the simple observation that each man sees his orange fall straight down. For the sailor, it falls from the crow's nest to the foot of the mast. We know this because that is what happens to us when we ride in trains or planes or cars. When you drop something, it just falls straight down. The same thing happens for the bridge walker, it falls from the bridge to a spot just beneath. But straight down is different for the two men!

And they will each see the other's orange behave in a strange manner. According to the man in the crow's nest, the bridge orange flies off backwards; while according to the bridge walker, the ship's orange scoots off forward. Each orange remembered where it was from!

As students make sense of this story, relating it to their experiences in cars or trains, they also can see how it would fit in an Aristotelian context. The boat's motion is a violent motion. To maintain it, you would need to continue to apply a force. The orange dropped from the crow's nest should shake off this violence and then fall more or less straight down—in the bridge framework—so it would not end up at the foot of the mast. Bruno's fix on the perfect memory of the orange was a break with the Aristotelian framework. You do not need to keep acting on the orange to keep it moving with the boat. That motion comes for free. In Bruno's story, the oranges' inertial motion is not the same as Aristotle's natural motion, and working on the differences helps students to think about what the concepts are saying and what they are not saying. The story offers a certain texture to the typically minimalist lines of equations. Now there is something to grab a hold of.

Bruno's story is not the end of the line with regard to the moon. There is lots of good physics left before you have proven that the moon orbits the Earth because of the force of gravity. Nevertheless, we can set the rest of the matter aside; for our interests are really pedagogical. The question we had set ourselves was: what do you teach when you don't teach the answer. And our answer has been: you teach several answers. Here is what Dewey has to say about problems and alternatives: "Thinking begins in what may fairly enough be called a forked-road situation, a situation which is ambiguous, which presents a dilemma, which proposes alternatives." And he continues with a lovely image: "In the suspense of uncertainty, we metaphorically climb a tree; we try to find some standpoint from which we may survey additional facts and, getting a more commanding view of the situation, may decide how the facts stand related to one another" (Dewey, 1997, p. 11).

A Ladder for Tree-climbers

We can now ask a further question: What do you test when you don't teach answers? Tests structurally support educational values. We are announcing to students what we hold to be important. Hence, the common refrain from students: "Do we have to know this for the test?" This is more or less straightforward in the context set by the logic of the material. If the primary purpose of schooling is to secure information . . . if what it means to be a good student is that you have learned what you have been told, then tests that hold you accountable for the material structurally support this understanding. But what if we are not teaching answers? Our test should still resonate with our values, but what will this look like?

We need a ladder to help students climb.

Consider D.Q. and Sancho's conversation about atoms. The first question was a natural sort of question in the context set by the logic of the material, determining a competency with certain aspects of the atom. But the second question was different. It focused not on an answer, but why we invoked an analogy. It was a question about our effort to understand; as such, it was an invitation to climb Dewey's tree. We want students to engage class discussions as they happen, and as we bring things together in a test, we want them to view and review the landscape of those discussions. In this instance, it concerned a fundamental aspect of how we should think about atoms and the relationship between the qualities of the world as we experience it and the qualities we attribute to the world beneath experience . . . in short, do atoms have color? By asking a question about an analogy, we direct students to how we make sense of things . . . how the facts stand in relation to ideas and theories that offer to explain the phenomena.

There is a line from Goethe that seems exactly right on this point: "Whatever it is that you have inherited from your father, you are going to have to earn it if it is to really belong to you" (in Vonnegut, 1981, p. 60). By reconstructing the issues that provoked important ideas, we enable students to earn these ideas, and so they can belong to them . . . can come to be a part of the way they understand their world.

This idea of structurally supporting educational values is important. The high school I work with in Baltimore values the connection between what you are learning in school and the issues and challenges of life in your community. People had lots of ideas about how to make this connection happen, from internships at public defender's offices, emergency rooms, and after-school programs to making sure public health issues are part of the curriculum in the biology course. It was difficult, however, to pull this off in the flow of the traditional school day. So they have revamped things. Regular courses take place 4 days a week, but Wednesdays are different. Students from the University of Maryland Law School come in and offer classes discussing different aspects of the law; teachers offer seminars on social issues, urban issues, and the like; seniors have a chance to work on the college application process; and students go off into the community on their internships. This certainly takes time away from regular classes, but it also makes clear their commitment to these other educational values.

We need not limit such structures to educational matters that are so close to content or the flow of the schedule. At the mid-point of this book, we spoke of the importance of listening. Is there a structure that one could put in place that would support listening better? Even though this is a subtle and highly individual matter, I think there is. It has to do with grades and how we give students feedback on their work.

Our discussion of assessment in Chapter three turned on the differences between the logic of the material and the logic of the actual exchange with students. As we traced the implications of this shift, we underlined the value of a different kind of feedback. Holding students accountable for arguments rather than answers opens the door to deeper analytical qualities, most especially what evidence supports a given theory and what issues are then raised. It is important for teachers to give ample feedback to students on the strengths and weaknesses of their explanations. To structurally support this extended feedback, teachers should be asked to write narrative reports on the progress of their students. Such narratives also structurally support listening because teachers find themselves having to write about the work of each student. As you write, you discover the sorts of items . . . comments made in class discussion, the character of the written work, their discipline, thoroughness, or clarity of expression . . . that support and make clear your evaluation. While I believe such narratives are a powerful tool in shaping a student's appreciation of the goals of an education, I recognize that not every system will readily accommodate this reform. In such cases, a similar end may be reached with a checklist of some variety that encompasses those habits and cognitive skills most relevant to a given discipline or course. The key moral of the story is this: If you want to be able to make thoughtful and insightful observations, then you need to have listened better. Structures work in powerful ways.

Interlude
Uncovering the Gods

The heart of Michels' critique was the notion that physics teaching was too often fragmented. It turns out that there is also a problem with fragments when we turn to the earliest chapters of science and natural philosophy. Take, for instance, the ancient Greek philosopher, Thales. Thales lived a long time ago, well before Socrates, Plato, and Aristotle. He was born in the seventh century BC. By tradition, he was the "father" of science, the first to pursue and engage the sort of questions that mark the sciences. Unfortunately, we have only a hint of his teachings, as with these two fragments. The first teaching is that in the beginning all you needed was water, that land and air and life could have teased themselves out from the waters (see Aristotle, *Metaphysics*, 983b 6–11, 17–27 cited in Barnes, 1987, p. 63). We can understand how Thales might have explained this notion. He might have pointed to the silt that accumulates at the mouths of rivers, as the way land could emerge from water. He might have pointed to the bubbles that emerge as you boil water, as the way air could have come from water. And he might have pointed to mosquito larvae and other insect life in small puddles, as a sign that water can give birth to living things. Here is a reasonable hypothesis about the beginnings of things drawn from the mechanisms of nature. This is a plausible notion for the "father" of science.

What else did Thales have to say? What was that other fragment?

Thales taught that the world is full of gods (see de Santillana, 1961, p. 23). This is curious, given that commonly we see science and the gods as pulling in opposite directions. Perhaps this is why it is rarely noted in accounts of the emergence of science in antiquity. But that is a mistake: our mistake. For Thales there was no tension between this observation and science. A fine classical scholar, W.K.C. Guthrie, explains why. When the ancients spoke of gods they did not necessarily mean what we mean. We tend to think of god as some sort of being and we offer attributes to describe his character. God is wise. God is love. God is forgiving. The ancients turned this around. They would say things like "love is a god." Loyalty, friendship, beauty . . . such things are gods (Guthrie, 1950, p. 10).

How should we understand this? Let's look at an example, friendship. When I form a friendship, I have not created friendship itself, but rather instanced it.

That is, a particular friend is simply an instance of the idea of friendship. Similarly, should the day come when for whatever reason this person is no longer a friend, friendship itself would not cease to be—only this particular instance. A flower can come into being and pass away. A sand castle can come into being and pass away. People, cars, pencils, they all have beginnings and ends. But not friendship. It neither comes into being, nor passes away. It is immortal. We may note here that Diogenes Laertius, who lived in the third century AD and about whom we know very little, wrote an account of the views and sayings of ancient Greeks, *Lives of the Philosophers*. In it he attributes to Thales this aphorism: When asked what is divine, Thales replied "What has neither beginning nor end" (in Barnes, 1987, p. 68). So we can see that while a given friend is human, friendship itself would be divine. Moreover, having a friend is a real thing and friendship is a real thing. We can feel its presence, even though it may not have weight or take up space. It makes a difference to have a friend, a difference we can feel. Friendship acts. It is real, but is "not there" in just that way that is a god's (Guthrie, 1950, pp. 10–11). Pulling this all together . . . to say that the world is full of gods is to sense that there is an agency that comes out of things themselves. It is to assert that there is a pattern out there; that the world can be understood. It and the complex net of all its wondrous happenings are not wanton or arbitrary. We can make sense of it. All we need do is uncover the gods.

Surely this is the well-rounded heart of science.

"D.Q., I'm really worried now. I would never have understood what Thales had been talking about . . . would never have made the connection between the gods and order within the world. A bit ago you went from a question about how astronauts can be weightless and yet gravity can still act on the moon to a discussion of Aristotle. Before that you started talking about atoms and before long you were discussing Parmenides and a Franklin printing press. You've told stories about Cuvier in order to understand Darwin and we've also heard about Huey Newton, the Mullah Nasrudin, James Hutton and John Playfair, Mitford and Thirlwall, Balzac . . . just a whole tumble of different voices to help us appreciate what's going on as scientists have tried to make sense of the world. Where did you get all of these stories? I can't imagine learning all of this stuff and if I don't know it, how could I teach? I would be awful."

"As your question is about stories, let me answer with a story. A wealthy landowner is riding across his estate. He rides past one of his barns and there against the side of the barn are three large circles and in the center of each is a bullet hole. Impressed, he calls out to one of his workers: 'Old man, who is the fine marksman who has hit the center of the targets each time?' The old man says: 'The one who fired the bullets is out there in the fields, but I am not sure he is a great marksman.' 'Why not?' said the landowner, 'He hit the center of the target each time.' 'It depends,' the old man replied, 'on whether you draw the circle first and then shoot; or shoot and then draw the circle.'"

"I have known where I was going, Sancho. I fired first and drew my target after. The various tales and analogies have come afterwards, as I searched for material that would highlight the deep issues within the material. Sometimes I would find it in science fiction, but most of the time I found it in the history of science."

"I don't know, D.Q."

"How about this, then, from David Hume. Hume was a Scotsman who lived across the latter half of the eighteenth century, a contemporary of Ben Franklin, say. And at one point in his work he invites the reader to imagine those great sailing vessels that plied the seas back then. Surely an extraordinary man must be responsible for their design, what with their many masts and sails and myriad ropes and pulleys. Yet, Hume continues, if you go and seek out this genius, you find an ordinary soul, a simple mechanic. How could this be? It is, he explains, the accumulated craft of ages. Each has copied the work of those before him, and perhaps added an improvement or two. After many trials, mistakes, corrections, and contemplations, the modern ship has emerged (Hume, 1948, part v, p. 39).

"I have been a teacher for a long, long time. There is no reason to believe that you would not similarly come up with a host of relevant tales and voices to explain the wonder in making sense of things. The key is to see this as your task, and not simply laying out the answer in easily digestible chunks."

"There must be more to it than that."

"Perhaps there are a few more things, Sancho. Mastery of content is an important quality for good teaching, but usually we have had the wrong content in mind. We are so intimidated by the sciences that we have assumed that what was needed was a clear grasp of the answer, when it was really a clear grasp of the question that was crucial. To know a lot of physics is great when it comes to teaching high school physics. But, if we have to choose between learning how to solve the differential equations involved in a compound pendulum or learning about the issues surrounding Galileo's first insights about the pendulum . . . then we should be choosing Galileo. It's Galileo that will capture the imagination. It's Galileo that will lead students to uncovering the gods. It's not that knowing those differential equations is a waste of time . . . but they are far less relevant to what should be happening in our classrooms."

"But how would I know what to look for?"

"By taking it seriously. Whatever you are teaching, think through what it is really saying about the world. Take it down to the most fundamental notions and try to connect as directly as you can to them. I can remember as a child trying to see if something was coming down from my tongue as I drank through a straw. I had figured that there must be something that would haul the soda up . . . like a bucket at a well. That's the kind of question you want to put before a class at the start of things . . . something that captures how extraordinary ordinary things are. When you then start to unfold the material, students are not only learning particular items, they are learning how to make sense of things. They're seeing how to tie things together and to trace an argument.

"*There's a nice example of this if we go back to Galileo and the pendulum. It's not uncommon for students to study pendulums in science classes. Typically, they are told that the period, the time it takes to swing back and forth, is independent of the size of the pendulum's swing.*"

"*I remember that, D.Q. As a pendulum slows down and swings less and less, it's not really slowing down.*"

"*That's right, Sancho. Strange as it may seem, it takes the same amount of time for a pendulum to go through a long swing back and forth and to just go back and forth a little bit. The 'speed' of the pendulum bob slows down as the sweep of the arc decreases, and the time stays a constant. But there is an obvious problem . . .*"

"*What's that?*"

"*The pendulum stops in the end.*"

"*Oh, right; so it must slow down.*"

"*Exactly. How can we go around saying the period of a pendulum is a constant, when it obviously isn't? People said this to Galileo when he first put forward this peculiar property of pendulums (see Matthews, 2000, ch. 5). He was undeterred. And, of course, he was right. There is something fundamentally true about the constant time notion, even though things don't actually happen that way.*"

"*That's a pretty curious use of the word 'true,' D.Q.*"

"*You bet it is, Sancho, and it gets at something at the very heart of physics.*"

"*Huh?*"

"*Everywhere you look in physics you run into this same curious break between good physics and what actually happens. We can see another lovely example in Galileo's work on the trajectory of projectiles, like cannon balls. He argued a projectile would move uniformly in the forward direction as it rises and falls subject to the force of gravity. The result would be a parabola.*"

"*It is not, and Galileo knew it was not.*"

"*The actual trajectory of a cannon ball lacks the symmetry of a parabola. It rises in an arc, but then drops rather precipitously—a pattern not far removed from the Aristotelian view—and scientists before Galileo had carefully analyzed this motion and given it sophisticated form.*"

"*Galileo knew this, too.*"

"*The problem was, Galileo explained, this work was too close to the phenomena. Its natural motion, its real motion, was parabolic, despite the fact that this is not what we see. What an extraordinary claim. We so often extol the virtues of careful observation in the sciences, and here is one of its most distinguished figures turning his back on experience. Galileo has denied a rival theory because it fit the data! From his perspective, the actual behavior reflected more than it should. And, of course, he was right. Air resistance so distorts the real motion as to make it un-natural (see Whewell, 1873, p. 331).*"

"*But this is taking us too far afield. The real point here is the way things open up when you frame them with basic questions. It changes the study of an item such as pendulums completely. It makes the data in the lab more intriguing.*"

It raises issues about the equations and their derivation. It opens the discussion to other things you already would have examined in class . . . are there similarly curious uses of 'true' in kinematics, for example? It just makes physics and the sciences more compelling.

"*Another thing worth noting here is the value of a deeper appreciation of the material. The theoretical mechanics course an undergraduate physics major might take would deal with compound pendulums and more complicated trajectories than just going back and forth and would do so with elegant mathematical treatments, but this is not what you need as a teacher. What you want are commentaries that would help you see issues like this curious property of pendulums . . . what the concepts really mean . . . what they say about the world and our efforts to make sense of things (Matthews, 2005; see also, Rosenblatt, 2004 and 2005). Your best bet here is to turn to the history and philosophy of the sciences.*"

"*I am still intimidated, D.Q., but I guess I have to trust that with time, if I kept working on what the material is really saying, I could build up a set of stories and questions that would carry a course of study. But how do you know if the kids will pay attention and engage with what you are talking about?*"

"*You're right; there's something else here, Sancho. When the teacher takes the material seriously, when you're not just moving from one page of the text to the next, then you set up the 'Peter Rabbit effect.'*"

"*Oh, you mean the kids rising to the challenge . . .*"

"*That's right. The most important step in teaching is getting students to buy into learning. There are any number of strategies you can pick up in a methods class about how to organize things. Breaking students into small groups, or having them post their musings and then take a 'gallery walk' around the room to compare various postings, for example. I have never been drawn to these routines. I start by trying to make sure I have something important to share.*"

"*Student alienation is real, but it's a thin veneer.*"

"*What do you mean, D.Q.?*"

"*A number of years ago I taught a physics class on Saturday mornings to some high school teachers. It was a good group and they asked if I would observe them teaching once or twice. So there I was observing a class when the teacher asked if I wouldn't take over. I was more than a bit surprised, but agreed. As it happened, they were looking at pendulums and learning about potential and kinetic energy.*

"*I stood at the front of the class and let the pendulum swing back and forth a bit. Then I asked if they knew who Michael Jordan was. They did and I went on to imagine a young twelve-year-old Michael Jordan playing in a junior league of some sort and his coach deciding that he had real potential. 'What would that mean?' I asked the class. Was he a great ball player at the age of twelve? No. If you had put him on the court in the NBA he wouldn't have been able to do anything. The quality he had was not yet there. It was real and we know it would come to be 'actualized'—but it wasn't there in an ordinary sense when he was twelve.*"

"*Neat. I never thought of that.*"

"The first person to talk about things being real, but not really there, I went on, was Aristotle. Aristotle lived a long time ago, back before the birth of Christ. And he thought seeds were really interesting . . . like acorns. Acorns come from oak trees, and if they catch-on and grow, they become oak trees. But they aren't oak trees. They're acorns. If you cut open an acorn, you won't find a tiny oak tree. It's there, but it's only there in potential.

"By the way, Sancho, what do you think happened when Von Leuwenhoek developed the microscope back in the early sixteenth century? They went looking for really tiny oak trees in acorns. It was just too hard to believe that something could be there and not there at the same time. They didn't find any. What about today? Where do you think modern science locates the 'oak-tree-to-be' in an acorn?"

"I don't know."

"It's the DNA, the genes."

"Oh, of course . . ."

"And then I asked the class: 'So how would you connect acorns and Michael Jordan to this pendulum swinging back and forth?' There was a pause, and then students began raising their hands and sharing their ideas. We had a lively discussion that was capped off by one of the students asking if they couldn't have their homework connected to this discussion instead of the assignment that had been on the board at the beginning of class. The teacher nodded, and we decided that a good assignment would be to explain how pendulums are like seeds.

"That's the 'Peter Rabbit effect.' Kids are ready for substantive work, for something beyond a steady stream of technical terms. That's what I meant when I said student alienation is just a thin veneer. If you go into class confident that you have something important to share, if you have thought your way through to what it's really saying about the world, then you can get the kids to take it on. You have treated them with respect, invited them to tackle what Aristotle had had to say, or Cuvier, or Darwin. This stuff is neat, but you can't just walk in with some heavy concept. You need Michael Jordan and acorns, and you need to have seen that what is really neat about potential energy is that it's there and not there at the same time—which is crazy.

"You have to work to get students to buy into learning, but you can do it, and the best way to do it is with a problem, a perplexity that comes from the core of the material. There's a lovely story the Nobel Prize laureate, I.I. Rabi, told about growing up. When he came home from school his mother would not ask him 'What did you learn today?' but instead 'Did you ask a good question?' Teachers need his mother's insight. We need to go beyond 'What material will I teach tomorrow?' We need to ask ourselves 'What are the fundamental questions in this material and what's a good way to ask them?'"

"Can you tell me any more about how you think your way through what you are going to teach, D.Q.?"

"Well, Sancho, a large part of that has to do with stories and that's the next chapter . . ."

Chapter 6

On Story

Let's suppose there is a break in the trees. We have been hiking now for some time. The break affords us a glimpse at the terrain we have covered. We have spoken of wonder, of the reach of reason, and of the role of perplexity. We have asserted the value of talk of a particular kind, of arguments rather than answers. This led us to distinguish between the systematic display of the material of the sort that you find in textbooks and the way material unfolds in a classroom filled with students of varying backgrounds and strengths. The logic of the exchange within the classroom set the framework for a discussion of assessment, and for a new slant on how student inquiry should be structured. This idea is to walk backwards with our students, engaging them directly in problems, taking cues as to what is substantive from the historical development of the material. That brought us to the preceding chapter where we examined more closely the practice of teaching when it is not organized around answers. And so we come now to a critical quality to our teaching: how do we support students in the effort to gain a coherent account of things? How do we move beyond the persistent practice of fracturing our instruction, what Michels called our "piecemeal" approach? How do we dwell on and make sense of things?

There is a charming Calvin and Hobbes cartoon where Calvin asks his father where the sun goes when it sets. Dad explains that it sets out West near Flagstaff, Arizona, adding that that is why the rocks there are so red. When Calvin replies that he thought the sun was really big, his father explains that if you hold a quarter up you can see that it's really only about that big. Calvin then asks how the sun can rise in the east, if it is landing in Arizona each night. To this Dad observes that it's about time for bed (Watterson, 1992, p. 115).

Calvin is clearly very bright and his push here is exactly the quality good teaching nurtures. But this story is really about Dad. It's a little like that story often told about George Washington and the cherry tree, and how honest the young George was. But that folk tale is really about the father who so valued George's honesty that he did not punish him for chopping down the cherished tree. Same thing here. Calvin's Dad is modeling great teaching, but how so? In the first place, he is listening to his son and answering his questions. More importantly, it's how he answers those questions. He answers in "tangible" ways—ways that make sense in a direct sort of way, like rocks becoming red because they are routinely close to the sun and so become sun-burned. So, instead of having to yield to the authority of some imposing account he didn't really understand, Calvin is put in a position to figure these things out and size-up their adequacy. If it doesn't make sense, if it doesn't fit all the data, then he comes back with another question.

We should not underestimate this last aspect. After all, that's where the joke comes in. When Dad says it is time for bed, he is shutting down the questioning. Up to then his answers invited Calvin to deal with the material, but he can't keep it up. In one sense, Dad is up against it because his answers are so outrageous, but in another sense, it is simply hard to answer questions and continue to invite even more questioning. This is such an important part of how we should be interacting with our students that it is worth taking the time to consider it more fully, especially as even though questioning is crucial to the growth of critical thinking, not all wisdom grows from this sort of exchange. Take the wisdom of Isaiah, for example.

The Old Testament prophet Isaiah lived across historical times. His teachings are set during the time when the people of ancient Israel were taken over by the Assyrian Empire, roughly from 742 BC to 687 BC. Curiously, there is a rather stunning historical break within the Book of Isaiah, and the last third of his teachings relate to a much later period, around the time of King Cyrus of Persia from 539 BC to 510 BC (*Oxford Annotated Bible*, 1962, p. 822). I mention these dates because this would mean that Isaiah had lived over 200 years, but the book says nothing about such a miracle. How can we explain it? The answer would seem to be that the book of his teachings reflects his voice, rather than his being. We can imagine a community of his followers dedicated to his teachings, nurturing his voice over the decades. And when, centuries later, there was a crisis, the continued relevance of his wisdom was clear; so clear that when the leader of this community spoke, he spoke with the voice of Isaiah.

We might add that such reverence for the wisdom of the elders is not limited to religious communities, nor is it a thing of the distant past. There is more than a touch of it in the practice of constitutional lawyers and Supreme Court judges who work to frame/constrain modern issues and understandings within the bounds set by the Founding Fathers.

The Book of Isaiah may then stand for us as the traditional view of wisdom, a view that contrasts sharply with the emergence of natural philosophy and the sciences in ancient Greece. We have already spoken of Thales, the father figure of the ancient Greek tradition of natural philosophy and science. Thales, as it happened, lived within the span of time embraced by the Book of Isaiah. Yet how different was his legacy. He is remembered far less for what he had to say than as the first of a series of thinkers, each of whom challenged the teachings of those who had come before. It is not his voice that was maintained over the generations, but his attitude toward critical discussion. Karl Popper, who understood criticism to be the vital core of the sciences, loved this story. At one point Popper imagines what Thales must have said to encourage his students to question, rather than defer: "This is how I see things—how I believe things are. Try to improve upon my teaching." Such a perspective leads to the notion that our efforts to find the truth are conjectural and that criticism is the only way to get nearer to the truth. It is the engine that powers the growth of our understanding (see especially "Back to the Presocratics" in Popper, 1963, p. 151).

Sadly, schooling typically has just the opposite effect. The older students get, the fewer questions they ask. They become less like the followers of Thales. Their work is more about learning what they have been told than ferreting out what it means about the world. It takes work to turn this around and get class to be filled with Calvins.

"But what kind of work is that, D.Q.? How do you foster questioning?"

"I think Calvin's dad is a good step forward. The 'tangible' quality of his answers is a kind of provocation. I had a really curious experience years ago in a course on the historical sciences, the same course where we would do Cuvier and Darwin. We were looking at bio-geography, the distribution of living things, and how the fossil record could suggest the contours of land masses in the distant past. It's a fascinating line of argument . . . maybe I can suggest how it works with the example of the Lystrosaurus. Have you ever seen a pygmy hippopotamus, Sancho?"

"I think so. They're a lot smaller than regular hippos, low to the ground and with big bellies."

"Fair enough, Sancho, and that's pretty much what the Lystrosaurus was like. Only it lived about 200 million years ago in places like South America, Antarctica, and Africa. And that's the rub."

"How so?"

"Well, that's a long hike, if you try to walk up into North America and then over the Rockies and across the Bering Strait, through Siberia and down to Africa, especially for an animal adapted for eating river grasses in tropical settings."

"Oh, I see, and it's not built to swim across the Atlantic, either, if it's like a pygmy hippo."

"Right. So how do we explain it? An interesting character, an Austrian geologist by the name of Suess, proposed that back in the day of the Lystrosaurus the Atlantic hadn't been there. Instead there was a giant continent, which he christened Gondwanaland. In this class, I was sketching Suess' ideas, but something was up. There was a kind of buzz in the class, and finally they asked me when I was going to stop pulling their leg. I was puzzled at first, and then realized that I had been talking about a guy named Dr. Suess, some strange animals, and an exotic land with a funny name. The fact that this guy was Dr. Suess and not Seuss had only underlined the spoof. It took me a while to convince them that it was all legit, but it was a nice example of how students can come to look at things sceptically. They weren't just writing things down. They were at the ready, and this episode was clearly a tease . . . even though I was being as straight as I could be."

"So, the key to fostering scepticism is to be outrageous?"

"Not just that, Sancho. If you are routinely asking students to explain why we would believe things . . . what are reasonable grounds for thinking something is the case . . . you set a different tone to study. Students become accustomed to evaluating whether something is plausible or puzzling. If you set the expectation that things can make sense, that your job is not simply to defer to the material in all of its obscurity, then their engagement is different, and their willingness to question rises and is at the ready. Being 'tangible,' laying things out in a way that invites them to make sense of things is the key. And it doesn't have to be as outrageous as the sun landing in Arizona or a geologist named Suess."

Thinking About Content

We have talked about the logic of the classroom as opposed to the logic of the material, a matter of listening better and of seeking to connect with the open mind of the student. I have put forward the notion of reconstructive inquiry and the value of exploring issues and structures deep within the material, issues and structures found in the historical development of the sciences—so that before you teach Newton, you would teach Aristotle; before you teach Darwin, you would teach Cuvier. We have seen the value of dwelling on the material and acknowledged how hard this is to do. And I have again underlined the value of scepticism and rational criticism. All in all, we have been talking about the practice of teaching, of how to think about what we should do as we walk into the classroom and invite students to engage in earnest study as they make sense of things.

In all this we have not really addressed the matter of content. There are a host of issues here: questions of depth vs. exposure, elective study vs. required sequences, courses that integrate topics across several disciplines vs. systematic explorations of a given discipline, and questions of rigor and the demands of accelerated and advanced courses. School systems across the country face an array of possibilities.

Recently, quite a number of school districts have switched to "physics first," inspired by the views of Leon Lederman, a Nobel Prize laureate in physics who has thrown himself very effectively into science education. The idea is that modern molecular biology really presupposes an appreciation of chemistry and that chemistry rests upon basic concepts of physics. So . . . physics first.

There is a real draw to Lederman's idea. There was a time when biology was much more descriptive. We knew lots of things about plants and animals, but it did not commonly push to matters of chemistry or physics. So you could study it on its own grounds, more or less.[1] Similarly, there was a time when chemistry was more descriptive, and it, too, could have been studied more or

---

1   There have always been connections between and among the sciences. In the eighteenth century, for example, Lavoisier tried to get at the way combustion would work inside of living things, and de LaMettrie wrote, *Man, A Machine*, where he explored the basic mechanical principles of our bodies and how we work.

less on its own; that is, it would not have presupposed as rich an appreciation of physics, of electrical forces and field theory, or the kinetic theory of heat, etc. Nevertheless, the conversation about physics first is too much about the material itself. We need to think about content in a different way, a way that is closer to the logic of the classroom.

In fact, given the research we considered in Chapter three on carry over, it would be surprising if any particular approach or sequence would distinguish itself as the right way to go. If students are not learning high school physics in a way that significantly boosts their performance in college introductory physics courses, for example, why would we anticipate that it would be a significant boost in terms of high school chemistry or biology courses? Various efforts to establish a "rational" sequence through the sciences have all been exercises in the logic of the material, a logic we have seen to be far removed from the logic of the classroom, especially a classroom where understanding is sought and secured. We have got to figure out the right way to teach, before we worry about curricular sequences.

Yet, content is a necessary part of the design and deliberation that goes into teaching. Let's suppose we're on the right track in terms of our practice, how should we think about content? Our work thus far suggests several key requirements in the shift from answers to arguments. We seek to dwell upon the material. There must be substantive issues that can be examined . . . this is the water in the classroom, and there must be alternative constructs that can be considered and evaluated. There's one more critical piece. We need to set things up so that students can make sense of things . . . so that it all stands together coherently . . . so that they can put a story together.

A Story's End

There are many animals that communicate: to signal danger, to claim territory, to call for a mate. Humans are not unique in these respects, but when it comes to story-telling, that's a different story. Story-telling is as close to the heart of being human as you can get; recall Barry Sanders' observation (Chapter one) about our very sense of self as reflected in the word "person," derived from the Latin "per-sonare," a sounding or telling through. We create ourselves in the act of telling stories. We also are released in the act of listening to stories— wandering lonely as a cloud with Wordsworth, taken by Don Quixote's fading dreams of chivalry to tilt at windmills or by Jules Verne around the globe in a mere 80 days, or again by Douglas Adams across the Milky Way.

However, these are not the qualities we seek just here at this moment. Story is also a natural whole. It stands by itself . . . as much as anything can. Hence the power of those memorable beginnings and ends, those openings and closings, whether it's Herman Melville who takes us from "Call me Ishmael," to ". . . and the great shroud of the sea rolled on as it rolled five thousand years ago." or Charles Dickens who takes us from "It was the best of times, it was the worst of times . . ." to "It is a far, far better thing I do than I have ever done; it is a far, far better rest that I go to than I have ever known." The quality we seek here is the quality that knits the whole into a single piece.

A story is more than a string of events. Ask any elementary school teacher and they will tell you this is precisely the struggle young children often have with learning what a story is. They confuse a story with a string of events or episodes and happenings, and then they say "The End." We might say to them that they need to pull things together so that there is an end, but what we mean by that is hard to explain. And for good reason. The end of a story doesn't just happen at the end. Somehow the idea of an end has to include setting things up so that we can see the end before it arrives. This is a curious bit. The end of a story is an "emergent property," and it is a difficult tune to catch. It's not really there in the events, but rather rests somewhere else. Earlier, when we were talking about atoms, we considered the relationship between words and letters. We offered the meaning of a word as an "emergent property." You can't get the meaning of a word from the meaning of its component letters. You also can't get the properties of a compound from the properties of its component elements. There is a corresponding emergent property in a story that is "above and beyond" its component events. This is what makes a story a story. Let's try to nail it down.

One way of looking at the nature of story is that there is a conflict and the end is its resolution. Another similar view looks for a significant change in a character. This is a somewhat ecological view: the character is not fitting in with his or her surroundings and so changes in order to make things viable. In his *Poetics*, Aristotle offered a different notion . . . that a story has a beginning, middle, and end (Aristotle, *Poetics*, Book 2, Chapter 4). This is a curious notion and I can still remember reading that and thinking that lots of things have beginnings, middles, and ends that are clearly not stories: the sentence "That is silly" for example. But I was the one who was silly. The key notion in Aristotle's observation is that tricky word "end." "End" carries a lot of different meanings. The end is the last in a sequence; yet we can reasonably ask the question "To what end?" where "end" is a matter of purpose, of intent, and not just the last item. Thus we could say without contradicting ourselves: "The end of a man's life is not his end."

Where does this reading of "end" take us? The end gives the story its point, its purpose. This is exactly the challenge when we think about our teaching: how can we set things up so that the string of classroom events, discussions, labs, and activities are not seen as end-less or as point-less? How do we grace our teaching with an end?

We have come to see that the key to good teaching is an echo of good story-telling. It is the framing of the material so that there is more going on than just a sequence of terms and definitions, labs and activities. I am reminded of the answer one student gave when asked by a researcher what she was doing during a lab exercise. She didn't know. She was just doing what it says . . . it's 8.5 . . .

and the next one we have to do is 8.6 (Osborne and Freyberg, 1985, p. 69). It's got to be more than this. So how do we pull that off? Again, how do we grace our teaching with an end?

This is where walking backwards, our third way, is so critical. The past, the historical development of concepts, affords us the critical material we need for our end.

We have touched upon this in our discussion of Cuvier and Darwin back in Chapter two, where in order to appreciate Darwin's arguments for evolution, we examined the work of Cuvier. This, too, was the heart of our discussion of Aristotle and Newton on the moon and whether it is falling, in the last chapter. In such units, I have argued, there are two objects of study: the phenomena, that is the things themselves, and the reasoned imagination, our explanations. Hence, students not only come to appreciate the contours of anatomy and the relationships between structure and function, they also come to see what these meant to Cuvier as he interpreted life and its history. We have shifted from answers to arguments. At the same time, these comparative frameworks set a natural end to study. We begin with one account; then introduce a second account. There is a *conflict*. The two different explanations point to different evidence and raise different issues. Students *resolve this conflict* by weighing the evidence and issues. As they do so, there is a *change in the character* of their understanding. Their work has an *end*. There is a story.

"D.Q.?"

"*Yes, Sancho, I know. This sketch is pretty abstract and bare. Why don't we take an example and see how material can be shaped into a story. We can pick a topic out of the proverbial hat. What do you say?*"

"*Good idea.*"

"*The nature of heat is a common topic in physics, chemistry, and biology classes. Does that sound like a good choice?*"

"*You bet; let's do it, D.Q.*"

On Making a Story Out of Heat

In today's classroom, the most important thing about heat is that it is a form of energy. Students are led to consider the nature of heat energy—that it is the disorderly motion of molecules—and the ways heat can be transferred from one body to another, via radiation, conduction, or convection (see, for example, the AAAS project, *Benchmarks for Science Literacy*, 1993, pp. 81–85). In such a classroom, the important thing about heat is the way it differs from other forms of energy, say chemical or mechanical energies, and then what we are led to see about the nature of energy itself; for example, that it is neither created nor destroyed. We can readily conjure up various ways of demonstrating these notions and there you have it.

But there is no story here. There is rather a chunk of an outline, a body of material with an elegance, a logic of its own; but nevertheless, it remains just "stuff." It is an answer. But if we exercise a Collingwood sensibility and seek the questions behind these answers, we find an intriguing set of notions, theories, and phenomena. This is the material that we want to work at.

In creating a story, we need a substantive issue where the answer is not obvious. This is Feynman's dictum, and trying to figure out the nature of heat certainly qualifies. We then need alternative understandings. That way we have a natural plot development, analogous to a character change in an "ordinary" tale. In the beginning, things were understood in such and such a fashion, but there were problems and issues that divided sensibilities. Then these differences were resolved with the emergence of a new understanding: The End. In the case of heat, the alternative we seek is not hard to find . . .

For over 2,000 years fire was a major analytical category of the sciences. It was one of four basic components of the world, along with earth, air, and water. Today, we would fail to find "fire" in the table of contents of any science text of the sort one sees in a university bookstore. Fire is no longer a major analytical category. It is not an element of our understanding of how the world is made or of why things are the way they are. It is merely a residue of activity, a form some energy takes as it moves from one sort to another. You eat food; it is processed and distributed to cells via the blood, and inside the cell it is "burned." This combustion releases chemical energy that is captured in little molecular packages that are then drawn upon for activities such as the contraction of a muscle in your hand as you type. Along the way, odd bits of energy are lost as heat. That's it.

Furthermore, I daresay "fire" would not appear in an index. It is not even a thing. Modern science has dismantled the flame and scattered its ashes. In a chemistry text we may study oxidation-reduction reactions to learn about the basic burning of fuel. In a physics text, we can explore black-body radiation in order to appreciate the incandescent glow given off by intensely hot bodies. In a third text, we examine statistical mechanics in order to appreciate the convection currents in the air surrounding a flame, and we turn to yet another text, this one on electromagnetic theory, to understand the light given off by the flame.

"D.Q.?"

"Yes, Sancho."

"I think I get the business about setting study up as a story, but what just happened here with the difference between a table of contents and an index?"

"No problem. It's just that typically, a table of contents in a textbook lays out the major concepts in that discipline; while an index itemizes the things that are examined. Fire has somehow been transformed from a major conceptual category to a non-event. The flame has been broken down into so many different parts that it has disappeared.

"Let me give you an example. The AAAS project, Benchmarks, that I have cited several times, lays out an extraordinary array of all the science topics that students should come to know by the time they finish elementary school, middle *school, and high school. It is quite a sweep of concepts and notions. Fire only appears as an item within the study of the history of science, not as an object of study directly. Moreover, what is important about this historical episode is that it illustrates such central concepts as the conservation of matter. There is no attention to the flame itself."*

"But I can remember some sort of triangle and how fire needs fuel and oxygen and something else."

"Yes, Sancho, there is that diagram out there somewhere, but not in our science classes. By the way, the third thing you need is a spark, a source of heat to get things going. The point is that somewhere along the line we changed our minds about fire, and now we don't really talk about it very much because it's too complicated; it involves too many different concepts. What you remember is really from conversations about fire safety. But let's return to the text . . ."

If we are going to frame our study of heat in such a way that students will forge a story, we need a beginning. In this case, because fire was an element in the first theories about the building blocks of nature, we can take things all the way back to ancient Greece. The idea of elements was a powerful notion. It was an effective way to make sense of the qualities of things. The elements—fire, earth, water, and air—had several contrasting properties. They were heavy or light, wet or dry, and hot or cold. Thus one could hazard a "chemical formula" for a substance based on these qualities. Blood, for example, would be a mixture of water, fire, and earth; since it was wet, warm, and when it dries leaves a gritty residue. And so it was that fire, as an element, came to occupy a central place in the world of ideas, just as it did in the world of ordinary experience.

In the course of the next 2,000 years, these notions were extended in various directions, but the basic Aristotelian framework remained. With regard to the element fire, one significant development was the separation into two aspects: a chemical substance, phlogiston, and a physical substance, caloric. Let's follow the discussion surrounding the physical face of the flame.

On Caloric

Heat has several striking qualities. For example, almost everything expands when heated. To explain this, heat was put forward as a material substance, called "caloric," that was the source of a repulsive force. So, since caloric would repel other caloric, as you added more heat to a substance its particles would push against one another more intently and the material would expand— a very clever explanation. In this way, there were two basic forces. Ordinary matter was the seat of gravity, a universal force of attraction, and heat or caloric was the seat of a universal force of repulsion (Dalton, 1808, p. 114; see also Fox, 1971). The volume of a body at a given temperature was the resolution of these two opposing forces.

There is an intriguing illustration of how the caloric theory explained heat phenomena that comes from a Cambridge physicist, J.B. Emmett. In the old days, before matches, blacksmiths could either keep their fires smoldering, which consumed lots of fuel, or they had to come up with a good way to start a fire. They did . . . an iron nail! If you strike a nail hard enough, it will glow red hot and can be used to ignite flammable material such as straw. Now here is the neat part. After the nail is red hot, you need to put it back into the fire for a while. If you just let the nail cool, you won't be able to pound the nail up to red hot again, no matter how hard you hit it (Emmett, 1820, p. 145)! For the caloric theory, this was straightforward. Pounding a nail drives out its caloric, and the surface becomes red hot. Putting it into the flame allows it to replenish its inner store, ready for the next occasion. Just cooling it means that there is not enough caloric inside to pound out next time to the point where it could become red hot again. That is, the heat is not *generated* by the pounding, but is released by the pounding from an inner store. Heat is a material substance.

There are other facets of the caloric theory, but let's move on to its alternative, where heat is not an elemental substance, but rather an activity. Most of the time when we talk about "things," we are talking about objects that have weight and take up space, such as a table or a person. But sometimes "things" are not at all thing-like. Ideas, feelings, numbers, patterns, and all sorts of gerunds— activities like running and playing—are also things. We can usefully represent these two notions of "thing" using the difference between a dancer and a dance. The modern understanding of heat—the kinetic theory of heat—takes heat to be a dance, not a dancer. It is the motional energy of the atoms and molecules inside of things. This is the domain of the standard account we find in science textbooks. But we have come to this point with a difference. Just like Cuvier before Darwin or Aristotle before Newton, the plausibility and effective insight of the prior understanding sets up a critical stance with the modern approach. We want to know why anyone would have opted for the kinetic theory, instead of the clarity and effectiveness of the caloric theory. A good start here is the work of an early-nineteenth-century scientist, John Herapath.

Herapath

Across the countryside of England there lies an ancient road, the Ridgeway, carved by the travels of the earliest Britons. Connecting such sacred sites as Stonehenge and Silbury Mound, the Ridgeway today is barely discernible in parts, a mere path across the fields, while elsewhere it lies beneath the asphalt of the motorway from London to Bristol. Why is it that the Ridgeway, or the Herepath as it is called in the West Country, has been treated so differently by history? Why should some parts lay obscure, abandoned to the margins, while other parts have been built upon again and again, remaining vital, though of course transformed?

As with one Herepath, so with another. John Herapath, also of the West Country, has left a similarly mixed legacy. Some of his work was built upon, some was not. What was at work here? What were the laws of commerce and traffic that determined what would be built upon and what left fallow?

Here is the general proposition. Born near the turn into the nineteenth century, Herapath threw himself into the debate over the nature of heat, and his entry effectively marked a new and important plateau for the conception of heat, not as an ethereal substance, but as a certain busy-ness within matter, a mode of motion.

Herapath's conception of heat as a dance directly opposed the then prevalent understanding of heat as a material substance. Other scientists had explored the connection between heat and the internal agitation of the particles of matter, but Herapath went far further than they had. He envisioned a chaotic molecular world, with a host of particles moving freely in straight lines and colliding with one another. These collisions, Herapath went on, may be taken to be perfectly elastic—that is, ideal collisions of the sort that would take place on the perfect billiard table. For Herapath, the pressure a gas exerts on the walls of a container would be the result of thousands of collisions, millions and millions of collisions, as the particles of the gas slam into the sides. By adding heat to the gas, raising its temperature, the particles would move more rapidly. There would therefore be more collisions and each collision would be harder, more forceful. Thus the pressure would increase. That is, for a given volume of gas, the pressure is directly proportional to the temperature. This is but one of the relationships between volume, pressure, and temperature that Herapath was able to derive from his model of heat as a dance (Herapath, 1816 and 1821).

The critical issue regarding the nature of heat is the difference between seeing heat as a material substance, a dancer, or as a form of energy, a dance. We want students to understand the profound differences between these frameworks. How do we do it? How might we engage students to explore this issue critically?

To begin with, we might simply talk about the differences between a dance and a dancer. Having explained what we intend by this distinction, we can ask: Is heat a dance or a dancer? We might then follow up with some observations. It looks as though heat takes up space, since when we add it to things, they expand. Moreover, we can touch heat—for example, you can feel it near a flame. And in ordinary discourse we speak of heat as flowing from one place to another, as if it were a fluid. These several observations suggest heat is a dancer. But is it?

If heat were really a dancer, wouldn't it have weight? This is an excellent question for students to explore, and how they would go about doing that is a critical part of the challenge. How could you test whether heat is a dance or a dancer?

"Can I give it a go, D.Q.?'

"Sure."

"I would take some water and weigh it. Then I would heat it and weigh it again."

"Good. I've done this with students many times and I can tell you what they consistently find. The water does not gain weight. In fact, it loses weight. So, what do you think?"

"It's possible that the heat has a kind of negative weight, but that sounds more like science fiction, like an anti-gravity device. I am surprised that it weighs less. I would have expected it to weigh the same. So I would repeat the experiment, and try it for different ranges of temperature change. You know, one beaker with a 10° change, and another with a 20° change, etc. That way I would see if it was just a bad measurement, or if there was a pattern."

"That's interesting. And what if you found that the greater the temperature change, the greater the loss in weight?"

"Then I would check to see if I still had the same amount of water, and I bet I wouldn't."

"Why's that, Sancho?"

"Because water evaporates and by adding heat, I bet the water evaporates more readily."

"O.K., but why?"

"Because when water evaporates it is pulling away. Adding heat makes it easier to do that for the same reasons that things expand when they are heated. If you think heat is a dancer, then adding heat means there is more of a push between particles. If you think it is a dance, then the particles are dancing faster and they break away."

"Excellent, and extra points for seeing that both dance and dancer can explain the loss of water. Where do we stand now?"

"If the loss of water matches the loss of weight, then the water did not gain weight as it was heated, and we can say that heat is not a dancer, but a dance."

"Very nice. By the way, can you think of a way to do this experiment that avoids this issue about evaporation?"

"No, not off hand."

"Having done this lab with students for a long time, I can recall another approach. You could have a reservoir of the hot water and another of the cold water and simply compare the weight of a cup of each."

"Oh, that's very clever. I'd like to try that one . . ."

In this example, Sancho designed his own experiment and then continued to engage the issue as he evaluated the results. How different this is from the standard practice in classrooms today. Textbooks are filled with activities, and the materials for these activities are often pre-packaged and arranged. You can even have trays with sheets where spaces for the different materials needed are outlined. Each group gets a tray and voila . . . they are ready to do what they are told.

What often happens when you work to set a problem before the class rather than a protocol is that students engage in what we might call theoretical tinkering, as they weigh the implications of their results . . . playing with one notion and another. This in turn often leads to follow-up experiments to push to a conclusion. We saw that in Sancho's suggestion for further experiments with beakers of water exposed to different amounts of heat. Here the student is elaborating the protocol in response to issues he has come to see. The lab is not a prescribed procedure, but a way to solve a problem. That is, instead of carefully delineating a procedure, we have defined a problem carefully enough that students could develop a procedure of their own. The alternative theoretical frameworks, dance and dancer, structured the play with ideas and pointed the experimental results in particular directions.

If you look back over the conversation between D.Q. and Sancho, another important feature becomes clear. By framing labs through problems rather than protocols, the fundamental nature of the activity changes, and the work of the teacher needs to change with it. The lab is no longer a witnessing; it is an investigation. Things don't just happen. When doing labs this way, the teacher needs to "work the room," to tease out critical thinking by talking with students about what they are trying and why. This goes back to John and his partner back in Chapter four. Their theoretical tinkering had led them to a non-standard interpretation. If the teacher had talked things through with them, they could have pushed their ideas and come to see the strengths of the standard account through follow-up experiments. Finally, the problem-solving strategies and arguments students use should become part of the public space of the classroom. Students could report on their work, or the teacher could summarize what he or she has seen. In this way the many individual and small group conversations become a way to highlight and reflect on the issues raised and the notions put forward.

On Reflection

We could readily continue our look at Herapath's work and the development of the kinetic theory, but we have done enough here to suggest what happens as we set things up so that students may compose a story about heat. The standard approach to instruction emphasizes the answer and opportunities for students to explore phenomena in light of the answer. Our approach adds to these a further critical ingredient: the judgement of the scientist. We see the inherent play in theory and explanatory frameworks. But this is more than a witnessing. Students weigh evidence, perform experiments, and evaluate arguments.

What we have so far is the core of a good unit of study, but there is more that can be done in two different regards. On the one hand, the examination of whether heat is a dance or a dancer sets up a host of related issues within the sciences. There is, for example, the notion of latent heat, the energy related to changes in state such as when ice melts. This was first understood as "latent" heat because it was heat or caloric within an object that was not hot. When you put ice in a drink, it will absorb a lot of heat from the drink, thus chilling it, without itself becoming hot. There is also the powerful notion of the conservation of energy as it expanded in the nineteenth century to become the first law of thermodynamics, when heat came to be seen as a dance, rather than as a dancer. These two episodes lend themselves to good labs or investigations and fall nicely within the dance vs. dancer framework.

There is more, however, to a strong unit of study than the core conceptual conflict, be it dance vs. dancer or design in Cuvier vs. Darwin. There is a value to setting the science itself in a broader context. A study of fire reminds us of the overwhelming centrality of fire in ancient society and so sets the stage for the centrality of fire in the ancients' theories of the world. Fire was a building block, a mainstay of things. As we then explore the subsequent dismantling of the flame to the point that it virtually disappears, different particular issues move front and center. Whether it's the blacksmith's nail or whether it's the weight of heat, students come to see the sorts of considerations that shape physical argument. The right answers of modern science are no longer seen as simple matters of fact, but rather they are appreciated as products of the well-formed imagination interacting with experience and physical principle.

Something else happens as well. The gaze of the students comes to take in a lot more of the landscape. The analytical frameworks of the sciences are seen as reasoned conclusions. But other frameworks can become important as well. A study of fire becomes a fascinating invitation to talk about the impact of technology in human history. This is a wonderful example of what I call the "Möbius effect", after the nineteenth century mathematician who found something interesting in a folded strip of paper. The Möbius strip is a loop with a twist in it, as in Figure 6.1:

What is so compelling about it is that it only has one side.

"D.Q.?"

"Yes, Sancho."

Figure 6.1 Möbius strip. Adapted from a photograph by David Benbennick from Wikipedia entry, subject to GNU Free Documentation license.

"How can a strip of paper only have one side? I mean, if you held the paper, wouldn't your fingers be touching opposite sides?"

"I'm glad you asked. Let's start with a simple notion of what a side is. Two points on a piece of paper are on the same side if you can draw a line from one to the other without lifting up your pencil. How's that?"

"Ah . . . O.K., I can see that. And if they're on opposite sides, you'd have to lift your pencil up to turn the paper over in order to draw the line."

"Exactly. What this does is define sidedness in terms of connectibility. A side is the sum of the points that are connectible. Good. So let's look at a Möbius strip. Because of the twist in the paper, I can draw a line from any point to any other point. If you were an ant, for example, you could walk this loop forever, inside and out, covering the whole thing. Isn't that sweet?"

"I get it . . . very nice. That's clever, the two sides are really just one side. But what then is the Möbius effect?"

"Let's return to the text for that, Sancho."

There is a tendency to separate the content of a scientific theory and its broader significance—to see them as two different sides. The Möbius effect denies that these should be separated (see F. Durrenmatt's fine play, *The Physicists*, 1964).

I applaud this "Möbius" sensibility. Science is not a mere calculus or formal system of inferences. It gives us an image of nature and of ourselves. It is important to address the issues raised by the material we teach, issues that clearly are not going to go away just by ignoring them. And ignoring them seems to be the favored strategy. Too often, we take an end-run around these issues.

As an aside, we may consider the host of issues surrounding evolution. There is a real problem here. You don't have to have lived in Tennessee in 1925, the year of the Scopes "monkey" trial to know there is a problem. Many people are very concerned about teaching evolution to our children. Part of what is going on here is the difficulty of reconciling the apparently competing claims for authority of science and Scripture. But something else is going on with evolution. It has been hard for people to buy what evolution seems to be saying about life, the universe, and everything else. How do we deal with these issues? For the most part, our biology texts reduce the matter to a question of the facts. Here is molecular biology; see how it works. If we allow this array of molecular entities to run loose for a long time, things will change. We don't need to call it evolution, or any particular theoretical framework. It is just the facts. No one, they seem to say, would deny transfer-RNA. So how can there be an issue?

What this really does, however, is leave our students out in the cold, caught between competing doctrines. The cost here is not only a heightened hostility between opposing camps, it also collapses the contours of evolution into the flat terrain of simple matters of fact.

However, evolution is not a "fact"; nor is it a fact that the moon is falling, or that heat is the motional energies of the atoms and molecules that make up materials. I mean this in a pedagogical sense. For our students to understand what we offer them, we need to give them a sense of where it comes from—what arguments carry it—and what issues it raises when we look at the world this way.

By unfolding the material in an historical manner, we allow students to see alternative approaches. This means we are routinely evaluating theories and connecting them to the problems they addressed and the evidence they used as support. And as we have seen, this shapes the material into a story. There are conflicts. The conflicts are resolved. There is a change in the character of our understanding. At the same time, this can also allow students to witness contemporary social issues in historical episodes.

Our purpose has been to explore what happens to content as we shape it into a story. Stories are not "fluff." They are not mere entertainment, a bit of comic relief from the press of more serious work. What we have been talking about is the central structuring framework for the material . . . that which changes it from a mere sequence of items into a coherent whole. The absence of story is, I am convinced, the single most deadening quality of today's classrooms. We are engaging students by reminding them that there is a test coming, sometimes a state-wide exam, as if this could carry the class. It can't. It doesn't. It never has. There is nothing so pointless as an endless sequence of items.

The Myth of Prometheus

So having determined a fundamental core to our study, we turn our gaze to the broader context . . . the impact of the mastery of fire, and for this we may turn to a powerful ancient tale, the myth of Prometheus. This tale is a great adventure, pitting gods against one another. Prometheus steals fire from Zeus and shares its secrets with humans. Enraged, Zeus punishes our hero by having him chained to a mountain top, arms outstretched, and everyday an eagle rips out his liver. Pretty extraordinary, but myths were not children's tales. They were not idle fancies, cartoon adventures in an age before television. They were the heart of ancient Greek culture. Looking at this myth as Thirlwall might have, we may ask: what was it really about?

As told by Hesiod, an early poet, the Prometheus saga is part of the great conflict between Zeus and the Olympian gods on the one hand and the waning, older gods, the Titans, on the other. These tales take us back to the beginnings of things and show us the imagination of the ancient Greek as it sought to understand how the world had come to be the way it was. This is a "titanic" conflict: whole mountains are hurled and great forces of nature unleashed. In the end, Zeus is the victor and a new world order is established. Strikingly, it was not a world designed for humankind. Quite the contrary. These gods acted on a scale beyond that of mere mortals. Our well-being is not at all the issue. Here is a perspective that takes life to be hard . . . always lying in the shadow of death and suffering, and the gods are indifferent—except for Prometheus (see Grote, 1844, vol. 1, pp. 73–79; Murray, 1940, pp. 19–27 and 87–88).

The myths of antiquity were an array of conceptual devices ready to be recast to meet new social and political demands (recall our discussion of Thirlwall in the interlude after Chapter three). We can see this in the way Aeschylus reworked the myth of Prometheus. For Aeschylus, Prometheus was not simply the god who had stolen fire and given it to humankind, he stood as the symbol of all the gifts that technology and science had offered: agriculture, navigation, astronomy, letters, and arithmetic. Here is what Eric Havelock had to say in the preface to his translation of Aeschylus' play on Prometheus: "Fire is no longer the instrument of the savage, used for cooking and warmth. It has become the 'technological flame' . . . no longer a scarcely approachable mystery, but an instrument—perhaps the chief one—of the applied sciences" (Havelock, 1968, p. 14). And we may note that though technology depends on invention and research, it must also be taught and expounded. And so, the god who stole fire is replaced by a new three-headed divinity—the inventor, the thinker, and the teacher.

What Aeschylus had caught is the underlying impact of the mastery of the flame. The history of technology offers a grand sweep of transforming developments from the first stone tools to the wireless Internet, but the mastery of the flame and of the forge was a revolution apart.

"Why is that, D.Q.?"

"There are a host of details to point to, Sancho, but perhaps the most suggestive item is the importance of the early communal fire. Think back to that era when fire was first coming under control and with it the appreciation of all that fire has to offer: warmth and light, protection from animals, and the pleasures of cooked food. Let's stop to consider just how hard it is to create a flame in the first place. I don't know if you've ever tried to rub two sticks together, Sancho, but it is very difficult to get things hot enough to start a fire. I even resorted to putting a wooden dowel in the bit of a power drill and still only got smoke when I pressed it down against another board. So it's not surprising that maintaining a fire once you've got it became a priority. So important, evidently, that it may have been the driving stimulus for the very idea of a civic space and civic responsibility. The Greek words for public building and public official both derive from the words for hearth and fire-tending" (Reclus, 1889, p. 229–230).

"Whoa. So the idea is that fire was so important and it was too much for an individual to maintain; so people had to come together to make sure there was plenty of wood and to build a shelter in case of rain. In effect, they had to set up a communal order. It must have been a real bummer to let the flame go out."

"You bet, but let's go back to the text now."

Here is a wonderful passage from an H.G. Wells novel, *The World Set Free.* Wells is speaking of life a quarter of a million years ago when the utmost man was a savage:

> He knew no future then, no kind of life except the life he led. He fled the cave-bear over rocks full of iron ore and the promise of sword and spear;

he froze to death upon a ledge of coal; he drank water muddy with the clay
that would one day make cups of porcelain . . .

(Wells, 1914, p. 2)

The irony that carries this passage is the juxtaposition of past and present, and
our appreciation of the promise that lay trapped within iron, coal, and clay.
Strikingly, the promise of iron, coal, and clay is released by the flame—in
foundries, in steam engines, and in kilns. The mastery of the flame captures the
difference between our past and our present. It is the beating of both sword
and plowshare, and all that they imply.

And beyond this, there was a profound shift in the way we thought of
ourselves. We became technological beings, *Homo faber*. We were now powerful
agents, transformers and makers, not simply husbanders of nature's bounty,
the way we had been before. This part of the myth is scary. The myth of
Prometheus is not simply an adventure; for Aeschylus, it is a tragedy. Things
are beyond our control; they're more complicated than we can foretell. Eric
Havelock makes a connection to events in our world, events of the twentieth
century, observing:

The nuclear theorists of forty years ago were just professors pursuing in
relative obscurity a mathematical dream, in service to the purest, the most
abstract type of science and, it seemed, the most useless. Did any of them,
in Cambridge or Copenhagen or Berlin or Moscow or Paris or New York,
foresee Hiroshima, and the hysteria of nations, and the naked power politics
of the bomb?

(Havelock, 1968, p. 16)

The Cold War was an instance of the technological flame, as are a whole
tumble of issues we face, from climate change and global warming to computer
fraud and identity theft. We are reminded that Mary Shelley's novel about
Dr. Frankenstein's monster was titled, *Frankenstein, or the Modern Prometheus*.
The story of technology always threatens to be a tragedy.

Here then is the fuller sweep of a study of fire. Its context is the impact of
technology on the human condition and the imagination, and at its core lies
the substantive matter of the character of fire as dance or dancer. This is a good
story. It is a framework that brings together anthropology, the history of
technology, the sciences, and their history. Readings for such a course could
include an array of wonderful texts . . . Eliade's *The Forge and the Crucible*,
Bachelard's *The Psychoanalysis of Fire*, Frazer's *The Golden Bough*, Gilbert
Murray on Aeschylus, various texts on the history of science by Stephen Brush
or Robert Fox, and many other items, like Faulkner's powerful short story, "Barn
Burning." And, at its heart is the invitation for the student to pull together a
story about the character of the flame.

Story as Content

From the beginning, I have emphasized the importance of right reasoning over right answers. So it is not surprising that when we start talking about content, I do not offer a particular sequence of courses or concepts. It's not biology or physics first. The conversation has been shifted to a different plane altogether. It's not the material itself, but how it is packaged. There's got to be a story. Story is about coherence, about things making sense.

There are two different lines of thinking here. One is that since reasoning is more important than the facts, we need to make sure that things unfold in keeping with arguments students can understand . . . hence the basic idea of story. The other comes out of the discussion of carry over. Too little is sticking because students are being taken through material too quickly. They need to be allowed to make sense of things . . . again, story. But that leaves us with a fundamental question: how do you know what to teach? Can it be anything?

The answer is straightforwardly, "No, not everything will work." Story sets a pretty severe set of conditions. The chief one is that things have to turn on a substantive matter . . . there's got to be water in the classroom . . . and you need to be able to get at these fundamental matters pretty directly. We saw that in the discussion of Cuvier and Darwin and the core notion of design. We saw it again in the discussion of qualities when we talked about the atom and little bits. And we have just seen it again in the differences between the caloric theory and the kinetic theory and the notion of heat as a dancer or a dance. Such stories are very different from the odd biographical piece, and different again from taking the more technical language out of the sciences and rendering it more colloquially. That might make things more approachable, more "friendly," if you will, but it is not what we have been talking about. Remember our interlude about Peter Rabbit and Plato, where relevance is not about "pop" culture, but about being substantial. What story does is bring fundamental concepts to the surface by highlighting how they have figured in the growth of the modern understanding.

There is another fundamental consequence of the shift this approach embraces. When you seek to make a story of the material, you move away from the outline that is the logic of the material, and so you move away from the survey course. The logic of the exchange, the "Möbius" principle, these things take you away from the discrete, chop-chop sequence that so often characterizes our science courses. We come to dwell more on essential matters and reach out horizontally to take in their consequences. The study of fire, which we have just sketched, takes in anthropology, a history of technology from the first forges where both sword and plowshare were hammered, to the industrial revolution, and the development of the modern understandings of both fire as flame and combustion and fire as heat. This is not a survey course, not an introduction to chemistry or physics, but it is instead a delightful foray into core ideas in the modern understanding.

One compelling consequence of the break from introductory survey courses is that you are no longer committed to the idea that there is a body of information out there your students need to have witnessed. So right away, a test is not rightly about catching them at what they do not know. Instead, it is about the character of their knowing.

"Can you play that out a bit, D.Q.?"

"You bet. Years ago, I had a student in physics who found that he really liked it. We had an internship program for seniors, so he decided to try to become an intern with the physics department of a local university. He came back from his interview really deflated. Somewhat reluctantly he explained to me that he had 'failed' his interview. He'd been asked about rotational momentum, and he didn't know anything about it. I tried to explain that it was the physicist who had 'failed.' How silly to have sought to catch him at what he did not know. The real issue is the quality of the knowing, and if that professor had talked to him about aspects of physics he had studied, then he would quickly have come to see how well-formed his judgement was.

"People do this all the time. It reminds me of that mindset Clarissa Hayward describes in her paper, where the idea of schooling is that you learn what the teacher tells you. But everything in this book challenges that approach. Schooling should be about nurturing a child's voice and critical judgement, not about knowing a given body of information. That's why I spoke about tests in terms of the character of a student's knowing. A test is a diagnostic tool. You give students an opportunity to share their understanding, chiefly through essays . . . expository writing. And what you are looking for is how well they have pulled things together; how coherent a story they can tell. What they expose are their cognitive skills."

"That makes sense to me, D.Q. By the way, what do you do when a student hasn't pulled together an effective story of the material?"

"This is a critical issue. It moves from the story we want to tell, which we might think of as the first round of teaching, to the second round, where it's all about what you do with students who didn't really get it. In terms of testing, I found there was one good thing you could do before the test. I would remind students that the test will have essay questions on the central ideas of our study and ask them what they think I will be asking. That really serves to get them to think more directly about the big picture and the major threads that ran through our study. After the test, I think it is important to discuss it right away, next class, even if you haven't graded their papers yet. The questions and the issues raised as they wrote about the questions will be on their minds. Then, when you have graded their papers, let students who didn't do well take the test over again. And encourage them to read the essays other students had written. Figuring out what's going on with 'higher-order thinking' is complicated and a second go at the test is a great opportunity for students who are struggling to practice at it, and get good at it.

"The key thing is to keep our eyes on what we are really trying to have students learn . . . those habits of mind and cognitive skills that inform critical thinking.

It's the rule of reason we are after . . . arguments, not answers. This is not an idle goal, like a New Year's resolution. The heart of this book has been to translate this goal into the practice of good teaching. It's been about how we should think about what we want to teach tomorrow. It examines how we should think about the material: how to frame it; about the wonder in the material, and how to pose questions that are both engaging and get at substantive matters. In this context, assessment is really about the habits of mind and cognitive skills you want to nurture: giving students a chance to explain themselves in class discussion and in written work. And then to diagnose how well they are thinking: what kind of story they can tell."

"I guess that's a hard row to hoe."

"To stay with your metaphor, Sancho, good teaching may be a difficult crop to grow, but the harvest is lovely."

We may close by going back to the heart of this discussion, the importance of story in teaching. There is an interesting nuance that comes from a brilliant study, *The Mirror and the Lamp*, by M.H. Abrams, which captured the differences between classic and romantic literature by looking at the role of the poet (Abrams, 1971). The earlier, classic poet held a mirror to nature and society. His art gave the scene a focus and an elegance, but he himself was transparent. The romantic poet, on the other hand, was the heart of the picture. The poem was the sensibilities of the poet. When Wordsworth wanders lonely as a cloud, the cloud we "see" is the poet's loneliness as he wanders across the countryside.

I think we can connect Abrams' thesis to the fundamental role of story in science teaching. The various stories we have told have been about making sense of things, whether it was me or a child I have driven to school . . . or some scientist, be it Aristotle, Cuvier, or Newton. It is what we found intriguing, and what we found satisfying. These have been stories about ideas more than people. What is on display is an argument, the act of making sense of things. Such stories are romantic, in that they display the sensibilities of scientific analysis. It's not the facts that matter, but how they are worked . . . the inferences they were seen to support.

In all of this, Thirlwall's work resonates. It was Thirlwall who modeled for us how to read material in a way that focused on the logic of the exchange. By focusing on what the myth meant to the story-teller and his audience, he invited the reader to see the material from within. Thirlwall read history as if it were romantic poetry. This is what story has to offer teaching in the sciences. Unlike the routine of textbooks and worksheets, of technical terms and diagrams, all on the outside, all classical to the hilt, stories as we have framed them, offer the sciences from within, modeling the creative effort to make sense of things.

Interlude

Why It's a Good Idea to Smack Your Lips When the Lord of the Manor is Around

Taking seriously our own dictum, that the material does not speak for itself, let's play with Chapter six a bit more. Here is a story. It concerns human nature, asking the most fundamental of questions: Are people good? You might not think that science could address such a question, but it is there when you push. Significantly, the story also proves to have a pressing relevance to everyday life in our schools.

Primate studies are not only hazardous; they are a logistical nightmare, especially back before air travel and the infrastructure of hotels and restaurants that has come with it. A long trek and stay in remote regions of Africa, Asia, or South America was hard to combine with a university career. So, not surprisingly, early studies of the behavior of apes and monkeys were of caged animals in such places as London's Regent's Park Zoo. The results were stunning. Apes were found to be both terribly violent and bisexual. We can conjure up our scientist of 100 years ago standing in Regent's Park, his back to the magnificent metropolis of London. The message at that time would have been clear. The essence of humanity, what we had inherited from our primate ancestry, was coarse, violent, and un-civil (Pfeiffer, 1972, p. 278). What, then, this scientist would have wondered, accounted for the civility of modern man? What power would be great enough to overwhelm our natural tendencies toward violence and open sexual license? Society. Social pressures made the modern Englishman civil and heterosexual, law-abiding, and monogamous. Lift the sanctions of organized society and we would revert to our inner, primate selves.

This is the very model of a scientific tale, is it not? An empirical study intimately related to the deepest questions about being human. The part of the tale I find most compelling is the way it reaches out to the exotic wilds of the savanna to make sense of our most mundane routines. There is a certain magic in connecting the behavior of primates in the wild to the way we stand in queue waiting to purchase a newspaper or board the No. 7 bus. There is a wonder here, a wonder not only about the roots of the human character, but also in the enterprise of making sense of things: just like Jesse's remark on the rain.

So we may ask: Are we innately good? The apes of the Regent's Park zoo seem to offer a pretty resounding "No." Yet, there was an important caveat here.

Such studies were of caged animals, an artificial setting, and so might well distort the natural character of primates. Maybe such studies are not a good window to our past and to our inherited inner selves. What are we really?

Among the first studies of primates in the wild was the work of Irven DeVore early in the 1950s (Pfeiffer, 1972, p. 286). DeVore went into the field to study baboons. Armed with a clipboard and pencil, he watched. After a relatively short while, he was accepted as little more than a curious sort of bush. Baboons, he discovered, form a remarkably complex social structure. The male elders fan out in a circle, foraging for seeds and other tidbits out in the tall grasses. Baboons are monkeys, not apes, and they cannot stand upright; but as they forage, they will regularly rise from their haunches and stretch out to their full height, taking a quick look around. There are enough members to the troop, so that at any given time several are actually scanning the environs, looking out for predators. In this lies the security of the group.

Following the troop one day, DeVore made a critical mistake. Coming over a rise, he startled a youngster who gave out a cry. Within moments DeVore found himself surrounded by an angry circle of adult baboons. This is the sort of story one is not supposed to be able to tell. Baboons are quite large. They spend their lives out in the savanna precisely because they are too large for life in the trees. Furthermore, though largely vegetarian, they do kill and eat meat, and are quite aggressive in defending themselves.

DeVore, however, was able to escape. Escape is not really the right word. He was able to apologize! He faced the angry baboons and he smacked his lips. Fantastic, isn't it! He had observed many conflicts among the members of the troop. Two baboons would claim the same food, the same bit of shade, or the same playmate, whatever. Yet, these conflicts never led to actual violence. Each baboon would try to intimidate the other into getting its own way. That's where the lip-smacking came in. DeVore decided it was the signal a baboon gave that it had been intimidated (Pfeiffer, 1972, p. 286).

It was the way they said: "I give."

It was that hands-up sort of gesture communicating that everything's O.K.—you go right ahead—my fault—no problem. That's exactly what DeVore wished to say to those angry baboons ready to tear him limb from limb, and it worked.

This is such an amazing story, and what I really love about it is what the baboons must have thought. We all know how pets have ways of communicating to their owners—going to the door and scratching at it or knocking over a food bowl. But here DeVore spoke in the baboon's language. It's as if Fido were simply to come over and say: "Hey, I'm hungry."

What does this story tell us? It gets directly at the difference between caged animals and animals in the wild. DeVore did not find baboons in the wild to be violent, as long as we distinguish between the violence of intimidation and the violence of physical beating. Why not? Because they had the ability to show deference.

Deference is the key to the whole structure of baboon society. In a pick-up game of football there is an elaborate process of working out who is going to be quarterback and what the play is, etc. But it is hard to believe that baboons work out who will do what for the coming day or week in some sort of huddle. It is far more plausible to suppose that they establish a hierarchy, a pecking order, through a myriad of individual conflicts resolved through intimidation. Without the ability to smack their lips, the baboons of the savanna would be driven to the violence of the caged ape. And of course, that is precisely what caging does—it deprives the animals an avenue for showing deference. They are always in each other's faces.

Deference is critical to the organization of social structures for the baboon, but what about humans? We would want to get at the equivalent of lip smacking, but the case with humans is far more complicated. We can talk and we negotiate across a far richer array of options than baboon society affords. How pervasive is deference? Do we defer in ways that we don't even realize? How often do we smack our lips?

This is an interesting idea, one worth exploring a bit further. To do so, we may look at a rather extraordinary series of developments in eighteenth century England to help us "see" deference in human societies more clearly. One more preliminary note: It is common to see the law as protecting individual rights, most especially property rights, so that, for example, it is against the law to steal. This story suggests that something else is going on at the same time. In this story, I lean heavily on an essay by Douglas Hay, "Property, Authority, and the Criminal Law," in a wonderful book, *Albion's Fatal Tree: Crime and Society in Eighteenth-Century England* (Hay *et al.*, 1975, pp. 17–64).

In the early decades of the eighteenth century, English law counted a small number of crimes as capital crimes, crimes for which the punishment was death, and few souls were executed. Across the century, however, the number of capital crimes increased to a remarkable degree. Where hardly any but the most egregious crimes, like murder and treason, had been punishable by death, now virtually all were. One might face the death penalty for poaching, or smuggling, for robbery, even for blackening one's face. Yet, and this is most stunning, the actual number of people executed did not increase proportionally. Indeed, it continued to be a very small number.

At first glance we might suppose this harsh regime had so intimidated the populace that they avoided committing crimes even of a minor sort—such as killing a rabbit on the lord's estate. But this is not so. The number of people arrested and charged with these crimes grew with the population. The threat of capital punishment did not deter the "criminal."

Now we have an intriguing problem. A host of "ordinary" crimes are made punishable by death. If the death rate does *not* rise, it seems reasonable to assume it is because the potential criminal thinks better of it, deterred by the enormity of the cost if he is caught. But then we discover that the number of crimes did not go down at all. In fact, as the population rose across the eighteenth century and as the category of capital crimes increased, so the number of people charged and convicted of capital crimes increased accordingly. When you stop to think about it, this is not surprising. Crimes such as poaching were not sport, but represented the efforts of people to cope with the scarcity and hardship characteristic of their place in society. Life was hard. They were on the edge.

The puzzle then becomes this: if the number of people committing capital crimes increased markedly, and they were convicted, how is it that the number of executions remained so small? In seeking an explanation, it is important to appreciate that a ruling elite is rarely ignorant, most especially the British aristocracy, which, after all, never suffered a French Revolution. It never suffered, that is, a dramatic redefinition of its power—economic or political.

The key to the puzzle is that having been convicted of a capital crime, there was a way you could escape execution. A character witness could come before the court and plead for mercy, urging that this episode be seen as an aberration. The convicted felon is really a fine soul, responsible, and dutiful, etc., but because of special circumstances, stress, family discord, whatever, had wandered from his or her accustomed, virtuous path. On the strength of this plea the court could suspend sentence. But whose judgement would carry sufficient weight in the eyes of the court? A mother? father? sister? friend? Hardly. The court would turn to the lord of the manor.

In the eighteenth century, before the Industrial Revolution, the economic life of England centered on the estates of the landed elite. Everyone, or almost so, worked directly or indirectly for the lord of the manor, as farmer or baker, blacksmith or candle-maker.

Now we may see the real purpose for expanding the number of capital crimes. It was to root deference into the everyday behavior of the people. It would have been clear to all that they would quite possibly one day be caught and convicted of a crime punishable by death. Their one way of survival was to make clear to the lord of the manor how very good they were, so that on that day he would speak in their behalf. And so they smiled, and they did as they were told. They knew their place, and they knew it rested on pleasing the lord.

This system worked, but it later fell apart, not through the violence of political revolution, but through profound changes in economic patterns. With the Industrial Revolution workers became unknown figures, anonymous operatives within the massive halls of industry. Now the lord of the manor could no longer speak in behalf of those who worked for him. This distorted the purpose of the law, which had never actually been to execute wrongdoers, and late-eighteenth and early-nineteenth-century judges found themselves with the awful task of choosing between the law and justice. If they convicted a soul for a petty crime, the punishment would be wholly disproportionate; but to refuse to convict so as to not have to execute, in the face of clear evidence, was to deny the law itself. From this crisis, came the notion of a "hanging" judge, that judge who adhered to the law; and from this crisis there also came a thoroughgoing reform of the law that tied the magnitude of the punishment to the nature of the crime.

The juxtaposition of these two stories yields this basic question: Why is it a good idea to smack your lips when the lord of the manor is around? This is exactly where you want to take the material. To answer this question, students will find themselves at a vantage point where they are evaluating the arguments within the tales and sifting through their own lives and experiences for relevant examples that support or illustrate their notions about the role of deference in establishing the social order.

This story uses more familiar experiences to inform our sense of the more removed. They are metaphors that clarify our appreciation of what lies within a reality that is hard for us to see. The straightforward "baboon-dynamic" of physical intimidation helps us see what was behind making so many "ordinary" crimes punishable by death. This, in turn, gives students a new lens for looking at the social structures that surround them, as they come to "see" the ubiquitous work society asks us to perform in order to sustain the social order. Take the matter of life at school.

Deference is a key aspect of life in a school. Teachers and students are finely tuned to degrees of decorum and respect in manners and dress. Take, for example, a discovery I made years and years ago. If students did not know I was around, they might well use language very different from the language of the classroom. When they realized I might have overheard them, they were quick to apologize. Now I could understand why I, the adult, should not use coarse or vulgar language in the classroom out of a regard for their youthful innocence, but why was it wrong for them to swear in my presence? Certainly, it was unlikely that it would be a source of corruption for me. It struck me that they were not apologizing for the language itself. They were apologizing for having acted their age. School requires them to be the six- or seven-year-olds they had been back in second grade when they learned to walk in a single file on the way to the library, or to wait politely when they wanted an adult's attention. After all, school is the only place where a sixteen-year-old child has to raise his hand to get permission to go to the bathroom. For them to speak their age pulls the mask off of the charade and challenges the politics of deference that otherwise prevail. A teacher's authority is a jealously guarded affair.

While this is everywhere the case, it is heightened in urban schools. Early on we noted an insightful paper by Clarissa Hayward and her observation that "obeying the rules" was different in urban and suburban settings. In suburbia, Hayward suggests, students are encouraged to see rules as nurturing behavior to make things work well and they are invited to look at things from the perspective of the community. In the city, students are expected to behave themselves . . . to follow the rules, and no questions asked (Hayward, 1999, p. 338–339). Good students do what they are told. Into this setting comes the matter of school uniforms.

Imagine a faculty meeting at an urban high school. The faculty was once again voicing its concerns about student behavior. There needed to be a real commitment by every adult to enforce all the rules. No one wanted to be the only one telling students to tuck their shirts in. Before long this conversation turns to earrings. Some kids were coming to school with earrings that were too big . . . but how could they draw the line on earring loop size? As the faculty struggled to get a handle on this issue, they began to wonder about just how they had come to such a bizarre place . . . earring size? The answer seemed to be that there was a lot at stake with uniforms. They were not just a way to keep a lid on adolescent urges to spend too much on their clothes. There was something about uniforms that had to do with kids making a commitment to their schooling. "Street" clothes somehow intrinsically spoke against school.

It was certainly the case that kids would go to extraordinary lengths not to be seen in their uniforms. Everyday they would wear their street clothes as they traveled back and forth from school, changing into their uniforms in bathrooms and corners of the hallways . . . even changing from one pair of sneakers to another. How can we understand this? There seems to be a culture war between mainstream middle-class culture represented by school and its uniforms and the street life of the inner city, as represented by popular culture and music videos. Students were caught in the middle and rules about apparel and having your shirt tucked in made the conflict explicit. Every day, in your clothes and your manner, you declared which side you were on. Would you defer? No wonder schools everywhere struggle with student compliance on uniforms, even to the point of working out the size of earring loops. By the way, the faculty settled on the size of a quarter.

These two stories about lip-smacking and capital punishment are exactly the sort of stories you would need to get students to see the larger picture and appreciate the tensions they feel and the forces that are pushing and pulling on them. And most critically, conversations that might flow from stories such as these are more likely to resolve the tensions than parsing a set of standards about the fine points of student dress. We need more stories and fewer rules. They are a powerful resource. There is an immediacy to baboons smacking their lips in the savanna and in eighteenth-century parliamentary statutes. Isn't that extraordinary? Their very distance somehow brings things closer. It provides a floor for conversation to stand upon, and things get worked out. Students see what is pushing them around and begin to appreciate what is really at stake. Instead of playing games with rules, they weigh their choices.

Chapter 7

STEM—A Promethean Program

"Life is hard," we may be tempted to say on occasion; but why "hard"? What is it about the sensation of hardness that lends itself to that other sense, that sense for difficulty, for challenge? For the great French scholar, Gaston Bachelard, the connection is immediate: "One has only to offer a tool to a child playing alone to observe how an inert, hard object incites a rivalry both immediate and lasting, a determined, crafty struggle for mastery" (Bachelard, 2002, p. 27). There is in all of us a draw to see in a rock or a closed wooden box a challenge that is rightly met by picking up a mallet or some other tool and "whacking" away at it. "Hard" is a good word. Too often we reserve the hard problems for the best and the brightest, and leave easy problems for the weaker students out of a concern for their self-esteem. But they, too, should have the pleasure of taking out that mallet, and we need to be sure that we give them a fair share of "hard" problems.

And so, hard work and tools emerge together in a basic struggle for mastery of the world around us. The story of technology is never far from hard work and struggle. Prometheus, inventor, thinker, and teacher, is also the first foreman.

The intimate connection between fire and tools rests upon the forge where both sword and plowshare were beaten into existence. But the story of fire and technology hardly stops there. Fast forward several millennia and coal-force and iron-force are being harnessed to produce steam-engine-force, and great manufactories cluster in the flats of Spittlefields and Manchester. Assembly lines and mass production cast a pall over the English countryside, even as they cast great iron bridges and railways.

In 1744 a small group of country squires and gentlemen in the neighborhood of provincial Manchester formed a Literary and Philosophical Society. Meeting fortnightly, they would gather to share farming practices, travelogues, and medicinal speculations. By the 1790s the Society had grown so that they added a curator to organize sessions and dabble in experiments. His name was John Dalton, the same John Dalton who would go on to develop in a significant way the modern chemical theory of the atom. One hundred years later this fledgling scientific community had become home to the University of Manchester and ᴕ a physics department headed by Ernst Rutherford. In his study, *Science in Victorian Manchester*, Robert Kargon, asked a simple question: How had this provincial outback come to be the home for such an outstanding collection of physicists? His answer was straightforward: look out any window. Here, as nowhere else, was the Industrial Revolution (Kargon, 1977). Here, steam and tool and hardness had taken root as nowhere else; and with it, not only great temples to Prometheus, but also hovels known as "back-to-backs" and cholera.

Manchester is a Promethean story, just as "Silicon Valley" is a Promethean story, a story about science, mathematics, technology, engineering, and work.

On Problem-Solving

Every discipline has a technical language that it uses to structure its take on the world. It might involve the difference between a third-person narrative and stream-of-consciousness in literary criticism, or the difference between natural motion and inertia that we discussed earlier; or yet again it might involve the differences between a social history of the role of women in the American West and an economic history of the 1930s.

There is a set of disciplines that are more especially problem-solving disciplines, where work focuses on being able to apply concepts in ways that take advantage of well-formed relationships. These several disciplines—we may abbreviate them with the acronym STEM, for science, technology, engineering, and mathematics—form a natural whole.

"What do you mean by that, D.Q.?"

"Everything is connected, Sancho, and we always pay a price for treating things separately. But we pay an especially big price when we cut up natural wholes. In fact, much scholarship is about competing claims for the right context through which to understand something. Take a poem, some would argue that the best way to understand it is through the life of the poet; while others might urge that the key is the tenor of the times, and still others argue the value of some theme reaching across the ages.

"More relevant to us in a text on education is the controversy over phonetics and whole language. Are you familiar with that, Sancho?"

"Only that it's about teaching reading."

"Yes and no. Many have seen it that way, as a question of how to teach reading, but it really isn't. Those who favor a whole language approach happily use phonetics. The real difference is over the separation of reading as a skill from a broader set of facilities with language, most especially story-telling. Whole language seeks to nurture the whole package, so that children would be telling stories and drawing pictures from stories they listened to, along with learning how to read. Given our discussion of story-telling in the last chapter, you can guess where my sympathies lie. There is a lot more to reading than just reading. The greater our sense for how stories work, the richer our engagement with the text, and the more we gain from it. We become more like Popper's 'searchlight' and

less a 'bucket.' That is, we play with possibilities as we read, speculate as we go along, and so become more alive to the twists and turns of the tale.

"It's sort of like this crazy thing that happened to me years and years ago. My family had gone to an amusement park. At one point I went on a roller coaster that my younger brother was not old enough to ride. He was disappointed, and to try to make up for it, I offered to ride with him on another roller coaster, one designed for younger kids. We climbed into our little two-seater car and set off. Fully expecting it to be a gentle imitation of the real thing, I sat back. But at our first turn, as we zipped along, I realized something was wrong. The car went way beyond where the lead wheels should have gripped the rails. Our car was broken and we might fly off the track at any turn. I didn't want to frighten my brother, so I didn't say anything; but I braced myself for the worst and kept my hands at the ready to grab him and anything else should the car break lose. It was the most harrowing ride of my life.

"Near the end of the ride, I noticed another car taking a turn the same way we had, and realized that our car wasn't broken after all. It had taken those turns by design. I didn't need to feign that mix of exhilaration and relief when the ride came to a close. My expectations had heightened that experience way beyond the ordinary ride. The same thing happens when you read: what you bring to it is critical.

"When teachers see the need for a whole language approach, it is not because they have rejected phonetics per se. It is out of a sense that there is more to the ride. It's the same thing with STEM. STEM opens things up. It steps back from the rush to cover the material and let's kids dwell."

"How so?"

"That's next, but let's turn things back over to the text for that."

What is STEM?

School districts across the country are investing in the promise of STEM. But we have long had schools that featured study in science, mathematics, engineering and technology . . . Lane Technical High School in Chicago, the Bronx High School of Science, and the Baltimore Polytechnic Institute, to name just a few. What's the difference between a STEM school and the many polytechnics, science schools, and vocational schools across the country? What's the deal with STEM?

As with many another simple question, this one opens onto a number of issues, but we can offer one observation straight off that suggests the depth of the transformation at the heart of STEM. STEM is not a particular body of material—that is, it is not defined by its content, like chemistry or computer programming. It is not a particular patch of science, technology, engineering, or mathematics. It's not their overlap. It's not an integrated program where you spend three weeks with one discipline and switch to another. It's a point of view, a style. It is a rethinking of how we teach that challenges traditional disciplinary boundaries. The borders that divide these several domains, like the borders that divide one state from another are like that line from Galen . . . there by convention. Da Vinci and Archimedes moved across them without skipping a beat. As such, STEM fits comfortably in the new science classroom we are describing, a classroom that nurtures student voice and takes the time for students to come to an understanding of the many aspects that bear on a given topic or issue.

There is a long and sober history of efforts to reform education in science, technology, engineering, and mathematics. Here, for example, is a ringing passage from Charles Eliot, president of Harvard, writing in 1898: "Effective power in action is the true end of education, rather than the storing up of information, or the cultivation of faculties which are mainly receptive, discriminating, or critical" (in DeBoer, 1991).

To this we may add a document from a century later: *The National Science Education Standards* of the National Research Council, which, as we have already noted, urges that there be:

- Less emphasis on the "acquisition of information" and more on "understanding and use of scientific knowledge, ideas, and inquiry processes."
- Less emphasis on activities that "demonstrate and verify science content" and more on those that "investigate and analyze science questions."
- Less emphasis on science "as exploration and experiment" and more on "argument and explanation." (NRC, 19)

Such passages call for a decided change at the deepest levels of the aims and practices of our classrooms. This is the call STEM has responded to . . . this is what STEM is about. The challenge in STEM is not: How many computers do we need? Or what additional sciences course should we offer? But how can you shape schooling so that it rises beyond rote memorization or the mastery of algorithms and actually empowers students? How do you teach to argument and understanding?

To Tinker

The heart of STEM reform is in the doing. If we would stand back a bit and look at schooling, so much of what we do is a matter of codes and schemas. Stand in a lower-school classroom. The array of symbols is staggering, from alphabets to maps to mathematical tables. And this is only magnified as you move through the grades. Being able to manipulate these codes with the appropriate algorithm is important, but of much greater value is actually to understand what you are doing.

I have banged on this drum before. Our interest here is how you can pull this off in labs and activities. Commonly, labs and activities are used to enable students to witness answers, like a dissection exercise where you identify the parts of a worm. In Chapter two we considered Osborne and Freyberg's criticisms of hands-on inquiry in their study, *Learning in Science*. Too often students don't understand the purpose of the activity, and they cope by doing and writing what they think the teacher wants. Osborne *et al.* offer several suggestions about how to meet this problem, all of them focused on clarity. But clarity is hard earned. It is not just a matter of getting the protocol right. Moving an activity from "hands-on" to "minds-on" is more difficult than being careful. We considered then of the importance of perplexity, of engaging students in something that was puzzling. Let's go back to that.

In a fascinating study called *The Forge and the Crucible* (1962), Mircea Eliade examined the earliest chapters of humankind's mastery of the flame and the technology that came with it. His gaze, however, was less on the beating of swords and plowshares than upon technology's impact on our imagination. Looking at the differences between alchemy and early modern chemistry, for example, Eliade urged that it is not what you do, but what you think you are doing that is important. This was brought home to me years ago at an evening performance of some music by Dave Brubeck. It was religious music, a mass, but I was there because I liked his jazz. For me, it was a concert. What Eliade was getting at was that even if a chemist and an alchemist performed the same procedures, there was a profound difference in what was happening. Each step along the way would have been conceived differently and the result would have had different meanings. The same is true in the classroom. As students work on a lab, there is a critical difference between those who are engaging a problem and those who are executing a protocol, even as they perform the same tasks.

This is where the approach put forward throughout this book provides STEM especially fertile soil. The great value of STEM is the place it gives to design and tinkering. "Walking backwards," "constructive inquiry," drawing upon basic issues in the development of the sciences, these come together nicely to frame labs and activities that take good advantage of the core sensibilities of STEM.

But we should first stop to consider what tinkering and design are all about. One evening some time ago, I discovered a small group of high school kids over in the lower school playing with blocks. It was a gentle, playful activity. It is not surprising that block-playing appealed to these older kids, but block-building is not what tinkering is about—at least it need not be.

It's a question of problems.

Playing with blocks or K-nex, or paints, can involve tinkering, but it can also be more idle. Not "idle" as in without value—not a Puritan idle—but idle as in, by happenstance, where something catches the fancy. Tinkering is more directed. It is a matter of focus. Tinkering is the manipulation of number, symbol, pattern, material, or concept with the solution to a puzzle in mind.

Tinkering is thus a positive, virtuous activity—a view that I suspect is not necessarily common. I was struck to discover that a dictionary definition of tinkering was essentially negative, suggesting unskillful or clumsy work, to bungle, and to be makeshift. There is little regard here for the successful solution of a problem by taking advantage of what is at hand or "do-able" at the moment.

Yet, this is a most important talent. Consider events during the Apollo 13 and 14 missions. In both of these missions there were malfunctions that endangered the mission and, in the case of Apollo 13, the crew. In both cases, the problems were solved by creative, ingenious maneuvers that took advantage of existing parts to scrape together a solution. For example, as they orbited the moon, the Apollo 14 computer signaled that the mission should be aborted. The crew, working with ground technicians, was able to determine that there was a hardware malfunction in a portion of the computer. A program designer on Earth, some 200,000 miles away, devised new programming that bypassed the faulty section of the computer on board the capsule and the crew was able to complete its mission. In a lovely essay, John Campbell likened this to what happens when a dog breaks a leg. The dog can reprogram itself and develop a three-legged gait that bypasses the faulty hardware. This, by the way, is why horses that break their legs most often are put down. They can't reprogram themselves and would suffer horribly as they tried to walk on all fours (Campbell, 1971, p. 6–7). The ability to tinker is a crucial step in the "evolution" of problem-solving.

A key part of tinkering is the puzzle. We have already talked about the importance of perplexity. Is there anything useful to be said about puzzles? Let me hazard a notion. Puzzles, a subset of perplexities, are a variation of a fine and well-formed notion—the anomaly. An anomaly is a working violation of our understanding of the way things ought to be. There is nothing inherently wrong with the thing itself, except that it contradicts a theory. The flight of an arrow was anomalous for Aristotle, but not for Galileo—nor for the archer. The fact that the sun was the source of such extraordinary amounts of energy and yet was not consumed was anomalous until the discovery of nuclear energies.

If we take this as reasonable, how does it connect to puzzles and to tinkering?

Puzzles provoke in the manner of anomalies, but they are not as tightly anchored to an explanatory framework. They may, for example, arise in the context of strategies within games where rules set the frame, rather than a theory. Puzzles seem, that is, to require a context, a body of common assumptions, rules of reasoning, or other notions about acceptable manipulations. A classic example is the longstanding challenge of geometric constructions, such as trisecting an angle or constructing a pentagon. One must use only a compass and a straight-edge, and, of course, one's creativity.

To tinker, therefore, involves a purposeful focus, a clarity of mission, and a solid sense for the rules of the game, whether it's Scrabble, geometry, or a particular happenstance, such as the breakdown of a piece of equipment on a space flight.

On Design

As we look at STEM, the companion to tinkering is design. There are several dimensions to design. For example, in a lovely essay on the panda's thumb,

Stephen J. Gould teases out an essential tension between design and tinkering. Pandas are remarkable creatures that resemble Walt Disney creations. There is an almost human quality to them as they sit, pick up a long bamboo shoot and strip it of its leaves by pulling the pole through their fists, and then eat the leaves. But, observed Gould, how is it possible for the panda to form a fist? Where did it get an opposable thumb?

The panda's thumb is not a thumb. Pandas have "regular" paws, with five modest digits around a pad. The apparent thumb is really an elongated wrist bone with muscles that enable it to move with a scissors-like motion. Gould uses this feature to tease out the differences between two basic perceptions of life. There are those who see life as designful, and there are those who see it as the product of a kind of tinkering, more "make-do" than carefully designed. For the one, life is a contrivance; for the other, it's a contraption (Gould, 1980, pp. 19–26). Cuvier's work is the very model of nature as contrivance; Darwin's the model of nature as contraption. Yet, to a degree, I digress, because this is not the dimension of design that is crucial to our discussion. It is not designfulness *per se*, but the process of design that is critical to the practice of the STEM classroom. Design is a verb in the STEM classroom, not a noun.

The importance of the design process marks a critical shift in the classroom. Let's look at labs and class activities. Instead of presenting students with a rather well-defined activity, students are invited to design their own inquiry into a rather well-defined problem or issue. Let's try an instance, picking up on our earlier discussion of the nature of gravity. There is a fairly common activity that becomes uncommonly rich if you shift the framing of the activity from protocols to problems. Students are often asked in physical science and physics courses to measure the acceleration of a ball rolling down a ramp. Then the teachers bring out the apparatus . . . stop watches, photo gates, Vernier sensors and calculators, all sorts of trappings, and students go about collecting the data. But what if we change the activity? Ask students if they can show whether the ball is accelerating down the ramp or coasting at a steady speed. Then, to make it more interesting, throw in this kicker: no watches. This makes explicit the shift from collecting data to making an argument.

How can you prove the ball's velocity is changing as it rolls down the ramp, if you don't time anything and so determine the velocity directly at any point? This proves to be a lovely challenge and students have designed a number of arguments.

"*Can I try?*"

"*Sure, Sancho. What would you do?*"

"*I think I would try to roll a marble down the full length of the ramp and see how far it rolled along the floor. Then I would let it roll from only half-way down the ramp and see how far it rolls. If it rolls just as far then that means the two had the same speed at the bottom of the ramp and there is no significant acceleration. But I don't think that would happen. The ball with the longer run down the ramp is going to have the longer run along the floor.*"

"This is a good experiment, Sancho, nicely designed. You are confident of the result. Can you point to any common experiences to lend support to your confidence?"

"I don't know, D.Q. . . ."

"What happens if you turn your experiment upside down?"

"Upside down? . . . You mean, if I roll the marbles up? Going up hill causes things to slow down. That's clearly acceleration. If I want the ball to rise higher, I have to throw it harder. That's like Skee Ball."

"Now put the two together."

"I don't understand, D.Q."

"What about a downward motion and an upward motion, like a ball rolling in a bowl?"

"O.K., I see. If you release a marble from one side of the bowl it rolls down and goes up the other side, like a pendulum."

"Yes, and if you release it from just half-way up the side of the bowl?"

"Oh, I see . . . the ball wouldn't rise as high, and since how high it rises is a function of how fast it is moving at the bottom, a marble dropped from higher up the bowl must be going faster at the bottom. That shows acceleration."

"Very good, Sancho, now let's get back to the text . . ."

There are several other good arguments showing the acceleration of a ball down a ramp. For example, you could put a wooden block on the track near the bottom of the ramp and see how far the marble pushes it. Here the push on the block operationally defines the magnitude of the velocity, just as the length of the run on the floor did in Sancho's first experiment.

When you are doing this sort of activity with a class and have as many as six or seven groups of students there are several things to keep in mind. You should have a tinkering table with all sorts of objects: wooden blocks, paper clips, cups, rubber bands, string, meter sticks, different size marbles. You want to foster speculative play. Make sure there are things there for solving the problem in lots of different ways. When a group solves the problem, ask them to find another solution. If another group is having trouble, send them over to a group that has solved the problem. When they see how it can be solved one way, they may well come up with other ways of their own. They're not in competition with each other, but with the problem itself. Then bring the whole group back together for a discussion. Compare arguments, talk about the relative strengths or weaknesses of different approaches. There's a lot to do here beyond just collecting the data from a sensor or whatever.

How Things Work and Why They Are the Way They Are

There is a large body of fascinating stuff that borders the sciences, but it's a restless border. We don't teach these things, but we can't quite put them down. They might appear in a box in a textbook, as an aside. It's the kind of thing that you see on the Discovery channel in programs like "MythBusters." It's the kind of thing Michels criticized . . . those technological applications that riddled old physics books. How things work. Why they are the way they are. It seems to me as I look back on my schooling, every time a teacher was absent they would have a coach or some member of the staff come in to cover, and every time they would talk to us about how automobile engines worked. It was a different day. If your television went on the blink, you would gently extract an array of tubes from the back of the set and head toward the store where you could test them, find the faulty one, and install the replacement yourself. A different day. When I was a kid learning about cars, there was a whole raft of things you could do for yourself. I would take the air filter off and check the valve on the carburetor, or see if the points in the distributor needed cleaning, or if the battery was low on water, or the gap in the spark plugs was clogged, etc. Nowadays, your tool kit has only one item, a cell phone to call for help. It was a different day.

We think about the world of science and technology differently today. It's more remote despite the fact that we are everywhere surrounded by it. Back in the middle of the nineteenth century, the Crystal Palace Exhibition, a hallmark event in Western culture, showcased the modern technology of the Industrial Revolution. It was a building of glass and steel. It displayed the great engines that drove England's economy, coal-driven steam engines and pumps. The middle of the nineteenth century was fascinated by its new technology. This fascination continued until well after World War II. Walt Disney, for example, could feature a documentary about science and technology, "Our Friend the Atom," on prime time on a Sunday evening. But it is not there now. The technology that surrounds us is a black box, and to be good with technology these days is to be adept at turning it on. In this sense, STEM is a throwback. It reconfigures the borders and invites students to make sense of the devices in their world.

The Project Itself

At a celebration marking the 75th anniversary of Park School a distinguished alumnus was invited to give a talk. Dr. Wolman is a most accomplished scientist and a member of the National Academy of Sciences. As he reflected back on his schooling, the single most significant moment was not that special science teacher he had had or anything like that. What stood out was the time the whole school built a garage. He described in detail the way the older students designed the garage and then acted as foremen in guiding its construction. Everybody played a part, all the way down to the kindergarten kids. Students dug and moved rocks, mixed cement, cut beams, hammered boards and shingles into place. They built a garage. That was a neat thing for students to do.

There is a simple, yet profound reward to working on projects. And the more responsibility you have, the more opportunity to give the project your own signature, the more satisfying the experience. Sadly, our schools rarely afford students such project work of any significant magnitude.

On a decidedly lesser scale, I too look back on a project as a key part of my early schooling. I took a class in ninth grade where we each designed and pursued a research project. I built a small wind tunnel using the fan from an old vacuum cleaner.

"*That sounds neat, D.Q. What did you do with it?*"

"*The idea was to study how airplanes worked. I was going to examine the air flow around models of wings and determine which design created the most lift.*"

"*Did you use wings from plastic airplane models?*"

"*No, Sancho, I made the wings out of wood. That way I could drill holes through them for the capillary tubes . . .*"

"*The what?*"

"*Let's see . . . do you know what happens if you blow across a straw?*"

"*No, should I?*"

"*Well, it's just that it's somewhat surprising. Blowing across the top of a straw draws the liquid up. It's the same sort of thing as driving down a highway and rolling the window down . . . any loose papers go flying out of the car.*"

"*You know, that never made any sense to me. You'd think the air would rush in and push things back . . .*"

"*Exactly, only that doesn't happen. If we go back to John Herapath and his idea that heat is a dance, then we can imagine molecules of air rushing about in every direction. But when you blow air across the straw, those molecules are moving together and they don't do as good a job of fanning out and rushing all about. As a result, they don't push up or down very effectively. Meanwhile, the air inside the straw is going about its regular business and now things are not well balanced. The air inside the straw is pushing up more effectively than the outside air is pushing down. It rises and is swept along with the rushing air. That means there is less push down on the liquid than there had been, and so the liquid rises.*"

"*You mean taking something as light as a little bit of air off of the top of the liquid is enough for it to rise? Earlier you dropped your keys on the floor and asked how long before they ended up in the clouds. This is just as strange. What is lifting the liquid?*"

"*Very good, Sancho. The liquid isn't really lifted up; it's pushed up. It's pushed up by very substantial air pressure that we rarely feel directly. We spend our lives at the bottom of a vast sea of air, tens of miles high. Even though air is light, the column of air above us is so great that it presses down with a weight of almost 15 pounds on every square inch. An ordinary linoleum floor tile 12 inches on a side is carrying the weight of 144×15, or approximately 2,000 pounds!*"

"*Whoa! You mean there's 2,000 pounds of pressure on each tile in this room? The floor would be crushed by that, wouldn't it? This room has got to be 30 feet on a side. That's 900 tiles, or 1,800,000 pounds!*"

"*Incredible isn't it, Sancho. How can this be true? How could an ordinary floor handle 2 million pounds of pressure?*"

"*I have no idea, D.Q.*"

"*Then let's see if we can figure it out. What happens if you push down on a balloon?*"

"*It squeezes out to the sides.*"

"*The air takes the pressure from the push and spreads it out in every direction. This is different from what happens with a set of blocks, for example. With the blocks, the weight simply pushes down. There's no general spreading out of the force. But when you increase air pressure, the push goes off in every direction, including back up.*"

"*O.K., I'm following you.*"

"*So what do you think the push is on the ceiling of this room?*"

"*. . . Is it the same as the push on the floor?*"

"*Yes, it is, Sancho, with a tiny adjustment for the actual weight of the air. That's why the floor above us doesn't collapse. Air pressure from below balances out the pressure from above. The floor only has to handle its own weight.*"

"*So, going back to airplanes and straws, if you reduce the downward push of the air, there is already a strong push upward and the difference is what lifts them . . . Very sweet.*"

"*Yes, Sancho, very sweet.*"

This conversation brings to the surface some of the central concepts of that project I worked on so long ago, concepts I had to work out alongside building the wind tunnel, testing whether the air flow was smooth, shaping the wing segments, drilling holes that would break cleanly through the surface and other varied tasks. The project was hands-on and minds-on, and I even had to make presentations about my project, sometimes before fairly large audiences. A neat thing for students to do.

As a teacher, I drew upon this experience many, many times. In the first place, I moved the basic format for labs in my classes from protocols to problems, precisely so that students could work out their own approaches and follow up on the issues raised. But I also sponsored independent projects, overseeing student work on all sorts of issues and objects. They built cloud chambers, studied Crookes' tubes, built model airplanes and tested how lift worked, and tried building vacuum pumps. One of my favorites involved a small group of students who were keen on environmental issues and energy conservation of an ecological sort. We talked about things for a while and our talk led to hydrogen as a fuel because lots of energy is released and the end product or waste is "mostly harmless"—it's water.

They began by generating hydrogen and oxygen using an electrolysis device . . . splitting water molecules with electricity. (We have already met with the basics of electrolysis in our discussion of teacher-led inquiry in Chapter four. There we saw a student, John, try to make sense of how electricity acted on things dissolved in water.) Electrolysis is deceptively straightforward. Electricity is breaking up the water molecules. Now usually when you break something the parts separate right there; so you would expect to find the hydrogen and oxygen both generated at the same spot . . . the spot where they get "zapped."

But, in fact, what happens is that hydrogen is generated at one wire or terminal, and the oxygen at the other, clear across the way. How this happens is its own neat puzzle and they worked at that for a while.

Now that they could generate hydrogen and oxygen, they explored what happens when you recombine them. They burned hydrogen. This, too, had many parts, as they worked on how they could ignite the hydrogen safely. But the real focus of their work became measuring the energies given off by the explosion. This was the problem at the heart of their project. They wanted some sense for the bookkeeping of energies in and energies out. The energy in was pretty straightforward; they measured the amount of electricity it takes to break up the water molecules and explored what the electricity was actually doing with individual molecules. The energy out was more complicated. To get at the mechanical energy, the push of the explosion, they ended up putting a small mix of hydrogen and oxygen in a plastic "baggy" and securing it to the bottom of a pan of water. Then they "zapped" the mix and measured how much water had spilled out and the work it would take to move that much water. They measured the temperature of the water before and after to get at that form of energy, and then went to a darkroom where they photographed the explosion to get at the light energy released, even putting some film in a black paper jacket to get at "light" beyond the visible spectrum. It was a delightful sequence of designs and tinkering that raised good issues and delightful explorations.

That wind tunnel blew across a lot of terrain.

So often we prepare students for tests, tests that we have already written, tests that come with the textbook or that we gave last year, or the standardized tests that have become so important since "No Child Left Behind." We prepare them for these tests by telling them what they need to know. Project work can be at the other end of the spectrum. Students are learning, but we aren't telling them. They are solving problems. Sometimes they are looking things up, but what they are really doing is poking and prodding, figuring things out. They are working out some design or some redesign so that they can get some clarity on what is going on and offer an explanation.

At the same time, we teachers have a lot of preparation to do with such projects. Some of that is getting materials together, but a larger part is helping to shape conversations so that students come to some testable hypothesis and a reasonable experimental design . . . no mean feat. That's why, as important and valuable as project work is, I rarely assigned projects within classes . . .

"What!"

"In the first place, Sancho, I mean projects that take a lot of time, like the project on hydrogen, not the sort of lab project that students would do in 2 or 3 hours. I was always jealous of the time lost to good class discussions and that give and take about ideas and arguments. That part was a little selfish, but there's another critical reason, one that takes us back to that basic business of listening. A good project sits right on the edge of what a student understands. It's driven by more than interest. It's driven by perplexity. Too often, we assign projects that might work well with a handful of students, but leave the others without any idea of what they might do . . . how they might tinker with the issue. Or, worse, we assign projects that are essentially about collecting information and don't involve any real problem-solving at all. Students simply go to the internet and cull a few passages from Wikipedia and the like. For a project really to do its work, you have got to talk things though with a student or small group of students and see what it is that sits out there on the edge and is do-able. And that is hard to do with an entire class. That's why the independent study format is so much better."

"What do you mean by independent study?"

"There are lots of ways to pull this off. That class I took where I built a wind tunnel was set up so that each of the 10 or so students could do long-term projects. If this isn't possible, you can offer extra credit within a class for a project. Students may become interested in some aspect of their study and want to push it further. One interesting way to pull off time for project work is to suspend the regular school day for a week, and have all the students engage in different projects. You can also do projects with students after school, or if you are lucky and there are open times during the school day, you can do an independent study in that 'free' time. An extension of this is the independent study class, where students sign-up for a class that is their project. The hydrogen project students met every day, and I almost always met with them. The important thing is that you have plenty of time to talk things through, until you have a pretty good idea of the shape of the project. In terms of assessment, a rubric for evaluating a project should focus on two broad considerations. There is first the mechanics at the heart of the design. Is this good science? Does it meet other specifications in terms of time or costs? Then there is the execution of the design. Here is the basic realm of tinkering. How have they coped with problems? Was there a prototype? In addition, there are matters worth attending to that are less directly connected to the material. Did the group work well as a group? Were responsibilities shared equitably? What kind of leadership did individuals display?

"It's also nice if you can structurally support the project. You might have your students present their findings to classes or at an assembly. Still better, you might have a day when students would present their projects to one another at a gathering, a conference or symposium. The key thing is that the project sits on that edge; that it's engaging; that it involves design and tinkering; and, of course, you have to not know the answer."

As we close this chapter, we can see how powerfully STEM invites a rethinking of the material we offer students, emphasizing as it does interdisciplinary work and projects marked by tinkering and design. By opening things up so dramatically there is a risk that teachers and students might lose their way. The logic of the material is not completely irrelevant. Things have to make sense. What structure is there within a course of study to scaffold real growth?

The answer is not surprising. It has to do with the capacity to dwell. The right kind of focus across disciplinary boundaries and the right kind of project foster the capacity to dwell, encouraging students to play with options, to make sense of things. There's a fragment from a letter by the young J. Robert Oppenheimer, who would later lead the Manhattan Project to build the atomic bomb, where you can hear just this note. Robert was off at university and writing his younger brother, Frank, who was taking up the sciences in his older brother's footsteps:

> And now a final word of advice: try to understand really, to your own satisfaction, thoroughly and honestly, the few things in which you are most interested; because it is only when you have learnt to do that, when you realize how hard and how very satisfying it is, that you will appreciate fully the more spectacular things like relativity and mechanistic biology.
>
> (in Bernstein, 2004, pp. 16–17)

That's what STEM is about, whether it's building a garage or a wind tunnel. There's water in that classroom and the kids are learning how to swim.

Interlude
Taking Measure of Things

Beyond the interdisciplinary aspect of STEM, beyond the renewed emphasis on design and tinkering, there is the basic program of having students engage with material in ways that foster their coming to make sense of it. Curiously, a steady diet of schooling often leaves students indifferent to the seeming contradictions or outrageous proportions of the modern understanding. Take a simple example: in a study of the historical sciences, I would point out to students something I found rather curious in the standard chart of the Earth's history. Reading it from the bottom up there is a sequence of periods, the Cambrian, the Ordovician, the Silurian, the Devonian, the Permian, etc.—a sequence of eight items—and then the last two, the Tertiary and the Quaternary. Since "tertiary" and "quaternary" derive from the Latin for three and four, I would simply ask: Why would you have a sequence that goes through eight items and then says "three, four"? When I would get rather flat expressions from the class, as if to say "What's the big deal?" I would then tell a little story . . .

Years ago, I visited Aldeburgh, an old English seaport town. Lovely and quaint, with clapboard homes along the North Sea coast and a main street with old shops, Aldeburgh had been a thriving seaport and shipbuilding town. For example, Sir Francis Drake's *The Golden Hind* was built here. Having walked along the beach, I turned from the sea and crossed the beach road. As I crossed the street I noted that it was 7th street. But the next street was not 6th. Instead it was 8th, and then 9th. No one would lay out a town starting with 7th, would they? What happened to one through six? The answer was not blowing in the wind. It lay in the sea. There, off shore, is the top of the old city hall. The sea has steadily crept up on this old town, and half of it lies buried beneath sea and sand.

At Aldeburgh history explains the seemingly wanton face of the town, and the same might be true of the chart of the Earth's history. Why don't we look at things a bit more closely . . .

Across the years of my teaching this has been a common thread, catching a seeming contradiction or something out of whack, and looking more closely at it. Sometimes it's a name out of place, such as Tertiary. Similarly, I was led to the work of Dr. Suess, which I discussed in Chapter six, because I found it curious that texts referred to the southern half of Pangaea as "Gondwanaland."

Where did that name come from, I wondered? And I found it had been envisioned long before plate tectonics and it opened a door on fascinating work in bio-geography. Sometimes it was a number, like the curious business of calling the freezing point of water 32° in the Fahrenheit scale. What was that about? This question came up so many times, I found myself playing with it and the result was something like this . . .

"Sancho, I wonder if you would help me out. I've written a short play; actually it's a rewrite of a small part of a Tom Stoppard play called Rosencrantz and Guildenstern Are Dead. *Would you read with me? There's a catch. The play will stop, but our conversation will carry on. O.K.?"*

"Sure, D.Q., I'm game."

"Let me set the scene. Two Elizabethans, that's us, are passing the time of day in a place without visible character. They are well dressed, hats, cloaks, and all. Each of them has a large leather money bag. D.Q.'s is nearly empty. Sancho's is nearly full. The reason being, they are betting on the toss of a coin. They have been doing so for some time. The run of 'heads' is impossible; yet Sancho betrays no surprise at all. He is, however, nice enough to feel a little embarrassed at taking so much of his friend's money. D.Q., on the other hand, is well alive to the oddity of it. He is not worried about the money, so much as the implications of this extraordinary run.

"He spins successive coins. Sancho studies each and calls out the result."

Sancho: *"Heads.*

"Heads.

"Heads.

"Heads."

D.Q.: *"There is an art to the building up of suspense."*

Sancho: *"Heads."*

D.Q.: *"Though it can be done by luck alone."*

Sancho: *"Heads. 76—love."*

D.Q.: *"A weaker man might be moved to re-examine his faith, if nothing else at least in the laws of probability."*

Sancho: *"Heads."*

D.Q.: *"But what are the chances that a conversation about thermometers would begin with flipping coins?"*

Sancho: *"Heads."*

D.Q.: *"I see. Then let me pose another question. Suppose we took three bowls of water. Then we put our . . ."*

Sancho: *"Heads."*

D.Q.: *"No, hands would be just fine. One hand in the bowl of hot water, and the other in the bowl of cold water."*

Sancho: *"Heads."*

D.Q.: *"Then we put both hands in the middle bowl where there is a mix of hot and cold water."*

Sancho: *"Heads, again."*

D.Q.: *"What do you think would happen?"*

Sancho: *"Heads?"*

D.Q.: *"No, hands. The hot hand would feel cold, wouldn't it? And the cold, hot?"*

Sancho: *"Hmm."*

D.Q.: *"Tails, was it, at last?"*

Sancho: *"No. It was heads, but I was just thinking about staring down at your hands in a bowl of water, and one felt cold and the other hot. It's enough to make your ... heads ... spin."*

D.Q.: *"Not very probable, is it?"*

Sancho: *"85 in a row. Broke my record."*

D.Q.: *"Is that all?"*

Sancho: *"What?"*

D.Q.: *"A new record. Is that as far as you are prepared to go? Surely, there is more. Let's try to make sense of this ... a syllogism. Major premise: probability is a factor that operates in the natural world. Minor premise: probability is not acting here. Conclusion: we are not in the natural world."*

Sancho: *"What is the matter with you? You are acting as if you lost your ... heads."*

D.Q.: *"The scientific approach to the examination of phenomena is a defense against the pure emotion of fear."*

Sancho: *"You shouldn't be afraid. If we just put our ... heads, no make that hands together in that bowl, then we could make things sensible again."*

D.Q.: *"That's it! Sensibility is the problem. We need to be brilliantly insensitive. Metallically insensitive, as in mercury. Quicksilver. No confusion in a thermometer."*

Sancho: *"In a what?"*

D.Q.: *"A thermometer."*

Sancho: *"Now I am afraid."*

D.Q.: *"Huh?"*

Sancho: *"I'm afraid I don't know what you are talking about."*

D.Q.: *"You know, the Fahrenheit thermometer, named after an early eighteenth century chap who figured out a way ... Oh, now I see. We're Elizabethan, aren't we? The thermometer hasn't happened yet. Needs must talk to someone about that."*

Sancho: *"Me?"*

D.Q.: *"Why not? But later; for now let's invent a thermometer. No, better still, let's assume one has been invented, and we need simply to set up a scale."*

Sancho: *"That's easy. Do you want a butcher's scale or a carpenter's?"*

D.Q.: *"Length will do just fine. No reason to fret about changes in weight when heat is added or subtracted."*

Sancho: *"Huh?"*

D.Q.: *"A thermometer measures the quality in a bowl of water that corresponds roughly to whether it feels hot or cold. That quality has been given a name, temperature."*

Sancho: *"But there is already a name for that, heat."*

D.Q.: *"Close but not quite. Heat is what is given off by a fire or something that is very hot. But not all things get hot the same way when they are exposed to heat. Some things, like metals, become hot quite readily when you heat them; while others, like water, are very slow off the mark. Though exposed to the same amount of heat, they come to different temperatures."*

Sancho: *"Hmm, but it was heat that made them hot in the first place. This temperature is just a nicety of degree or some such."*

D.Q.: *"Very nice. Heat is an agent; temperature a quality, and thermometer a device for measuring that quality. But we still have our problem?"*

Sancho: *"Heads?"*

D.Q.: *"No, how to establish a scale. Lots of things change size when exposed to heat. Metals, for instance, do this with great regularity. If I start with a column of mercury and add heat, the column will expand. But I need a framework. What, for example, would I call this temperature, right here, now?"*

Sancho: *"Well, it is pleasant enough, but rather hot all in all."*

D.Q.: *"Yes, but I had in mind a numerical scale with a nice zero and another point that would be a good round number like 100."*

Sancho: *"What happened to Fahrenheit?"*

D.Q.: *"This is getting out of hand. You allude, I take it, to the curious role of 32 and 212 in the Fahrenheit scale. But surely this is not where Fahrenheit began. Let us maintain our sanity, however much we suspect it to be without warrant. Fahrenheit was the first to set a scale in the measure of temperature in a way that would enable any earnest soul to produce data that was universally recognizable. He did so in a 'rational' way. His was a centigrade scale, and he needed to set the scale in a way that almost anyone could do it for themselves. What do you think he used for his zero and his 100?"*

Sancho: *"Ah, but I see now that I have come to the end of my script and I have to answer your question. Hmmm, I haven't any idea."*

D.Q.: *"A Fahrenheit 0° is really cold, since it is 32° below freezing. What is out there that the good soul, Fahrenheit, could have used to mark such cold?"*

Sancho: *"I don't know. What is colder than snow and ice?"*

D.Q.: *"Have you ever wondered why people sprinkle salt on icy streets and sidewalks?"*

Sancho: *"The salt melts them, but come to think of it I don't know why."*

D.Q.: *"Think of it this way. Salt water freezes at a lower temperature than pure water. It also boils at a higher temperature. It seems the salt just gets in the way of things."*

Sancho: *"That's it, then. Something colder than snow or ice would be salt water freezing."*

D.Q.: *"You bet. In particular, 0° Fahrenheit is the temperature at which the salt water of the Atlantic Ocean freezes. Halfway there to our scale. What about the other end. What could he have used to set his 100° mark?"*

Sancho: *"I can't think of anything in particular. It's a hot day when it is 100°. It's also pretty close to our body temperature."*

D.Q.: *"As a matter of fact, that's it. Over time, people shifted to more readily reproducible results within a lab and with the increased accuracy it became clear that Fahrenheit's 100 had to be adjusted to 98.6. But in the beginning it was a centigrade scale."*

Sancho: *"That's neat."*

D.Q.: *"I think so, too, Sancho."*

We can break from this little dialogue. The point was that with STEM-like sensibilities there are lots of activities and conversations that take students back to basic questions about the reasons for things; about how things work and why they are the way they are.

Chapter 8

On the Politics of Learning

Consider a rational soul coming across some of the items we have touched upon in this book:

- The idea that water evaporates, despite the evident fact that it is a heavy body—what could make it go up?
- The idea that the Earth is a planet, despite the fact that we can neither see nor feel it move.
- The idea that those two dark rocks had been vertebrae of a long extinct, huge animal, despite the fact that they simply looked like two rocks.
- The idea that life has evolved, despite the evident fact that cats give birth to kittens and dogs to puppies . . . despite the evident fact that seeds work, that life reproduces itself with striking regularity.

What do we expect a student to do with these? In each, the critical reader should require an argument to be convinced: a well-reasoned argument, supported by appropriate evidence that connects with what he or she already knows. Without such arguments, why would they "buy" these claims? Yet they do.

Such is the authority of the sciences in our culture.

We live in an age where the image of science has been formed by the fantasy of space exploration, by the magic of medical technology, and by the specter of nuclear explosion. It is a crowded image, as profile overlays profile. Science is Voyager photographs of the rings of Saturn and electron micrographs of the extraordinary geometry of the smallest matter. It is also pesticides that leave fields barren and threaten aquifers; it is holes in the ozone layer and plumes of radiation above the ruins of the Chernobyl nuclear power plant. On another plane, science is both the gentle and affecting sensibilities of Einstein and the passionless calculations of a Mr. Spock. With all this, it is a commanding image; so much so that it is a commonplace to speak of the authority of science in our society, an authority registered in everything from advertising to the consultant in the courtroom. Everywhere one turns, the authoritative scientific study impresses its weight upon some decision.

Science teaching shares in this complex and commanding image, and this is a problem.

A Note on the Nature of Science

It is clear that "science as a body of knowledge" is a substantial part of how we look at the sciences. The holdings in any university library are ample testament to that. In this regard, such compendiums of scientific information as the *Handbook of Chemistry and Physics* come to mind, with their extraordinary arrays of tables and data. Densities, half-lives of isotopes, vapor pressures . . . if it can be measured and given a number, then it figures in a scientific table somewhere.

Yet, this seems somehow off. Science does not aim at the accumulation of data. Just as the end of man is not his death, even though his life ends in death; so, science may in fact end up with lots of information, but that is not its end. Its end is to explain the world around us: what it is, how it works, and how it has come to be the way it is. Science is an effort to understand. This is the great value of the popular literature that surrounds the sciences. Think of the essays of Stephen J. Gould or Loren Eiseley, of Carl Sagan or Stephen Hawking. These come much closer to capturing what science is than the *Handbook*.

As we link science to a body of understanding rather than a body of information, we need to be careful. We would not want to privilege any particular understandings. That is, we would not want to say that in order to be scientific one must have a particular understanding of a given set of phenomena. If we make science equal to a set of theories—evolution, quantum mechanics, relativity, plate tectonics, etc.—then we would have the awkward problem that science would have neither a significant past nor a promising future, since change has been so central to the sciences.

Science is the effort to understand, not a particular understanding. That is, it is the going, and not the getting there. Science is a process, a method for making sense of the world. You may recall that passage from John Dewey saying that teaching in the sciences needed to be more about its method and less about its answers. But what sort of process is it? In the opening essay of *Conjectures and Refutations*, Karl Popper examines the foundations of the scientific revolution and the subsequent Age of Enlightenment. It is a powerful essay and gives us a useful handle on this question of the methods of the sciences.

Popper begins with the great movement of liberation that started in the Renaissance, a movement inspired by a profoundly optimistic view of humankind's power to discern truth and acquire understanding. At heart here was the firm conviction that the truth is manifest. Man could know the truth and the truth would set him free. No longer would we need to defer to the authority of the way things were, to the authority of tradition, for fear that any bold change would lead to chaos. The vision of a new society could rest on a foundation made solid by reason. Change and a new society could rest on a foundation made solid by the truth (Popper, 1963; see also Michel Foucault's *The Birth of the Clinic*, 1973, which captures the vision and enthusiasm of these sensibilities at their peak in the years immediately following the French Revolution).

This new-found confidence rested upon the striking success of the sciences. There was an extraordinary burst of accomplishment in the seventeenth century, led by such substantive figures as Kepler, Galileo, Descartes, Leibniz, and Newton. But what of the methods of the sciences? For Popper, the answer is critical thinking. Science involves the basic enterprise of offering hypotheses and then testing them. Key here is the role of falsification, and though trying to capture all of what goes on in the sciences in a single framework is complicated, I think Popper is the right place to begin. There is a distinctive asymmetry to things. We can never establish the truth of a proposition; that would take an infinite number of tests. But we can establish the falsity of a proposition; that only takes one test. It only takes one black swan to prove that all swans are not white. Critical thinking, then, is the search to falsify a credible hypothesis: hence the title of Popper's book, *Conjectures and Refutations*. There is, then, a persistent critical strain to the sciences, a continuous push to test the adequacy of theory.

Of all the things we teach, surely these critical sensibilities would be the most central. Are we teaching them? Sadly, the answer is largely no.

Research on Reading

There is a problem. It has to do with how students read and, in particular, with how they read science texts. Studies of what is involved when a student sits down to read have underlined just how complex a set of tasks this is. Research has uncovered a broad range of considerations. Some have examined the brain and how many bits of information can be stored in short-term memory before they are processed to another level. Some have examined the mind and ideas, and the influence of particular belief systems that students bring to the text. Still others have examined the value of different study strategies.

In one study, Yore, Craig, and Maguire (1998) put forward a grid of some 60 items in a model of "meta-cognition" for science reading—that is, of what is going on in the head of an efficient and successful science reader. One of the key elements in their model is that the successful reader "evaluates science texts for plausibility, completeness, and interconnectedness by verifying the textual message against prior knowledge, evidence, and observed reality and by assessing the logic and patterns of argumentation" (Yore *et al.*, 1998, p. 34).

These qualities are the very core of reading and reasoning in the sciences, and what a complex set of analytical skills and sensibilities they represent. This is hardly the suspension of disbelief Coleridge had talked about. Students need to be critics, and disbelief is everywhere. They must evaluate the logical qualities of the argument that is being made. They must also draw upon their experience and their sense of the way things are in order to challenge the claims being made. When this doesn't take place, what we have is but an imitation of science. And sadly, Yore, Craig, and Maguire found that our schools are rife with imitation.

Research suggests that this sort of critical engagement and evaluation does not often take place. In an interesting study, Norris and Phillips (1994) asked high school students with strong academic records to evaluate various statements within popular science articles. They found that these students frequently reduced the ambiguity and subtlety of various arguments and inferences within these articles to simple, declarative truths. Instead of collapsing arguments to simple propositions, they should be pushing at the boundaries of these claims—challenging whether they work or whether they do not. In another study, Craig and Yore (1996) found that 70 percent of the middle school students they interviewed ascribed greater authority to printed science ideas than to their own knowledge and experience. Here again, students are deferring to the text, instead of challenging it.

Our students seem to be reading non-fiction as they would a novel or short story. This is an important failing. A critical scepticism is at the heart of the sciences. Our students are virtual "Aristotelians" who would rather not drop a weight out of a window, if it might contradict the word of their text. I know that there are those who see science as a body of knowledge. If students are learning the information, that's what we want. Remember the urgings of Shea about the authority of 200 years of scientific scrutiny . . . otherwise, wouldn't we be wasting our time simply reinventing the wheel? But I am all for wheels, especially the reinvented kind. The act of reinventing is the act of ownership. It is at the heart of reconstructive inquiry.

On Criticism and Deference

Yore, Craig, and Maguire (1998) offer the notion that students have weak critical skills because they have an "absolutist" view of science, where science is a body of established truths. They argue that this inaccurate conception of the nature of science leads students to see science as "The Truth," and so it overrules their own experiences and ideas. If we go back to that set of notions at the start of this chapter, evaporation, that the Earth is a planet, etc., we can see how hard it is to be a student. Here are central notions in the sciences, and yet they are stridently counterintuitive and hardly connect to everyday experience at all. What can you do when you are surrounded by authoritative constructs that just don't make sense?

It is quite possible that students have this "absolutist" view of the sciences. Yet, there is another hypothesis that I find more enticing: it is to see the lack of critical, independent judgement in our students in terms of the politics of the classroom. Deference is a political act; recall the story about lip-smacking. In this case, it is deference to a text. A student's approach to a science text,

I suspect, has less to do with how he or she understands the nature of science than how they understand the nature of being a student. If you see as your task when reading a science text to get the facts straight and make sure you are comfortable with new technical terms, then I bet you treat your history text the same way—not because history has the same "absolutist" authority as the sciences within our culture, but because this is how you play the game. This is what it means to be a student.

There is a natural tension here. We want our students to have a serious regard for the material we lay out in our texts and classes. They should not dismiss the material out of hand. Yet, a critical distance that allows for analysis and evaluation is clearly central to the sceptical rationalism of the sciences. This tension is made far more complicated by another body of research about misconceptions and alternative conceptions. There is an extensive body of research—our favorite here is Osborne and Freyberg (1985)—that illustrates just how difficult it is to get students to change their private notions, recall those two students doing the experiment with batteries and water and the question of the bubbles in Chapter four. Students somehow fend off the reason within scientific constructs and hold onto their own views. Some texts have taken this research to heart and have explicitly addressed common misunderstandings. Yet even these fail to effectively touch students' private ideas. According to Alvermann and Hynd (1989), the text alone is not enough to challenge the private understanding. Teachers need, they continue, to draw a direct bead on these notions everywhere and to subject them to critical scrutiny in order to make progress.

Thus we come to a rather remarkable bind. Research at once suggests both that students are not paying sufficient attention to the text (and so they do not change their private misconceptions) and that they defer too readily to what they read (and so fail to engage critically the claims that are made). These conclusions are virtually contradictory.

"D.Q., can you run that by me one more time?"

"Sure. Students appear to think that science is always right and it is pointless to question it. So you would think that they would simply agree with everything that science offers. But they don't. They rather stubbornly hold on to their own ideas about things. Somehow the whole process is like a game. You play. There are rules. But it's not what you really think."

"But aren't these two sides of the same coin? Both fall in place if we assume students are not trying very hard. They don't let their science books touch their own sense of things and they don't subject them to any scrutiny because they simply don't care."

"Implicit in your idea, Sancho, is a kind of conspiracy theory with the basic premise that anytime falsehood defeats truth, the contest must have been unfair. There must have been a conspiracy. Since science texts lay out the material in a clear and logical fashion, for students to fail to appreciate this material must mean they are willfully closing their eyes. They are not letting it change their private notions. They are not caring enough.

"Yet, this will not solve our problem. In these studies (Norris and Phillips, 1994 and Yore et al., 1998) efforts were made to link these behaviors to grades and other indices of earnest engagement, but with no success. The best and most earnest students were equally as guilty as others less accomplished or committed. The dilemma remains. Students defer too readily to their texts and at the same time do not change their basic conceptions. And so we return to our question: how are we to understand what is happening in our classrooms?

"There's another option. We can turn the conspiracy theory on its head. Rather than suggest these behaviors stem from a refusal to learn, perhaps they stem from our success. Perhaps, it is what we are teaching them.

"If we look back over this book thus far, what are the leading features that strike us? From the story about Pete and the light of the moon to Yager's count of technical terms, from Osborne and Freyberg's gap between what is presented by a teacher and what students think to the critique of the TIMSS report that our teaching is a mile wide and an inch deep, what are we nurturing in our classrooms? It would appear to be this manifest pedagogical truth: we routinely teach right answers that are essentially outside the ken of our students. As Finley observed: 'science texts typically fail to include the reasoning that supports scientific beliefs . . .' (1991). If this is so, what does it say about what it means to be successful? In order to cope, students must suspend their criticism. To go back to our introductory list of notions, students must accept and become facile with evaporation, with the idea that the Earth is a planet, etc., without becoming convinced rationally why one would believe such things. I go back to my son and the idea that the moon doesn't shine with its own light, but reflects the light of the sun. Their schooling is more 'mimetic' than critical, more a matter of manipulating propositions that have been given to them than the evaluation of their standing on critical grounds.

"In short, to be a successful science student, one must deny precisely those critical instincts that are the hallmark of the sciences."

On Habits of Mind

We can push this a bit further. Students learn more than their times tables and the causes of the Civil War in our classrooms. Along with the content come habits of mind. These sensibilities are a little like clouds: they're hard to delineate precisely, but they're real and substantive. Recall, in Chapter three, our discussion with Gerald Goldin of cognitive skills and the need for assessment to seek this deeper analytical surface. We can appreciate the weight, the significance of habits of mind, in a study of an epoch far removed in space and time, the Middle Ages. In his masterly *History of the Inductive Sciences* (1837), the Victorian scientist, William Whewell, put his finger on a key aspect of the Middle Ages. It is common to see the Middle Ages as a stagnant era where things fell apart, especially in the sciences. There is, for example, the story of a scholarly text on the history of astronomy that was divided into three parts:

astronomy in antiquity, in the Middle Ages, and in the modern era. The section on the Middle Ages consisted of a single blank page! Yet Whewell argued this was not generally the case. The Middle Ages were a time of great creativity. It nurtured the development of parliamentary government, of schools and universities, of changes in agricultural practices, and of various technologies, such as glass-making—and most especially for Whewell, it nurtured the development of cathedrals, notable both as institutions in the organization of the Catholic Church and for the brilliance of their architecture. This was no dark age. The lights, urged Whewell, had not been turned off. So why was there so little progress in the sciences?

This is a much better question.

The answer Whewell offered had to do with the analytical habits of mind characteristic of the day. Scholarship across the Middle Ages was dominated by a "commentatorial spirit" that focused on gaining a richer appreciation of the wisdom of a text. Such an approach sees the text as authoritative and the task of the scholar is to uncover the fullness of the wisdom it contains. We can see here the same critical sensibilities that would have informed the disciples of Isaiah, as opposed to those of the disciples of Thales (see Chapter six).

Perhaps we can appreciate the heart of the commentatorial spirit by considering its alternative. Take, for example, the story of Eve and the Serpent in the Garden of Eden.

Some time ago, a leading scientist visited our high school. Rather than present a lecture on his work, which I assume he felt would be too technical and dry for his audience, he chose to discuss reasoning in the sciences. He illustrated the differences between science and other ways of thinking by tracing what he would do, as a scientist, with the story of Eve and the Serpent. Since in this tale, Eve and the Serpent have several conversations, he would first go to the zoo and study snakes to see if they talk. They don't, and so he concluded the story is false.

This is very much not the commentatorial spirit. I do not offer it as especially insightful on the character of science, but it serves a useful purpose. Who would have thought that the point of this story was that snakes talk? When I first heard this story, I understood that snakes don't really talk. The snake was a device. When we consider how rich the story of the Garden of Eden is, when we think of the profound issues this tale raises, as it links the fruit of the Tree of Knowledge to the Fall of Mankind, then we can appreciate how many forms there are to wisdom and the appeal of the commentatorial spirit. To deny the value or insight of this tale because snakes don't talk is to very much miss the point. But the question remains: is there something in this approach to scholarship that is antithetical to science?

There is. And though George Grote's *History of Greece* might seem an unlikely source for an answer to Whewell's question, his study of the emergence of critical thought in antiquity is just what the proverbial doctor ordered.

The March of Mind

You will recall our discussion of the two classical historians, Mitford and Thirlwall. Mitford's *History* was of the events of mythical Greece, while Thirlwall's was of the spirit that informed the mind of the myth-makers. So for Mitford the real Hercules had been a hero who wielded the sword of justice at a time when government was too weak; while for Thirlwall Hercules was a conceptual device whose mighty arm explained to the ancients how communities had first been established and then later would be invoked to justify a new civil order. Let us turn now to another great classical historian, George Grote.

As we turn to Grote, we turn from Thirlwall's Cambridge to London. These two places offer rich images . . . the cloister and the market place. There is Thirlwall's Trinity College with its magnificent Wren library, fine ancient buildings, and ancient traditions walled in medieval isolation. And there is Victorian London with its omnibuses; whose children are Oliver and the Artful Dodger. The London buildings are different, the noise is different, the air is different, and it was all owned by Commerce.

There is more to the contrast than physical feature. Grote and Thirlwall are a marvelously matched pair, spanning the currents of Victorian life and letters. Grote, the young "utilitarian," met to discuss the new social philosophy of Bentham, James Mill, and Ricardo, while Thirlwall hosted dinners with Coleridge and Carlyle. One a banker, the other a churchman, they seem almost to divide Victorian life between them. But let us turn to Grote's *History*.

Writing neither about the events of ancient myth nor the mind of the myth-maker, Grote examined the telling and retelling of these ancient stories. He wrote about the processes whereby myth had been distilled and transformed into the critical thought of such later scholars as Herodotus, Thucydides, and Plato. All peoples have had a body of myth, tales that explained how the world came to be the way it was. But only in ancient Greece did that body of story-telling give way to non-fiction. This is the story that Grote tells, and the reworking of ancient myth in the commentaries of post-legendary times was the core of his tale. Since the tensions between the commentatorial spirit and critical thinking are the very core of the problem facing students in a science class, let's take a moment to follow Grote's study.

Consider this delightful instance of commentary regarding Hercules and the Kalydonian boar hunt. This expedition had been one of the four great aggregate dramas of heroic myth, along with the adventures of the Argonauts, the siege against Thebes, and the Trojan War. The question raised by Ephorus (third century BC) was: why hadn't Hercules participated? Ephorus decided that Hercules must have been busy elsewhere at the time (Grote, 1869, vol. 1, p. 142).

This question and the answer Ephorus offers are fully predicated upon the reality of the mythical world in all its detail. Any collection of heroes would have necessarily included Hercules. The fact that he was not a part of the boar hunt requires some explanation. Grote sees this sort of commentary as typical of a class of ancient scholars he labels as "logographers." The logographer, the "mapper" of the word, was a compiler. In bringing a body of tales together, he made evident their myriad inconsistencies, and so was led to the further task of reconciling the many points of difference and contradiction, choosing one version over another and introducing modifications (Grote, 1869, vol. 1, pp. 142 and 364–376).

A closely related body of commentary was guided more directly by moral sensibilities. This was the criticism of the poet or the dramatist. Apollodorus (second century BC), for example, thought it truly unjust that Hercules had avenged himself upon the sons of Neleus, while Neleus, the actual offender, escaped with his life. So, he altered the tale, claiming the passage in the *Iliad* was spurious (Grote, 1869, vol. 1, pp. 110 and 154).

A third approach was that of the historian. What sets apart the commentaries of Herodotus, Thucydides, Pausanius, Strabo, and others was their jaundiced eye. Their scepticism led them to question particular details. A lovely instance of this comes from Plutarch (*circa* 100 AD). In one of Hercules' many exploits, he visits a friend, Alcmaeon, only to find him distraught over the recent death of his wife, Alkestis. Hercules proceeds to rescue Alkestis by defeating Thanatos (Death) in a wrestling match. In Plutarch, instead of this wrestling match, we find a reference to the medical skills of Hercules, as illustrated by his cure of the deathly ill Alkestis—a far cry from the traditional tale (Grote, 1869, vol. 1, p. 381)!

These several commentaries on Hercules have provided us with three distinct veins of criticism: that of the complier, the moralist, and the historian. Stretching across centuries, it is important to note the central importance of myth to ancient society. We may see these stories as charming fancies and children's tales, but to the ancient Greek they were the core of serious belief. When it was realized that they could not be accepted as they presented themselves, the effort to fashion an understanding became the leading edge in the emergence of critical thought.

The tale Grote tells is a noble one. At first, reconciling discrepancies and divergent traditions, commentators came to apply their own sensibilities as to propriety and plausibility. Mankind had begun to emerge from the open credulity of the mythological mind. This scrutiny of myth, argued Grote, was uniquely Greek. Every nation has had its mythology, but only in ancient Greece did myth become the fertile soil for the growth of criticism. The march of mind had begun.

Key to this progress was "the habit of attending to, recording and combining, positive and present facts" (Grote, 1869, vol. 1, p. 352). Such "present facts" isolated the outrageous proportions of legend and guided its rationalization. This is a subtle matter. Both poet and logographer believed the mythical past had been real. It had not, however, been an ordinary reality. To borrow a lovely expression from the poet Pindar: the present was only half brother to the past. It was the historian who stood upon the planks of the present order of things.

For Grote, the progress from credulity to criticism was fused with the progress from religious faith and superstition to science. Both involved the same dynamic: the application of positive and present facts. This progress is nicely illustrated in commentaries on the legend of Deukalion. Unremitting rains sent by Zeus to punish the corrupt laid the whole of Greece under water, except its highest mountain tops where a few souls, led by Deukalion, found refuge. The devastated world was repopulated, the legend continues, by Deukalion and his wife who cast stones over their heads, the stones turning into men. Justin (second century AD) accepted the rains, but denied the miracle of casting stones into people by casting Deukalion as a king who gave shelter to refugees from the storm. Aristotle (fourth century BC) took a different tack, denying the religious character of the legend by denying the flood had been a divine judgement inflicted against a wicked race. The flood waters had been the result of periodic atmospheric cycles! No room here for divine punishment. In both of these accounts, Grote saw the testing of the past against a standard set by the present, a testing that left no room for faith (Grote, 1869, vol. 1, pp. 96–8).

These are the same views, by the way, offered by the great geologist, Charles Lyell, in an early chapter of his *Principles of Geology*. He observes that "in a rude state of society, all calamities are regarded by the people as judgements of God on the wickedness of man" (Lyell, 1837, vol. 1, pp. 24–25). As mankind emerged from this rude state, however, it shook off this superstition, replacing the wrath of God with the uniformity of natural causes. Thus it "often rejects the fabulous tales of former times, on the ground of their being irreconcilable with the experience of more enlightened ages" (Lyell, 1837, vol. 1, pp. 81–82). For Lyell, as for Grote, in history and in science, mankind's progress has been a progress of criticism over credulity, of present experience over faith.

Whose Fault Is It?

Combining Whewell, Grote, and Lyell, we can see how the commentatorial spirit was antithetical to growth in the sciences. Like the work of the ancient logographer and poet, the commentatorial spirit essentially works within the authority of the text. The historian and the scientist, however, keep the text at a greater remove because of the authority of reason and the present order of things. We can appreciate, therefore, the lack of growth of science across the Middle Ages. The authority of Aristotle was virtually complete; so much so that seeming contradictions between his views and experience would push the medieval scholar toward ever more subtle interpretations of the text.

How does this help us with our original problem about the way students read science books? In our view, the too-ready deference of students to the authority of their text stems not from their indifference, but instead from habits of mind their schooling has nurtured. With Whewell and Grote we can see why this would have been the case. Whose fault is it when a student doesn't understand?

Whose fault is it when they can't make sense of what a teacher or a text has told them? Or when they don't get the same answer their text gives? If it is always their fault, are we not teaching them to act like Aristotelians? Isn't the commentatorial spirit exactly what Osborne and Freyberg show us in the work of children, as they try to reconcile what the teacher is saying with what they are doing?

Here is a further reply to Shea's remarks on the National Research Council's *National Science Education Standards* (see the discussion in Chapter five). Shea asks if it really makes sense to lead students to doubt the atomic structure of matter, the chemical formula for water, or the shape and size of the Earth. Such ideas are tried and true. Why question them? But questioning such notions is not about dismissing their significance. It is about empowering students as independent thinkers. This also echoes our discussion of labs and projects, where I emphasized framing them with careful consideration of the problem rather than a careful delineation of the protocol.

Whewell's analysis is compelling, and it underlines that habits of mind, however vague, can be taught . . . cultivated across an era. What of our own era? On a scale that carries from Whewell's commentatorial spirit and Grote's logographer on the one hand across to the sceptical reaches of Lyell and Grote, where should we locate ourselves?

The answer, for now, is at the commentatorial end. Standardized testing and teaching to such tests is only the most evident sign of these sensibilities and educational values. To move from this end of the spectrum will take concerted effort, an effort not only to change educational policy but to reach beneath the surface of such sensibilities to get at a pervasive cultural perspective. It is a perspective we may characterize as "the black box" . . . a metaphor for all those things in our world we depend upon and use all of the time, but have no idea how they work.

Two centuries ago, at the height of the Industrial Revolution, sensibilities were very different. Though working people had few resources, they pooled them together, a penny at a time, to form subscription libraries and Mechanics Institutes. These institutions reflected a vision that valued a mastery of how things worked (Kelly, 1957). There were publishing ventures such as the Home Library of Science and Dr. Dionysius Lardner's Cabinet of Science, which brought authoritative texts in the sciences to "everyman's" home. And beyond this, the Society for the Diffusion of Useful Knowledge sold penny tracts from pushcarts that told the story of hydrodynamics, electricity, celestial mechanics, and the whole host of scientific wonders (New, 1961). It was a different day.

If we are genuinely to turn things around in our schools, teaching will need to nurture the promise of making sense of things. It will need to nurture humility in the face of complexity, and yet confidence, as well, that things can be understood. It will need to nurture voice. And above all, it will need to work to keep Jesse's wonder alive.

So, What is It That We Can Do?

The immediate suggestion would seem to be this: we should not underestimate how hard it is to get where we want to go and how complex the politics of learning are. Our students are coping in earnest, and we need to attend carefully to what we are teaching them and rewarding them for. We need to teach in a way that invites students to be critical, that allows students to urge that their text must be wrong when it says something that contradicts their sense of things. We need to allow students to set down the trappings of "student-ness" as they exercise the critical judgement of the scientist or historian. We need to teach in a way that encourages students to offer their views on the way things must be and to take them seriously . . . tracing their consequences and testing them where possible. All of which can be seen in that lovely—simple and direct—observation made by Richard Feynman about the character of effective science teaching: "the first thing really is, before you begin you must not know the answer" (Feynman, 1999, p. 106).

There is a tension between right answers and right reasoning. We want our students to build an effective understanding of modern science and this requires a solid foundation . . . but it should be a foundation anchored in understanding and critical habits of mind, not in particular matters of fact and technical terms. Consider the way we teach reading. We may have in mind that children should be reading Dickens, Ellison, or Shakespeare by the time they reach high school or college. But we do not get them there by teaching them the vocabulary they will need then. We offer them good stories. Over time these stories grow richer and more complex, moving children toward more demanding work. That is what we should be doing in the sciences. Each level should tell its own story, taking on the deepest issues, pushing the material, and nurturing students' critical reasoning. It's a matter of students building an understanding of their world, not preparing them so that they may be given one.

The End . . . Almost

As we have seen, ends are curious things. We began with Jesse's wonder at what could hold the rain up and we have since then considered a host of items, including brief forays into Cuvier's paleontology, Aristotle's physics, Herapath's kinetic theory, and a goodly measure of ancient Greece. As we began with Jesse, so we have ended with the classroom and the demands we lay upon our students. It is time to stop and let students have the last word.

Last Interlude
Let the Kids Have the Last Word

A high school senior recently spent the last several weeks of the school year as an intern in an elementary school. At one point she worked in a kindergarten classroom with a new teacher. It was pretty rough. The teacher seemed to be yelling at the kids all the time, and the student spent a lot of her time talking to kids who had just been yelled at, trying to calm them down and get them back on track and able to do their work. After about a week, another more experienced teacher invited her to work in her classroom. The difference was like night and day. This teacher never raised her voice. She spoke directly to the children, looking them in the eye. She didn't talk down to them, the senior explained, but she made herself clear. The class was so much calmer. The kids worked more, and they enjoyed it.

As it happened, another senior also spent time in two different kindergarten classrooms. At one school, she wrote:

> Every child has an assigned desk and chair with his or her name on it. They come in the morning, sit down, and begin to copy and answer a question from the board . . . When it is work time, they are expected to work. When it is play time, they are expected to play. The teacher seemed afraid to let things get out of control, and with twenty-five kids and only one of her, I don't blame her.

In contrast, at the other school there were two teachers in the classroom and students began the day sitting in a circle on the carpet facing one another.

> They played games and sang songs. If one child didn't want to do a certain activity, they would be encouraged, not forced. As a result, they seemed more relaxed. They were more comfortable with themselves and each other. To me they seemed happier and more eager to learn and to come to school each day. And it's not just because of the songs and the games. It's because the two teachers celebrated each individual student and his or her ideas and encouraged the rest of the class to do the same. They treated the children as colleagues, not burdens.

Finally, this senior closed her essay by talking about her own schooling:

> From teachers who always respected me, I have learned to respect myself. From teachers who wanted to learn about me and the way my mind works, I have learned more about myself. I will guard this self-understanding and self-respect with me throughout the rest of my life, and I will be a more self-sufficient adult than someone who never had understanding teachers in high school.

What a lovely observation . . . that from the adults around her taking an interest in how she understood things, "how her mind works," she learned to respect herself.

Let me close with one last student essay. It was written as a final reflection on his 4 years of high school. You will see that it is a very different sort of piece. I offer it virtually as it was written, with but a few minor changes:

> It hasn't rain in weeks and it is coming down like crazy today. It's this heat. I have no air conditioning, car and house alike, and when I go to roll up the windows in the front seat, left down for weeks the passenger seat window won't roll up! Rain is streaming into the car onto the little electric buttons and fuzzy seats. The window in the back seat, broken by a thief three months ago (he stole two coats), also lets rain into the metal ash tray and onto the buttons. My sisters lost the tape so I can't tape trash bags to cover the hole. I'm slamming them into the doors. My shoe is broken (and my sisters lost the tape). The older one, Candace, refuses to tie her shoes. She loses a shoe string a week (she's 21). So I find my broken shoes stripped of their strings. I'm standing barefoot in the rain rending garbage bags and slamming them into the door. The force of the closing door pushes the bags away billowing before they make contact. My hair is matted and I'm sweating in the rain. I slam the door and the bag flies, I slam the door and the bag flies. There the bag sits in the mud, rain smacking it, next to my bare feet, I lean against the car, and the rain pours in, and I think what can I tell the school? Tomorrow, tomorrow is the last day.
>
> It's hot in my room as I type this, sweat is pooling in my back even against my wet shirt. My car is collecting water, my blue seats, my tiny silver electronic buttons, my school papers, and clothes, and I think what can I tell school? I wish I had more patience and more time. I wish I could say this with more eloquence, and less desperation, but I wanted to thank you.
>
> Please don't take this lightly because I sure don't. In fact it disturbs me, on some deep and personal philosophically intuitive level. My god, please, I assure you this is no petty act of deference like for so many others. Unfortunately for you dear faculty you never took my ninth grade course, but perhaps you've read Darwin's *The Voyage of the Beagle* where he tells the story of the three slaves asked by Fitz Roy, "Do you enjoy being a

slave?" and they all reply yes because, of course, a slave is not free to respond with anything else. This is what I assume the main body of the essays will be (and knowing these people personally some are sure to be). "The last thing we ask you to do is tell us whether you like us or not, then you may go." My god, the only answer drilled in us for the past five years is yes, yes, yes, sure, will do, OK. This is, of course, the mechanics of school. You tell us to do something and we are successful when we do it. Probably most will not be so conscious about it, but certainly subconsciously. It would be unkind (and so tongues are bound in intimidation), but completely out of place for a student to point fingers, blame, and complain. A student doesn't complain, blame, bitch, or moan. A successful student says "yes" and does what he is told. Do you think after four years it would be so easy to change roles so quickly and compact this into an essay? No, preposterous.

So please, when I tell you how much I appreciate your institution don't take it as idle talk, nor a matter of politeness, as you pass me my four years here at the dinner table and I nod and say "thank you" for edict's sake. My gratitude is beyond sincerity (any fool can be deluded sincere). It is unbiased and reluctant.

My conception of school is that it is a vice. As one of my teachers said, a course is a course (obstacle, that is). One day in class, he quoted Vonnegut, "It's great to have a club. Everyone should have a club." I thought he was speaking about something to beat people with for a few minutes, until the rest of his lecture started losing coherence, and yet I find that true as well. Any club is a club; you can use any organization to beat people with. Chuang Tzu, the Taoist philosopher, has a parable that goes something like this: "Wrestlers begin their matches in good sport and fairness, but by the end their faces are grimaced and they pull hair committed to victory. A feast begins in celebration and good order, but ends in drunkenness and disarray. Thus things started off with the best of intentions, end in meanness."

Everyday I have things I'd love to do, activities I believe are filled with merit, and everyday I have things which need to be taken care of, cleaned up. Everyday it is raining, somewhere, into my car window, like it's doing right now. So I sure as hell don't appreciate people pushing me around and asking me to do more, and it's especially insulting when I find it valueless. So you can see why it's so damn perplexing. Look at me, sweating like a hog, soaking my seats, to try to convey my appreciation.

That was certainly my impression when I came to the school. I expected to be pushed around. But I found instead that what teachers demanded was reasonable. They left many things in front of me, gave me resources and opportunity with none of the bullying that seemed so synonymous with any school. I can't remember the line of the school's philosophy, but it might go something like ". . . belief that students have the natural inclination to learn." I'd like to thank you for this line. For not clubbing me. I find it completely unique for a school. There are other ways you could run the school. I am certain pushing kids is more efficient in some ways, but don't stop what you're doing. I think you're doing it exactly right.

That's really all I wanted to say, however clumsy. Please forgive spelling and grammar. Tomorrow, I'll drive this in, in my moist car.

I find this to be a wholly remarkable piece, and yet it is quite straightforward. There is a politics to learning, as to any institution. We would do well to remember as we teach what it had been like to be a student. Let us invite students to learn and set our bullying aside.

Finally, as we began our study running across a parking lot to the kindergarten with Jesse in the rain, so we may end with a senior getting into his car in the rain . . . Oh and

"Good-bye, Sancho."

References

Abbott, B. and Costello, L. (1952). Abbott and Costello loafing. Retrieved from www.youtube.com [accessed July 16, 2010].

Abrams, M.H. (1971). *The mirror and the lamp: Romantic theory and the critical tradition.* New York: Oxford University Press.

Alberts, B. (2004). Letter from Dr. Bruce Alberts, President of the National Academy of Sciences to the California State Board of Education, March 4, 2004. Retrieved from http://science.nsta.org/nstaexpress/lettertocaliffromgerry.htm [accessed July 16, 2010].

Alvermann, D. and Hynd, C. (1989). Effects of prior knowledge activation modes and text structure on nonscience majors' comprehension of physics. *Journal of Educational Research* 83(2), 97–102.

American Association for the Advancement of Science (1989). *Science for all Americans: A project 2061 report on literacy goals in science, mathematics and technology.* Washington, DC.

American Association for the Advancement of Science (1993). *Benchmarks for science literacy.* New York: Oxford University Press.

Aristotle (1939). *On the heavens.* (W.K.C. Guthrie, Trans.). Cambridge: Harvard University Press.

Aristotle (1957). *Aristotle's politics and poetics.* (B. Jowett and T. Twining, Trans.). New York: The Viking Press.

Bachelard, G. (2002). *Earth and reveries of will.* Dallas, TX: Dallas Institute of Publications.

Balzac, H. (1906). *The wild ass's skin.* (E. Marriage, Trans.). London: J.M. Dent & Sons.

Barnes, J. (1987). *Early Greek philosophy.* New York: Penguin Books.

Berg, T. and Brouwer, W. (1991). Teacher awareness of student alternate conceptions about rotational motion and gravity. *Journal of Research in Science Teaching* 28(I), 3–18.

Bernstein, J. (2004). *Oppenheimer: Portrait of an enigma.* Chicago: Ivan R. Dee.

Black, P., Harrison, C., Lee, C., Marshall, B. and William, D. (2004). The nature and value of formative assessment for learning. Retrieved from http://kcl.ac.uk/content/1/c4/73/57/formative.pdf [accessed July 16, 2010].

Bloom, B. (1984). *Taxonomy of educational objectives.* Boston: Allyn & Bacon.

Bolte, J. (1966). Background factors and success in college physics. *Journal of Research in Science Teaching* 4, 74–78.

Bradbury, R. (1953). *Fahrenheit 451.* New York: Ballantine Books.

Campbell, J. (1971). Bargain spacement. *Analog: Science Fiction, Science Fact* 87(4), 4–7 and 176–178.

Coleman, W. (1964). *Georges Cuvier: Zoologist.* Cambridge, MA: Harvard University Press.

Coleridge, S.T. (1894). *Biographia literaria.* London: G. Bell & Sons. (Original work published 1817).

Collingwood, R.G. (1939). *An autobiography.* London: Oxford University Press.

Craig, M. and Yore, L. (1996). Middle school students' awareness of strategies for resolving comprehension difficulties in science reading. *Journal of Research and Development in Education* 29(4), 226–238.

Crichton, M. (1990). *Jurassic park.* New York: Random House.

Cuvier, G. (1813). *Essay on the theory of the Earth.* Edinburgh: William Blackwood.

Dalton, J. (1964). *A new system of chemical philosophy.* New York: The Citadel Press. (Original published 1808).

Darwin, C. (1845). *Journal of researches into the history and geology of the countries visited during the voyage of H.M.S. Beagle round the world, under the command of Capt. Fitz Roy, R.A.* London: John Murray. Retrieved from http://Darwin-online.org.uk [accessed July 16, 2010].

Darwin, C. (1964). *On the origin of species by means of natural selection.* Cambridge: Harvard University Press. (Original published 1859).

Dewey, J. (1964). Ethical principles underlying education. In R. Archambault (Ed.), *John Dewey on education* (pp. 108–138). Chicago: University of Chicago Press. (Original published 1897).

Dewey, J. (1964) Science as subject-matter and as method. In R. Archambault (Ed.). *John Dewey on education* (pp. 182–192). Chicago: University of Chicago Press. (Original published 1910).

Dewey, J. (1997). *How we think.* Mineola, NY: Dover Publications. (Original published 1909).

Durrenmatt, F. (1964). *The physicists.* (J. Kirkup, Trans.). New York: Grove Press.

Eastman, D. (1982). *Now I know: The story of dinosaurs.* New York: Troll Associates.

Eckert, P. (1989). *Jocks and burnouts: Social categories and identity in the high school.* New York: Teachers College Press.

Eliade, M. (1962). *The forge and the crucible.* Chicago: University of Chicago Press.

Emmett, J.B. (1820–1821). Researches into the Mathematical Principles of Chemical Philosophy. *Annals of Philosophy* 16, 137–145, 180–188, 351–358 and 1 n.s. 81–88.

Fesperman, D. (2004). Mother upset about conditions at Hickey. *Baltimore Sun.* July 2, 2004.

Feynman, R. (1999). The role of scientific culture in modern society. In J. Robbins (Ed.). *The pleasure of finding things out.* Cambridge, MA: Perseus Books.

Finger, J., Dillon, J., and Corbin, F. (1965). Performance in introductory college physics and previous instruction in physics. *Journal of Research in Science Teaching* 3, 61–65.

Finley, F. (1991). Why students have trouble learning from science texts. In C. Santa and D. Alvermann (Eds.). *Science learning: Processes and applications.* Newark, DE: International Reading Association.

Foucault, M. (1973). *The birth of the clinic.* (A.M. Sheridan Smith, Trans.). London: Tavistock Publications.

Fox, R. (1971). *The caloric theory of gases.* New York: Oxford University Press.

Gess-Newsome, J. and Lederman, N. (Eds.) (2001). *Examining pedagogical content knowledge: The construct and its implications for science teaching.* Amsterdam: Springer Netherlands.

Goldin, G. (1992). Toward an assessment framework for school mathematics. In R. Lesh and S. Lamon (Eds.). *Assessment of authentic performance in school mathematics.* Washington, DC: American Association for the Advancement of Science Press.

Gould, S. (1980). *The panda's thumb.* New York: W.W Norton & Co.

Grote, G. (1869). *A history of Greece: From the earliest period to the close of the generation contemporary with Alexander the Great.* London: John Murray.

Guthrie, W.K.C. (1950). *The Greek philosophers: From Thales to Aristotle.* New York: Harper & Row.

Hart, G. and Cottle, P. (1993). Academic backgrounds and achievement in college physics. *Physics Teacher* 31(8), 470–475.

Havelock, E. (1968). *Prometheus, with a translation of Aeschylus' Prometheus bound.* Seattle, WA: University of Washington Press.

Hay, D., Linebaugh, P., Rule, J.G., Thompson, E.P. and Winslow, C. (1975). *Albion's fatal tree: Crime and society in eighteenth-century England.* New York: Pantheon Books.

Hayward, C. (1999). 'The environment': Power, pedagogy, and American urban schooling. *The Urban Review* 31(4), 331–357.

Herapath, J. (1816). On the physical properties of gases. *Annals of Philosophy* 56–60.

Herapath, J. (1821). On the causes, laws, phenomena of heat, gases, gravitation. *Annals of Philosophy* 9, 273–293.

Herapath, J. (1847). *Mathematical physics: or the mathematical principles of natural philosophy with a development of the causes of heat, gaseous electricity, etc.* London: Whitaker.

Hevesi, D. (1989). Huey Newton symbolized the rising black anger of a generation. *The New York Times.* August 23, 1989.

Hume, D. (1948). *Dialogues concerning natural religion.* New York: Hafner Publishing Co. (Original published 1779).

Huxley, T.H. (1907). *Aphorisms and reflections from the works of T. H. Huxley.* (H. Huxley, Ed.). London: Macmillan & Co.

International Association for the Evaluation of Educational Achievement. (1996). *Third international mathematics and science study.* Boston, MA: Center for the Study of Testing, Evaluation, and Educational Policy.

Kargon, R. (1977). *Science in Victorian Manchester.* Baltimore, MD: The Johns Hopkins University Press.

Kelly, T. (1957). *George Birkbeck: Pioneer of adult education.* Liverpool: Liverpool University Press.

Kohn, A. (2002). The dangerous myth of grade inflation. *The Chronicle of Higher Education.* November 8, 2002.

Kuhn, T. (1957). *The Copernican revolution: Planetary astronomy in the development of western thought.* Cambridge, MA: Harvard University Press.

Kuhn, T. (1962). *The structure of scientific revolutions.* Chicago: The University of Chicago Press.

Lakatos, I. (1970). Falsification and the methodology of scientific research programmes. In I. Lakatos and A. Musgrave (Eds.). *Criticism and the growth of knowledge.* Cambridge: Cambridge University Press.

Lijnse, P. (2000). Didactics of science: The forgotten dimension in science education research? In R. Millar, J. Leach and J. Osborne (Eds.). *Improving science education: The contribution of research* (pp. 308–326). Philadelphia: Open University Press.

Lucretius. (1968). *The way things are: The de rerum natura of Titus Lucretius Carus.* (R. Humphries, Trans.). Bloomington, IN: Indiana University Press.

Luria, A. (1974). *Cognitive development, its cultural and social foundations.* (M. Lopez-Morillas and L. Solataroff, Trans.). Cambridge, MA Harvard University Press.

Lyell, C. (1837). *Principles of geology.* (5th English edition). Philadelphia: James Kay, Jun. & Brother.

Macaulay, D. (1979). *Motel of the mysteries.* New York: Houghton Mifflin.

McCloskey, M., Caramazza, A. and Green, B. (1980). Curvilinear motion in the absence of external force: Naïve beliefs about the motion of objects. *Science* 210, 1139–1141.

Matthews, M. (2000). *Time for science education: How teaching the history and philosophy of pendulum motion can contribute to science literacy.* New York: Kluwer Academic/Plenum Publishers.

Matthews, M., Gauld, C. and Stinner, A. (Eds.) (2005). *The pendulum: Scientific, historical, philosophical and educational perspectives.* Dordrecht, The Netherlands: Springer.

May, H. and Metzger, B. (Eds.) (1962). *The Oxford annotated Holy Bible: Revised standard version.* New York: Oxford University Press.

Michels, W. (1958). The teaching of elementary physics. *Scientific American* 198, 56–64.

Mitford, W. (1808). *The history of Greece.* London: T. Cadell & W. Davies.

Moorehead, A. (1970). *Darwin and the Beagle.* New York: Harper & Row.

Murray, G. (1964). *Aeschylus, the creator of tragedy.* Oxford: Clarendon Press.

National Institute for Direct Instruction (n.d.). About direct instruction (DI). Retrieved from www.nifdi.org/15/about-di [accessed July 12, 2010].

National Research Council (1996). *National science education standards.* Washington, DC: National Academy Press.

National Research Council (2002). *Learning and understanding: Improving advanced study of mathematics and science in U.S. high schools.* Washington, DC: National Academy Press.

Neufeld, S. (2006). Schools to drop studio course. *Baltimore Sun.* February 16, 2006.

New, C. (1961). *The life of Henry Brougham to 1830.* London: Clarendon Press.

Norris, S. and Phillips, L. (1994). Interpreting pragmatic meaning when reading popular reports of science. *Journal of Research in Science Teaching* 31(9), 947–967.

Osborne, R. (1982). Science education: where do we start? *Australian Science Teachers Journal* 28(1), 21–30.

Osborne, R. and Freyberg, P. (Eds.) (1985). *Learning in science.* Auckland, NZ: Heinemann.

Penner, D. (2001). Cognition, computers and synthetic science: Building knowledge and meaning through modeling. In W. Secada (Ed.). *Review of Research in Education #25* (pp. 1–35). Washington, DC: American Educational Research Association.

Pfeiffer, J. (1972). *The emergence of man.* New York: Harper & Row.

Pinker, S. (1994). *The language instinct.* Cambridge: Harvard University Press.

Plato (1956). *Protagoras and Meno.* (W.K.C. Guthrie, Trans.). New York: Penguin Books.

Playfair, J. (1822). *The works of John Playfair.* Edinburgh: A. Constable & Co.

Popper, K. (1963). *Conjectures and refutations.* London: Routledge & Kegan Paul.

Popper, K. (1972). *Objective knowledge: An evolutionary approach.* Oxford: Clarendon Press.

Potter, B. (1995). *Tales of Peter Rabbit.* South Norwalk, Conn.: ABDO Publishing Company. (Original published 1902).

Rauch, H-G. (1974). *En masse.* New York: Macmillan Publishing Co.

Reclus, E. (1907). Fire. In *Encyclopaedia Britannica.* (11th edition). New York: The Werner Company.

Rosenblatt, L. (2004). Those puzzling pendulums. *The Science Teacher* 71(10), 38–41.

Rosenblatt, L. (2005). The poet and the pendulum. In M. Matthews, C. Gauld, and A. Stinner (Eds.). *The pendulum: Its place in science, culture, and pedagogy.* Dordrecht, the Netherlands: Springer.

Rudwick, M. (1972). *The meaning of fossils: Episodes in the history of palaeontology.* New York: American Elsevier.

Sadler, P. and Tai, R. (2001). Success in introductory college physics: The role of high school preparation. *Science Education* 85, 111–136.

Sanders, B. (1994). *A is for ox.* New York: Vintage Books.

Santillana, G. de (1961). *The origins of scientific thought: From Anaximander to Proclus, 600 B.C. to 300 A.D.* Chicago: University of Chicago Press.

Schwartz, M., Sadler, P., Sonnert, G. and Tai, R. (2009). Depth versus breadth: How content coverage in high school course relates to later success in college science coursework. *Science Education* 93, 798–826.

Sedgwick, A. (1969). *A discourse on the studies of the university.* New York: Humanities Press. (Original published 1833).

Shah, I. (1973). *The exploits of the incomparable Mulla Nasrudin.* London: Pan Books.

Shea, J. (1998). More progress (???) on science education standards. *Journal of Geoscience Education* March, 1998.

Snow, C.P. (1959). *The two cultures and the scientific revolution.* New York: Cambridge University Press.

Stoppard, T. (1967). *Rosencrantz and Guildenstern are dead.* New York: Grove Press.

Tai, R., Sadler, P., and Mintzes, J. (2006). Factors influencing college science success. *Journal of College Science Teaching* 35(8), 56–60.

Tennyson, A. (1850). In Memoriam. In M. Abrams *et al.* (Eds.) *The Norton anthology of English literature* (2, pp. 750–70). New York: W.W. Norton & Company.

Thirlwall, C. (1855). *The history of Greece.* London: Longman, Brown, Green, & Longmans.

Vonnegut, K. (1981). Roots. In *Palm Sunday: An autobiographical collage* (pp. 18–60). New York: Dell Publishing Co.

Watterson, W. (1992). *The indispensable Calvin and Hobbes.* Kansas City, MO: Andrews & McMeel.

Wells, H.G. (1914). *The world set free.* London: Macmillan & Company.

Whewell, W. (1837). *The history of the inductive sciences, from the earliest to the present time.* London: J.W. Parker & Son.

Wiggins, G. and McTighe, J. (1998). *Understanding by design.* Alexandria, VA: ASCD.

William, D., Lee, C. and Black, P. (2004). Teachers developing assessment for learning: Impact on student achievement. *Assessment in Education* 11(1), 49–65.

Yager, R. (1983). The importance of terminology in teaching K–12 science. *Journal of Research in Science Teaching* 20, 577–588.

Yore, L., Craig, M. and Maguire, T. (1998). Index of reading awareness. *Journal of Research in Science Teaching* 35(I), 27–51.

Index

Note: The three central themes of this book are presented in bold type to assist the reader in locating the key topics of the sub-title: Content, Pedagogy, and the Nature of Science.